GRAMOPH

CW01510408

EDITORIAL

Phone 020 7738 5454

email gramophone@markallengroup.com

EDITOR AND PUBLISHER Martin Cullingford
DEPUTY EDITOR Sarah Kirkup / 020 7501 6365
REVIEWS EDITOR Tim Parry / 020 7501 6367
ONLINE CONTENT EDITOR James McCarthy
SUB-EDITOR David Threasher / 020 7501 6370
SUB-EDITOR Marija Đurić Speare
ART DIRECTOR Dinah Lone / 020 7501 6689
'GRAMOPHONE PRESENTS ... MOZART'
ART EDITOR Veesun Ho
PICTURE EDITOR Sunita Sharma-Gibson
AUDIO EDITOR Andrew Everard
EDITORIAL ADMINISTRATOR Libby McPhee
EDITOR-IN-CHIEF James Jolly
WITH THANKS TO Lucy Parry

ADVERTISING

Phone 020 7738 5454

email gramophone.ads@markallengroup.com

COMMERCIAL MANAGER
Esther Zuke / 020 7501 6368
SENIOR ACCOUNT MANAGER
James McMahon / 07967 169001

SUBSCRIPTIONS AND BACK ISSUES

0800 137201 **(UK)** +44 (0)1722 716997 **(overseas)**
subscriptions@markallengroup.com

PUBLISHING

Phone 020 7738 5454

HEAD OF MARKETING
John Barnett / 020 7501 6233
GROUP INSTITUTIONAL SALES MANAGER Jas Atwal
PRODUCTION DIRECTOR
Richard Hamshere / 01722 716997
PRODUCTION MANAGER
Kyri Apessolou
CIRCULATION DIRECTOR
Sally Boettcher / 01722 716997
SUBSCRIPTIONS MANAGER
Bethany Foy / 01722 716997
EDITORIAL DIRECTOR Martin Cullingford
MANAGING DIRECTOR Paul Geoghegan
CHIEF EXECUTIVE OFFICER Ben Allen
CHAIRMAN Mark Allen

MA Music Leisure & Travel

Part of

Mark Allen

GRAMOPHONE is published by
MA Music Leisure & Travel Ltd, St Jude's Church,
Dulwich Road, London SE24 0PB, United Kingdom.
gramophone.co.uk
email **gramophone@markallengroup.com** or
subscriptions@markallengroup.com
ISSN 0017-310X.

This special Mahler edition of *Gramophone* is published in July,
and available in shops from July 27. Every effort has been
made to ensure the accuracy of statements in this magazine but
we cannot accept responsibility for errors or omissions, or for
matters arising from clerical or printers' errors, or an
advertiser not completing his contract. We have made every
effort to secure permission to use copyright material. Where
material has been used inadvertently or we have been unable
to trace the copyright owner, acknowledgement will be made
in a future issue.

Printed in England by Pensord Press

recycle
When you have finished with
this magazine please recycle it.

Founded in 1923 by Sir Compton Mackenzie and Christopher Stone as
'an organ of candid opinion for the numerous possessors of gramophones'

Mahler: music at its most profound

'Now that Gustav Mahler looms over musical life much as Beethoven and Wagner once must have done, it is difficult to credit the neglect following his premature death,' wrote David Gutman in his Collection on Mahler's Tenth Symphony, one of the articles reproduced in this special edition dedicated to the composer's music. 'For almost 50 years Mahler has seemed special, not just because of the breadth and power of his output, but also because of his place in popular imagination as a man at the junction of two centuries and two eras – the Romantic and the modern.'

These observations perhaps get the heart of why Mahler's music means so much to audiences a century after his death. It *is* special, and its profound power to open before us extraordinary expanses of emotional and spiritual insight – from sadness to beauty, and from acceptance to hope – has not been rivalled by any composer since. And if Mahler straddles epochs, well perhaps that ability to convey the wisdom of earlier eras to an ever-turbulent today, is what defines all great art. And Mahler *is* great art. To hear a Mahler symphony, or be drawn into the sound world of his songs, is to experience music at its most transcendent. In an age of ever-increasing immediacy and short attention spans, listening to Mahler is also somewhat counter-cultural – but that's all the more reason to explore it, seek to better understand it, and to pass it on to others.

That's what the greatest musicians have been doing for a century now, a century during which Mahler's music gradually but progressively came to be as celebrated as it is by audiences today. Over the pages that follow, we reprint some of the most illuminating interviews our writers have conducted with the leading authorities on Mahler's works, and in which they share their journeys. What strikes me as I read them is just how personal their answers are; this isn't music about which you can be detached, and analysis – of which you'll find plenty – only gets you so far. We also hear from some of *Gramophone*'s greatest writers as they respond – not always positively! – to what they hear, and leave you with recommended recordings to explore for yourselves. Preparing this special edition of *Gramophone* has been a real privilege – I hope you enjoy it.
martin.cullingford@ markallengroup.com

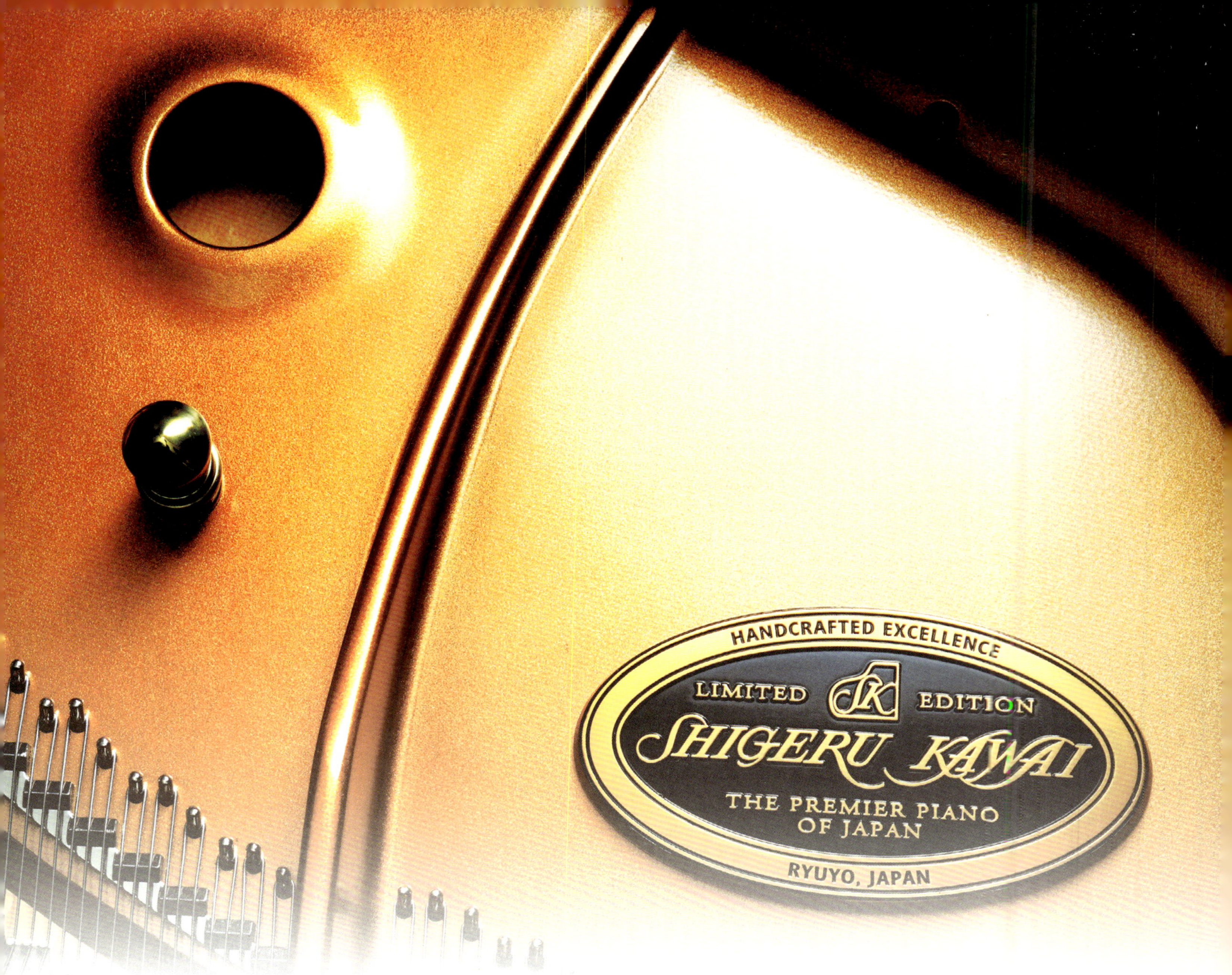

GRAMOPHONE PRESENTS...
MAHLER

GUSTAV MAHLER: *a life*

Driven by ambition and genius, Mahler's life was one of success and sadness. **Jeremy Nicholas** recounts the career of one of the greatest of all symphonists.

'**T**hin, fidgety, short, with a high, steep forehead, long dark hair and deeply penetrating bespectacled eyes' – that was how the conductor Bruno Walter, Mahler's one-time assistant, described him. He was also sadistic, a manic-depressive, an egomaniac, one of music's great despots, a neurotic with a mother fixation (according to Freud, who analysed him) and undoubtedly a genius. As with his music, people either loved him or hated him. 'The dedicated Mahlerians,' wrote Harold Schonberg, 'regard [those who dislike his music] the way St Paul regarded the Heathen. It is hard to think of a composer who arouses equal loyalty. The worship of Mahler amounts almost to a religion … Mahler's [music] stirs something imbedded in the subconscious and his admirers approach him mystically.'

A DIFFICULT CHILDHOOD

His tragic childhood stalked him for the whole of his life. His grandmother had been a ribbon seller, going from house to house selling her wares; his father had transcended these humble origins and was the owner of a small brandy distillery, married to the daughter of a wealthy soap manufacturer. It was an ill-tempered, badly matched marriage, one where the young Mahler frequently witnessed the brutality and abuse meted out on a long-suffering mother by an ambitious father. Of their 12 children, five died in infancy of diphtheria; Mahler's beloved younger brother Ernst died from hydrocardia aged

12; his oldest sister died of a brain tumour after a brief, unhappy marriage; another sister was subject to fantasies that she was dying; another brother was a simpleton in his youth and a forger in his adult life while yet another, Otto, a humble musician, committed suicide rather than accept the mediocrity that fate had assigned him.

When he was six, Mahler discovered a piano in the attic of his grandmother's house. Four years later he gave his first solo piano recital and aged 15 he enrolled at the Vienna Conservatoire. Here he not only developed as a pianist but won prizes for his compositions and discovered a talent for conducting. His professors noticed already the diligence and single-minded application that marked his professional career.

THE RISE OF THE CONDUCTOR

Within a short space of time, conducting and composition took over his entire life with a totality that left little time for anything else. Realising he could not make a living as a composer writing the sort of music he dreamt of, he took up conducting, first in Bad Hall, Austria, then a permanent position in Laibach (now Ljubljana). In 1882 he moved on to Olmütz and the next year to Vienna and Kassel – the traditional path of the aspiring conductor, moving from opera house to opera house, slowly building a reputation. In 1885 he was in Prague, then got a break in Leipzig working in harness with another brilliant young conductor, Arthur Nikisch. In one season Mahler conducted over 200 performances, apart from editing a Weber opera, falling in love with the wife of Weber's grandson and finishing his First Symphony. One thing that Mahler had in abundance all his life was energy, something he inherited from his mother. From his father came his drive and tenacity. His next step was to take over the Royal Opera House in Budapest from 1886 to 1888. Here he built up a fine company that won the praise of Brahms. When he moved on to Hamburg, Tchaikovsky himself allowed Mahler to conduct *Eugene Onegin* in his stead. 'The conductor here is not of the usual kind, but a man of genius who would give his life to conduct the first performance.' wrote Tchaikovsky.

OPERA AND STRICT DISCIPLINE

Then, in 1897, Mahler quietly converted to Catholicism. Shortly afterwards he got the position he yearned for. With the enthusiastic backing of Brahms, he became artistic director of the Vienna Opera and soon after of the Vienna Philharmonic. He remained at the opera for 10 years and in that decade raised its fortunes to a height which some say has never been equalled since. Here he reigned as king, choosing the repertory, singers, staging many of the productions himself and overseeing every aspect of life in the opera house; he engaged the great stage designer Alfred Roller and experimented with lighting and stage effects: this was Mahler's Wagnerian idealism put into practice – combining all the arts of the music theatre in a single man's

vision. Above all he moulded the orchestra into one of the finest in the world. The players respected him as a musician but hated him as a man, for Mahler's quest for perfection and intolerance of anything smacking of second-best was implemented by an uncompromising martinet. He was the sort who'd pick on individual players and reduce them to tears – he even disciplined the audience, forbidding latecomers to enter during the first act. But every work that he laid his hands on came up 'Herrlich wie am ersten Tag', as they say in Vienna – 'Glorious as on the first day' – and he did it all at a profit.

> *He reigned as king, choosing the repertory, singers, staging many of the productions himself and overseeing every aspect of life*

Inevitably, he made enemies. Not just because of his despotic methods and lack of social niceties – he had no small talk and was nervous among people – but because he was a Jew and a genius. He was merciless with his tongue, with his contempt for those who opposed him and with his anger at those who failed to match his standards.

MARRIAGE AND FATHERHOOD

In 1901 he married the step-daughter of the avant-garde Viennese artist Carl Moll, Alma Schindler. She was beautiful, well-read and a composer in her own right, having studied under Zemlinsky, Schoenberg's teacher. It was a remarkable marriage but one in which Mahler demanded complete freedom. His wife was to be mother, wife and

Mahler with his wife Alma, a composer in her own right

PHOTOGRAPHY: THE TULLY POTTER COLLECTION, LEBRECHT MUSIC ARTS / BRIDGEMAN IMAGES

Mahler at his desk; (below) the Vienna Opera House where he stayed for 10 years, raising its fortunes to a height which some say has never been equalled since

amanuensis; she was to give up her composing and be totally subservient to his whims. The first five years of his marriage saw Mahler at the height of his powers and at his happiest. He continued to compose as he had during the previous decade

> *Each symphony was vaster in scale than its predecessor; each one was met with hostility, misunderstanding and vituperation.*

in the one form to which he aspired and (to his austere way of thinking) in the purest, highest form of musical expression – the orchestral symphony. By 1906 he had completed the Fifth, Sixth and Seventh symphonies. Each one was vaster in scale than its predecessor; each one was met with hostility, misunderstanding and vituperation. Mahler was impervious to all around him, convinced that 'my time will come'.

GRIEF AND ILLNESS

Then personal tragedy hit him. One of his little daughters died from scarlet fever. Mahler went insane with grief and forever after carried around with him the guilt that he had been responsible in part for his child's death, guilt for tempting fate: in 1903 he had composed a set of songs using poems by Rückert entitled *Kindertotenlieder* – 'Songs on the Death of Children'.

In 1907 he decided to leave Vienna and, the same year, was told he had a serious heart condition. The remaining three years of his life were focused on America. He first went to the Metropolitan Opera for two full seasons. Indifferent performances and the presence of Arturo Toscanini led to friction and more unhappiness. Worse came when he took over the conductorship of the New York Philharmonic in 1909. The audience disliked him, the orchestra loathed him, the critics reached for their poisoned pens. The feeling was entirely mutual. The Philharmonic, in Mahler's words, was 'the true American orchestra – without talent and phlegmatic'. The orchestra board was dominated by 10 wealthy American women. 'You cannot imagine what Mr Mahler has suffered,' Alma Mahler told the press. 'In Vienna my husband was all-powerful. Even the Emperor did not dictate to him, but in New York he had 10 ladies ordering him around like puppet.'

In September 1910 he was in Munich to conduct the premiere of his mammoth Eighth Symphony, which met with overwhelming success, one of the few triumphs he ever witnessed as a composer. He returned to New York in late 1910 but early the next year collapsed under the strain of 65 rigorous concerts. An infection set in which serum treatments in Paris did nothing to alleviate. In a nursing home in Vienna, he died of pneumonia aged 50. **G**

A *Mahlerian* ODYSSEY

*In 2010 we embarked on one of our most ambitious interview projects to date
– to talk to 11 leading Mahler conductors about one symphony - plus
Das Lied von der Erde - each. Michael McManus took up the challange*

Eleven symphonic works. Eleven articles. Eleven leading conductors. Ever a man ahead of his time, Gustav Mahler played into the hands of an era that trades on anniversaries by dying a few weeks short of his 51st birthday. The 2010-11 concert season therefore forms a neat arch from the 150th anniversary of his birth to the 100th anniversary of his death. The musical schedules of the world are consequently packed to the brim with Mahler projects, Mahler celebrations and Mahler odysseys. These 11 maestros' articles gave me my own personal odyssey. Some of the conductors I knew already, others not, but it was crucial they should all trust me as I sought to meld their (sometimes highly) individual contributions into a coherent series. I cannot imagine there has been a larger single project in the history of *Gramophone*.

The odyssey even took me to Leipzig, for a stunning concert by the Gewandhaus Orchestra that ended with Mahler's First Symphony and a riveting meeting with Riccardo Chailly. In truth my odyssey began long ago, when a teacher called John Falconer used the last hour before the autumn half term in 1983 for one of his customary attempts to instil some culture into his restless charges. He deserves recognition: he has cost me thousands of pounds and opened up for me a world of infinite reward. He played the first three movements of Mahler's First Symphony. I was hooked. Within a year I had acquired numerous LPs of Mahler's music and within two years I had heard and met Claudio Abbado, Klaus Tennstedt and Leonard Bernstein, as they paid their homages to the Mahlerian canon. I used to think I would grow out of Mahler, as I hoped to grow out of teenage angst. It has never happened. As these pieces demonstrate, there is more to Mahler than highly subjective projections of anxiety and grotesquerie. The most serious and

accomplished musicians of our time continue to devote themselves to solving the existential and musical conundrums he created.

Audiences have their own reasons for loving the music of Mahler but conductors have a strong affinity with him because they see him as one of their own – as a leading member of the Conductors' Union. His concerns about transparency of sound, his reworking of the music for different orchestras and different acoustics, his concern over dynamic markings – a century after his death, all these qualities are commending Mahler to a new generation of conductors, which makes taking the views of some of today's finest Mahler maestros about 'one of their own' all the more fascinating.

It is a shame that Chailly's insights into the First Symphony and almost everyone's baleful observations about the Seventh had to end up on the cutting room floor. I grew more fascinated by that ugly duckling of the series as my odyssey went on, making a point of asking everyone about it. Far from expressing surprise at Valery Gergiev's fear of the piece, they all agreed with him. Mariss Jansons is pleased with his new recording of it, he says, because he and the piece have now come to an arrangement, an understanding. No one else may like what happens when they get together, but they are OK.

I am smiling as I type. For all my life I have loved music and admired musicians. Above all else, my companions on that journey have been Mahler's symphonies. I don't know why, but to use Mariss Jansons's metaphor, when I listen to them it is like looking into the mirror. I find myself, with all my moods, quirks and imperfections. This odyssey has greatly deepened my appreciation of works I already knew and loved so well. I hope you will enjoy reading these pieces as much as I enjoyed collecting and editing them. A little odyssey for everyone, perhaps.

Sir Charles Mackerras

on the work that started as a Titanic tone poem

This symphony was the one to which Mahler attached the greatest importance – he conducted more performances himself of this than he did of any of his other, later works. Originally it had five movements but the original second movement, 'Blumine', was soon cut out because it didn't really match thematically with the rest of the work. The other four movements are united by a descending fourth motif – it runs right through all of them.

The opening of the piece is a huge nature description, with that long, long octave played by the strings, then the first appearance of the descending fourth motif in the woodwind. The sounds of nature – cuckoos – and the quick fanfares from the offstage hunting horns are completely unrelated to the general tempo. When the movement hits a faster tempo we have the first reference to one of the *Wayfarer* songs – 'Ging heut' Morgen übers Feld' – which provides the main theme of the *allegro* part of the movement. Two more songs from that cycle of four are quoted subsequently, one in the Trio of the *Scherzo* and one in the middle of the extraordinary third movement. The third movement has a lot of cheeky, almost evil, music in it. The harmonies are grotesque and the orchestration is very harsh. I believe Mahler had in his mind the funeral cortège of a hunter, with animals walking behind the coffin, rejoicing in the fact he has died. Very unusually, the movement begins with a solo double bass, playing a theme we know as 'Frère Jacques'. This turns into a 'round', as the instruments come in one after another. On top of that there is a peculiar parody on the oboe, then on the E flat clarinet. Again, the tone is harsh, almost ugly. It's an extremely strange movement which was violently attacked by the critics at the time, especially in Vienna, for they believed such things were not appropriate in a symphony. They could be very conservative and believed a symphony must be a very classical piece of music, within which any description of nature or actions was unsuitable. César Franck was even denounced for using a cor anglais in his symphony.

For the last movement an even bigger orchestra is required. It takes us from Inferno to Paradise, starting off in an infernal way, using that motif, up or down a fourth. Sometimes the motif is used as a menacing call but later on it is used as a soft, gentle, noble theme going into a chorale theme, which Mahler uses very cleverly. The first time it comes, it is stated very softly in the brass, which sometimes are muted. Mahler was always changing the orchestration in his pieces, and there are versions of this piece that have the horns muted in this passage and also others where they are open horns, playing very quietly. It is a most remarkable sound. The call starts off in C major then suddenly shifts up a tone to D major, the main key of the symphony. It is one of the great moments of the symphony. At the very end the chorale theme comes back and Mahler writes that the horn-players should all stand up and make the greatest possible noise. This effect is used more often in jazz bands these

days. I once conducted the piece at the Aspen Festival in Colorado, where a horn colloquy was also going on. In the final rehearsal and the performance we had about 30 horns playing this in unison.

The music gets faster and faster, leading to a tremendous climax, as we go through F minor to D flat major, via C major to D major. On our recording, to double the horns, we had our eight horn players re-record the passage, so they could double themselves up.

He seemed always to be changing his mind about how things should go

I very much like Bruno Walter's recording of the piece. He knew Mahler and understood what his music really meant. He brings out all the beauties and subtleties of Mahler's music. There is also a very interesting interview with him on the CD, in which he talks about how Mahler behaved with orchestras. He seemed always to be changing his mind about how things should go and kept on altering the orchestration in order to make the music clearer. Mahler wrote huge works but he also had a kind of mania about clarity. Everything had to be audible. He wanted the listener to hear every instrument and relish every detail.

▶ Sir Charles Mackerras's recording of Mahler's Symphony No 1 with the Royal Liverpool Philharmonic Orchestra is available as a download from Warner Classics

Sir Charles Mackerras: relishing Mahler's multiple horn parts

Mariss Jansons

on Mahler's mighty Resurrection Symphony

Mahler is one of the most significant composers in the world, in all of history. The questions he sets out in his works are enormous. Why is his music so popular? It's because in his music there is everything. It's universal. You find nature, sarcasm, love, hatred, the grotesque, tragedy and comedy. Like finding his own face in a mirror, every listener can find something to relate to, a bridge into the content of the music. There is something for everyone – and people find echoes of their own fears, doubts and suffering.

The Second Symphony is typical of how he puts for himself and for listeners the big questions. What is life? Why are we living? What will be next? Is there an afterlife? The piece questions a lot, then he describes the mood of the human soul and in the last movement he answers the questions he raises in the first movement. His answer is the *Auferstehung* – the resurrection – because he believes we live many, many lives. That first movement is a funeral march for the hero of the First Symphony and that heroic element is very typical of Mahler, in almost all his symphonies. Who is the hero? Man, Mahler himself. In this respect Shostakovich is very close to him, for Shostakovich is another composer who represents himself as the hero in his own music. Mahler never observes from a distance. He is 'inside' every situation. He wrote at the time that he imagined himself in his own coffin. Then we go through the moments of life. The second movement recalls nice, beautiful moments. These are nice memories. The third movement raises more philosophical questions. It's based on Mahler's own song about St Anthony of Padua preaching to the fishes, which of course is really addressed to human beings. The movement is full of phantoms and darkness. The fishes listen, then they forget. They don't learn. This is Mahler's view of human beings. The conclusion is that you can tell people what you want. You can preach, you can tell people how to live, what not to do, but the reaction is nothing. Satire, sarcasm and irony are there in the form he used, and Mahler believed only a few people would understand his message.

The conclusion is very modern. In the 21st century our technical development is so advanced and our scientists have achieved so much, so our spiritual development too should be at such a very high level, but the development of the heart and soul is far behind. People can fly to the moon but spiritually they are at a low level, because we don't learn from our mistakes and we don't take care of our spiritual development. It's interesting that he should put such a light melody – almost a street melody – into such a serious and philosophical symphony, but that is typical of his use of the grotesque. In the fourth movement, 'Urlicht', we are dealing with very deep music from the soul, and the love of God. This should be sung in a childlike voice, to capture the innocence and pure soul of a child. This was Mahler's credo – true honesty can be found in how a child reacts. The fifth movement is an incredible fantasy. There is a

Mariss Jansons: Mahler in the mirror

frightful, terrifying march of the dead, then comes the big call – God and judgement. This is – or should be – the softest entrance by a choir in all musical literature. The chorus speaks with God and prays, with a special optimism. Here is the answer. Everybody is waiting for God's judgement, then it doesn't happen. In that movement, everyone is equal. There is no judgement in the end for him. Everything is calm. This is very special – you are in another world already, and you start a new,

> *This should be the softest choral entrance in musical literature*

different life, like a child. Such music could only be written by a genius and only Mozart could compose this quickly.

The latest edition from Universal corrects another 500 or so mistakes. There are instances where it is possible Mahler himself made a mistake, which every human being can do. There is no clear evidence either way and only Mahler could have given a definitive answer. Even in Beethoven there are mistakes and my old teacher used to say 'we don't correct this, because we are happy to repeat the mistake of a genius'. It's really important to establish what Mahler really wanted, but he was polishing this symphony right up until the last performance he gave of it, in Paris in 1910. We can take account of the changes he made but with Mahler there are no ultimate answers.

▶ Mariss Jansons's Mahler Symphony No 2 recordings include with the Oslo Philharmonic Orchestra (Chandos) , with the Bavarian Radio Symphony Orchestra (BR Klassik) and with the Royal Concertgebouw Orchestra (RCO Live)

Lorin Maazel

on the depiction of innocence in Mahler's choral Third

I don't believe in verbalising music. Music is a language of its own, which exists because you can express in it what cannot be expressed in words. Look how Berlioz failed – and he was a marvellous stylist, a master of the French language. Great writers such as Thomas Mann, Aldous Huxley and George Bernard Shaw have all tried. They wrote fantastic prose; but for a musician, what music is about cannot be adequately described in words. At the end of a performance, anything that is said can shatter that very, very delicate, vulnerable shell that has been created during the performance.

Mahler suffers greatly from being subjected to sentimental mediocrities, with heart-on-sleeve performances that stretch, pull and exaggerate the music. The inner balance of the music is forever being challenged, much to its detriment. So many interpreters see in Mahler a self-pitying person, grappling with the monsters of destiny and so forth. This is nonsense. He wrote music the way he heard it, because he had to write it. He tried to find the right notes for images of a musical nature.

If you eliminate the sentimental, which I don't think has any place in his music, there are certainly elements that one can characterise. There is the martial, the funereal, the bucolic, the insouciant, the light-hearted and the hopeful. He was a hopeful person, and the end of this symphony, in D major, is in a sense trying to say, 'I, Gustav, like everybody else, have looked into the abyss and what I see there is frightening, but now I must reaffirm my belief in life'. It is very much like Beethoven, who was a great reaffirmer. He looks to that moment in his symphonies where he can say, 'yes, what I have depicted – voids, abysses, chasms – does exist, but I believe, somehow, in some dimension, it's going to work out for the better'.

The reversal comes in the last movement of the Ninth Symphony. He knew he was dying. He has used up all his positive energy and it is aggressive. He is angry, shaking his fist at destiny, before finally accepting his fate. In the first movement of the Third Symphony there are three elements – martial, bucolic and insouciant. His tongue-in-cheek writing is so undervalued. He had a marvellous sense of humour, there's no doubt about it, poking fun, very often at himself. The second movement floats along, with little filigree semiquavers and sweet, innocent, semi-naive tunes, but these tunes are not really simplistic. They are deliberately stated as directly as possible in order to create a contrast with moments when he gets angry about things or feels he has to make a statement.

Probably the most delightful music in the symphony comes in the third movement. It is full of lightness and sweetness. The posthorn solo is so typical of Mahler's love of calls. The calls he heard as a child in what used to be Czechoslovakia played an important role in his musical development. He created an aesthetic around the call that is his own. The fourth movement is a world unto itself. The fifth movement – 'Bimm Bamm' – again contains music you might call simplistic. It isn't. He had

the courage of great composers, to place very direct, uncomplicated music within a larger, more sophisticated frame. Both he and Beethoven had that extraordinary courage. One should be not be writing to please one's colleagues but in response to an inner imperative. The text here is incredibly innocent and yet also highly sophisticated, because it lays the groundwork for the last movement, with its interruptions of faraway sounds, heard through the ether, as though from another world. In the end all of that is banished, the great tune comes back and we feel good about life. It reaffirms the meaning of life and the significance of our having lived.

Mahler had the courage of great composers

As with Beethoven, each movement can stand on its own. That they are strung together to form a symphony is almost accidental. Mahler was a doubter – as all great thinkers are – and wrestled with the problems of eternity and the afterlife. These problems cannot be resolved to anyone's total satisfaction. There is a lot of fist-shaking at destiny on the part of the Beethovens and Mahlers, as if to say, 'it may be that you will have the final word, but I am still alive and kicking and have a few things to say'.

▶ Lorin Maazel s recordings of Mahler's Symphony No 3 include with the Vienna Philharmonic Orchestra on Sony, with the Philharmonia on Signum Classics, and a live New York Philharmonic performance available as a download

Lorin Maazel: eliminating the sentimental

David Zinman

on the symphony he considers Mahler's most perfect

Mahler came to regard the Fourth Symphony as the closing work in a quartet of works, although there are still seeds of it left in the Fifth Symphony. The music in the Fourth is all derived from the wonderful song in the last movement. He had been thinking about that song – 'The Heavenly Life' – for a long time and within that song he had found the seeds for many ideas he had already used in the Third Symphony. Something about that song really spoke to him and obsessed him. In fact he originally included the song itself in the Third Symphony, but then he replaced it with the Bell Song – 'What the Child Tells Me' – immediately before the closing *Adagio*. This song had been hanging around for a long time and it spawned both the Third and the Fourth symphonies.

Consequently, the Fourth is very unusual, in that it was composed backwards, with the last movement composed first and everything else in the piece then relating thematically to this heavenly finale. Maybe the first three movements therefore describe a heavenly life on Earth. The first movement could describe a man with much cheerfulness and delight in his life – all touchingly human. Then comes the second movement, with Death striking up a dance. This is a very childish view of Death and the fears that we have, with Death fiddling very wildly on an out-of-tune violin. Then the third movement – the most wonderful movement of the piece – is like a very beautiful painting of St Ursula, who appears by name in the finale. So the entire piece is very much a continuation of the Third Symphony, with all those programmatic titles for movements – 'What the Flowers Tell Me', 'What God Tells Me', 'What Nature Tells Me' and so forth.

What makes the piece so wonderful is its classical form – only four movements, played by a very small orchestra, without trombones and tuba. It is in a way an odd one out, providing contrast but also continuation. These little motifs that appear in the Third and the Fourth symphonies are very beautifully developed. For me, it is the one truly perfect symphony he ever wrote, and also the most misunderstood, because he tried to go back to a world of purity and naivety, where music is just music and music speaks directly, just as a child speaks. I think that there's a lot written about his ideas about the importance of naivety in life.

This is the most folk-like of his works and I think it's my favourite of them all. The first recording I got to know was the amazing Szell recording – I also like his Sixth Symphony very much – but I think my first recollection of hearing Mahler was hearing Mitropoulos rehearsing in New York. Even though the last movement of the Ninth is something I shall always cherish and adore, the Fourth is something even greater for me. The appearance of Heaven at the end is so wonderful, and he makes such a noise with such small means.

What is very fascinating in this symphony is the manner in which he uses *Klangfarben*: for the first time the voices come out

The slow movement is just universal, timeless and beautiful

of one another, and various distances of voice and sound are written into the piece. There is such sophistication, and he was at his most sophisticated as a conductor at that time. It's a study for a composer, to see how Mahler balances everything and ensures that all the detail comes out. He was beset with problems at his opera house at the time, but then he happened to meet Alma who, let's say, changed him for a time.

There are many attempts at this symphony, and the hardest aspect is finding the ideal voice from the singer in the last movement. That's very hard, because some who have a wonderful top have a feeble low register and some who have a feeble top have a wonderful low register. The Bernstein recording tries a boy soprano and that doesn't work either. It's one of those things where you want to get to the core of it and find the perfect solution and you never quite do. This symphony is a very special work and I will carry on attempting to get to its heart for as long as I live. There is something about that slow movement which is just universal, timeless and beautiful. It's perfect – the one truly still centre that Mahler found.

▶ David Zinman's recording of Mahler's Symphony No 4 with the Zürich Tonhalle Orchestra is available on RCA Red Seal

David Zinman: finding a favourite in the Fourth

Sir Simon Rattle

on the symphony made famous by a film

The Fifth was almost the last Mahler symphony I came to grips with. I always found it peculiarly difficult. I first heard it when my father went to America in the early 1960s and came back with a copy of Bruno Walter's really astonishing recording with the New York Philharmonic. It's the fastest performance you could ever hear and I wasn't to realise then that Walter had very much his own performing ideas. My first impression when I subsequently heard it live was that it didn't sound like the same piece at all. At first, as a teenager and a young man, I couldn't understand why the piece as a whole seemed to keep failing, but that is exactly the point. This is a piece desperately longing for a conclusion and one attempt after another fails. You must hear it through to the end; it was a totally new type of symphony.

Before my inaugural concert in Berlin I had conducted the symphony quite a lot, but it seemed the ideal piece for that special occasion, in combination with Tom Adès's *Asyla*. The two pieces possess similar wildness. The music itself seems to be trying to find a way out of a predicament, and that was something entirely new in the symphonic form. Rather as in *Tristan und Isolde*, the final reaching of the goal is put off and put off. It's really in three movements, not five. The opening two movements start with a funeral march, which is interrupted by eruptions of rage and anger. These two movements together represent an attempt to deal with the fact of death, and an attempt to break away from darkness.

I am very grateful to have been able to hear Mahler's piano roll recording of the first movement. You can hear him swinging every rhythm in the Viennese style, which is so different from the German tradition. Of all Mahler's symphonies, this is the one most rooted in Viennese rhythms. This makes it much tougher to play. You don't play what you see in the score. You have to play what it means.

The middle movement is really one huge development section. The first horn part in this movement is written as a separate part, for a solo, obbligato horn, so I do believe the player should be placed separately from the horn section. Otherwise the orchestra ends up waiting for the horn. This seems to be something Mahler did and it turns it into a different piece, accentuating the dialogues between the horn and the strings. There is a dangerous, dark side to this movement too, despite all the exuberance, as the Viennese waltz finally loses its innocence.

By the time I was a teenager, performances of the *Adagietto* were down to half-tempo. This must be the only time in musical history that a film, *Death in Venice*, has affected how people perform a piece of classical music. Let's hope there will soon be a generation that can put Dirk Bogarde out of its mind. Leonard Bernstein was a great, great Mahler conductor but I do believe he misread Mahler's intentions in this movement. It's Mahler's declaration of love for his wife Alma, sung with

Sir Simon Rattle: getting to grips with the Fifth

words that cannot be written. It is also the basis of the finale, so these two movements also are really one long movement. The themes come back, in different forms and shapes. The finale has its shadows but it's really the last symphonic movement Mahler wrote where there is complete joy – unalloyed exaltation.

Mahler tried to repeat this in the Seventh Symphony but by then he was a very different person. It's a great tribute to Haydn, the other great composer who could capture good humour in profound music. It was not so long since Brahms's Fourth

I do believe Bernstein misread Mahler's intentions in the Adagietto

Symphony and many people were still amazed, almost insulted, by a symphony that ended tragically. The critic Hanslick likened that piece to being hit over the head for 45 minutes by two very intelligent men. That is what Mahler was up against.

Mahler was trying to find another style in this piece. He had recently devoted himself to the study of counterpoint and he found the scoring of this piece very hard. He revised it many times. I recently conducted *Tristan* in Vienna and the librarian loaned me Mahler's copy of the score for the first week of rehearsals. There were so many detailed markings – he really was the most intensely practical musician – that it was like having Mahler in the room with me.

▶ Sir Simon Rattle's recording of Mahler's Symphony No 5 with the Berlin Philharmonic Orchestra is available on Warner Classics

Christoph Eschenbach

on the controversies of the 'tragic' Symphony

The Fifth and Seventh symphonies both contain glorious statements of joy, and Mahler evidently felt he needed to write something between those pieces that gave a view on the tragic, negative side of life. It is a perfect piece for live recording, because then you really have everyone on the edge of their seats. It is an amazing symphony, so full of power, and the first movement in particular blows you away, thanks to that march rhythm right at the outset. The struggle from that A minor opening to the conclusion of the movement in A major is really titanic, with moments of extraordinary contemplation on the way – marked grazioso. Very characteristic is Mahler's use of the cowbells – they speak of loneliness, of mountains, of being with nature. The last shimmer of life comes not from man but from animals.

In my live performances and my recordings I have the *Scherzo* second, for two reasons. First of all I think it works in terms of the emotional logic of the piece. The demonic dance of the *Scherzo* carries on the sheer power of the opening movement. The march rhythm of the first movement is inverted – the emphasis is now on the upbeat and the switch to a 3/4 rhythm represents another attitude, a rebellion against the 4/4 of the preceding movement. The *sforzatos* on the third beat make this march a double opponent of the one that went before. There is a second reason too. To my mind, there is a crucial tonal clue in the fact the *Andante* ends in E flat major, which should be followed by the parallel, related key of C minor – the beginning of the finale.

We don't know for sure why Mahler changed his mind about the order of these movements. Numerous authorities have written on the matter but there is no definitive answer. My belief is there may have been practical reasons. Orchestras at that time may well have struggled to play this music, and to have two such unrelentingly powerful movements together may have been too much for them technically. Mahler may also have been influenced by advice from someone else, as Bruckner so often was, though Bruckner was of course tormented by self-doubt, which was a problem Mahler never had. I just believe the original way is preferable. The *Scherzo* is such a rebellious and rough piece, with a Trio that comes twice and has the unusual marking *altväterisch* – like an elderly father. I imagine an old man, uttering opinions and dancing awkwardly. There is also that marking of *grazioso* – implying a certain sympathy with old age.

Mahler wrote only wonderful slow movements but this *Andante* is one of the most wonderful. There are such beautiful, *cantabile* moments, especially when the music slips into C major and everything seems to stand still. No one can breathe any more. Even the passionate climax with the cowbells is *cantabile*. Everything is wonderfully balanced and the finale emerges naturally from this, with its unusually long introduction before the main subject appears.

There are also discussions about the third hammer-blow. I

Christoph Eschenbach: trying to solve the Sixth's paradoxes

fully accept Mahler's decision to leave it out. If you look at the score carefully, the two other hammer-blows are each followed by an incredible struggle. You are hit by a hammer – by destiny – and it is a phenomenon from outside our realm of understanding.

It is an amazing symphony, so full of power

Twice we make every effort to struggle back against Fate. I believe Mahler excised the third hammer-blow because he didn't want to make a final, pessimistic statement, which might have been interpreted as the death of symphonic creation in general. He already had it in mind to write a Seventh Symphony, which would be followed by the glorious Eighth, *Das Lied von der Erde*, the Ninth. So this was not the end.

Shostakovich wrote highly personal music too but he never captured all the facets of life in the same way. Many people wonder why Mahler wrote such tragic music when he was at the height of his powers. We can never understand the soul and thought-processes of such a genius but I believe this music demonstrates how full of force and energy he was. For him, this was the right time to write this music. Furthermore, he had reasons to sense a not-so-happy future ahead. He had already experienced some big fights at the Vienna State Opera and anti-semitism had begun to manifest itself. Out of all that burst this volcano of tragic force.

▶ Christoph Eschenbach's recording of Mahler's Symphony No 6 with the Philadelphia Orchestra is available on Ondine

PHOTOGRAPHY: LUCA PIVA

Valery Gergiev

on the work considered the cycle's most problematic

Conducting Mahler's Symphony No 7 was for me the scariest project of all. Listening to historical recordings of this piece 20 or even 30 years ago did not inspire me to think I wanted to conduct it. Listening to symphonies such as No 1 or No 5 as a student, it's far easier to understand the link with previous symphonic experience. Both No 7 and No 8 are especially scary for anyone who wants to record them as part of a lasting legacy. This symphony doesn't need rescuing as such, but it does not defend itself easily in the manner, say, of Symphony No 5 or Symphony No 2. They are shaped very well. They are organic and simply work, with ecstatic endings following a great build-up.

It has a strange, unusual shape, which is the key to it.

The Seventh I conducted first with the Rotterdam orchestra and then with the Mariinsky orchestra. I felt far from 100 per cent clear and far from 100 per cent prepared – not because I hadn't attempted to prepare myself but because the piece is so enigmatic. It has a strange, unusual shape, which is the key to it. You have to work very hard at shaping it. This is not really about tempi – it's more about working with light and shadow and different levels of power. It is essential not to tire your public too early. You start to feel exhausted yourself and worry about the orchestra too. The first movement is so immense you really need to know what to do with the second movement. It's not just about tempo, I repeat – it's about maintaining a sense of direction, line and proportion. Intuition plays an essential role. If it was just a question of technique, there would have been hundreds of successful interpretations of this music. If there is *Nachtmusik*, my view is that there must also be counterbalance, with a lot of sun and daylight and straightforward energy. Some should sound jubilant, but the balance is between different images that are peculiar to this symphony. I started to believe in it only after the live recording with the LSO. Having decided, together with the musicians and the management, that we were going to perform this entire cycle across one season, I was not allowed to think any work was not as good as the others. So I spent the maximum amount of time on this one, trying to make it work, focusing efforts on individual elements within the symphony. It just had to sound right.

I have to shape some vast pieces, in the opera house especially, and I have learnt the importance of shape. As a rule, you certainly don't expect to record No 7 more than once. The symphony is full of repetitions, especially in the Rondo-Finale, and it's crucial to decide how aggressive and bombastic you make that movement. Sometimes you have a sombre face, sometimes you have a smile. I took certain risks and urged the musicians to think again about the character of each movement, especially that last one. We know sometimes one composer can change dramatically from one composition to another. It is more tricky when a single composition has these divisions within it – for instance, *Siegfried* was composed at different

times and the two *Nachtmusik* episodes in this piece were written a year before the rest of the symphony – but for me that was not an obstacle. For me the terrible thought was that we might play, say, the first five or eight minutes of the final movement and I would find myself thinking, 'it's over, it didn't work again'. That's a very fearful thought, because a conductor has to be his own fiercest critic. You have to feel it's moving, becoming more and more focused on one goal, namely the end of the piece. You must feel a natural sense, like climbing Everest, and you mustn't break the natural line. In that finale, you have to be seriously focused on a dangerously slow tempo, with all those solos for unusual instruments. The temptation is always to exaggerate.

I have been conducting for 30 years and, even so, in this music I have to call upon all my resources and all my experience. This sort of orchestral challenge can destroy anyone. In symphonies Nos 7 and 8 I was charged with extra excitement, but also extra fear, like walking on a high wire. One wrong movement and you go down. I dread this symphony. If any conductor says No 7 is a rather dangerous composition, I will just say 'yes, yes, yes!'

▶ Valery Gergiev's recording of Mahler's Symphony No 7 with the London Symphony Orchestra is available on LSO Live

Valery Gergiev: dreads the danger of the Seventh

Michael Tilson Thomas

on the so-called Symphony of a Thousand

In the Seventh Symphony, Mahler was pursuing strategies of discontinuity – harmonically, polyphonically and schematically – notably in the last movement. So with this mastery of turning on a dime fully at his command, now he sets off to write this big new piece. The big problem with the whole piece is that the forces are so vast that it's very easy for it all to become quite thick and quite fat. Considering the wonderful, mercurial wit and humour, this is the kind of piece that requires rapier thrusts, whereas the actual forces you have to work with are more like a blunt instrument.

The first movement is a big exposition, including perhaps the longest, most continuous burst of up-tempo music Mahler ever wrote. The imagery is of cloudscapes and bursts of light and little ensembles of heavenly hosts. There is one slower, more dirge-like contrast with sly, expressive violin solos but this burst of exultant energy is combined with contrapuntal mastery that makes it extraordinary to think Mahler once admitted he hardly ever turned up to his counterpoint classes and just squeaked by with passing grades. In this movement, the challenge is to get this wonderfully inspiring and entertaining music, so inherently full of surprise and brilliance, to sound with enough clarity and enough shape. You have to lighten things up and balance them very carefully. Otherwise you lose the wonderful way the vocal group is used to create very particular colours and the organist underscores certain, craggy themes. There is a quality of astonishment, too, as each key area is introduced – harking right back to those dramatic modulations in the First Symphony.

The piece proceeds through an astonishing coda, in which the tempo doubles. It's important the first movement should end with that breathless feeling, because we are about to turn a corner into another language altogether, with a remarkably restrained and extremely mournful, simple little tune in the winds, which is duly transformed into the radiant, major-key power of the Chorus Mysticus at the end. The harmony here is pungent, with little shades of nuance the players must achieve without upsetting the overall mood of hushed sadness. Then there is a sudden outburst of sound, with the orchestra playing absolutely full out, especially the horns, the cellos and others in the middle range of the orchestra. The mood is reminiscent of the raw emotion in parts of the slow movements in the Fourth and Sixth symphonies and we are on the road to the 'Abschied' in *Das Lied von der Erde*.

Then we have all the high jinks. If you want to appreciate fully the wry genius of Mahler in approaching this text, you just have to compare this with Schumann's reverential, lyrical setting of the same words. Mahler observes this with all the observational skill of a genre painter. Pater Ecstaticus is this great, enamoured, swashbuckling character, then Pater Profundus is the nearest thing Mahler ever wrote to a Wagner villain role, very much in the Alberich or Hagen mould. There's great wildness in the music. Then we are into the first

The forces you have to work with are like a blunt instrument

appearance of the angels and a kind of street music. These are not delicate little choristers he's asking for here – these are really street kids, taunting us with edgy irreverence. The music in this section is full of humour. It's like a game, full of frothy laughter and, after the angels and all the tremolos and trills and the sense of an electric, atmospheric event, comes Dr Marianus.

This is a classic example of where many performances go off the rails, because it's clear from Mahler's markings that, whatever tempo you're at as you come out of the angel ensemble, you must slow down gradually to the final hymn of Marianus ('Jungfrau…'). That leads us beyond the realm of words and into the 'Ewig Weibliche' theme, with harmoniums and harps. It is the most daringly sentimental evocation of salon music he ever used.

Then we come to my favourite part of the piece – the ensemble with the great sinner ladies. Suddenly we are up a mountain, at a tea party with these three martyr ladies – these three old broads, who obviously get together regularly and reminisce about their wonderful old days of suffering. The twinkle in the music tells us their memories are predominantly happy – oh, remember those jackals? – and they sing a spectacular canon. It's so charming and they are so enjoying one another's company. Then comes Gretchen, bright and innocent, with another clear instruction to sing quietly and affectingly. This symphony mustn't degenerate into a *Schreifest*. Ultimately the message of the piece is that the majesty of this simple girl's love matches the entire majesty of Heaven.

▶ Michael Tilson Thomas's recording of Mahler's Symphony No 8 with the San Francisco Symphony Orchestra is available on the San Francisco Symphony label

Michael Tilson Thomas: marshalling Mahler's massive forces

Kent Nagano

on Mahler's Lieder-Symphony, the Song of the Earth

What exactly is this piece? A symphony? Some kind of opera? I don't find it so much of an opera. It has a special conception and it doesn't fit into any familiar structure. It is strongly tied to Lieder, with texts that have lyrical, *cantabile* characteristics. It is a Lieder-Symphony. People had been asking, is the symphony still possible? Is it still relevant? Mahler's response was to create a refined new form, using the idea of Lieder. In previous Mahler symphonies associated with Lieder, such as the Third and Fourth, only part of the work had taken the form of a Lied, but here all six movements do.

The texts are from outside the Western tradition and strongly influenced by China, which makes the music naturally confrontational. The Eighth Symphony was already an opening to such cultural confrontation, with its two very disparate parts. Part 1 is liturgical, based upon Christian texts, whereas Part 2 is spiritual-secular, with man presented as an individual. This all rather mirrors the old idea of a world divided between an *Abendland* – where the sun is setting – and a *Morgenland*, where it then rises. This tension was especially fashionable as the 19th century turned into the 20th. Many writers were influenced by it. Goethe – a major European figure – had strong ties with the East. Rückert, whose texts Mahler also set, was a professor of Oriental languages as well as a writer, with a profound interest in the Orient. Schiller wrote a version of *Turandot* and, in France, Ravel and Debussy had an obvious fascination with Asia. Throughout all his music, Mahler was striving to find something universal, avoiding exotic stereotypes such as *Butterfly*. In the words he sets in *Das Lied von der Erde*, he is once again seeking loftier ideas in words, and his music again takes us through numerous important aspects of the lifetime of a man or mankind. In the First Symphony we have nature and the sense of wandering. The Second brings resurrection and in the Third, nature again, while the Fourth contrasts the *Irdisch* with the *Himmlisch* and the Seventh deals with the idea of destiny. Highlighted through all his great works is this sense of the phases of life, a single human being's struggle with identity, all ultimately culminating in a confrontation with death. In *Das Lied* he explores these ideas from the perspective of a world that includes both the Orient and the Occident. The result is a breakthrough in what we mean by 'symphony'. Mahler used Asian texts as an opening, not a limitation, combining them with mainly but not exclusively Western harmonies and structures. The world is eternal, he tells us, but the individual will perish. It is one the most progressive of his works and takes us forward into the 20th century.

Mahler did rewrite and revise his scores, so would he have rewritten or revised this piece had he lived to rehearse it and hear it performed? We cannot be certain but I am not sure he would have changed it much. There is a lot of *forte*, especially in the first song, but *forte* is not all about decibel output. It can

Kent Nagano: seeking transparency in the orchestration

mean stronger rather than louder and, in any case, most of the music in this piece does not consist of *tutti*. There are long, delicate passages of chamber music. Mahler would have reworked the piece but I am not sure the result would have been a smaller orchestra or a slimming-down of the orchestration. This was written at the time of *Gurrelieder* and after the operas of Wagner, so Mahler knew the benefits of a broad orchestral palette, with the colours and textures it makes possible.

His music takes us through aspects of the lifetime of a man or mankind

Our recording is drawn from live performances and I asked the orchestra to play very transparently. This doesn't mean light dynamics from the point of view of the listener, but I did want to avoid congestion. My choice of a baritone (Christian Gerhaher) rather than a mezzo was not 'political'. I felt it was important for the concept of this particular performance that we should have collaborators who had a strong, mature relationship with Lieder. In this piece, the colours and nuances can change, even within an eight-bar phrase. The orchestrations must sound natural and organic, and I needed singers who could shade the music in the same manner. Christian Gerhaher and I had long talks about this, before we even began rehearsals. We were exploring together aspects of beauty, but that should not be confused with 'pretty'. Beauty can be profoundly disturbing, and distinctly 'not pretty'!

▶ Kent Nagano's recording of Mahler's Das Lied von der Erde with the Montreal Symphony Orchestra is available on Sony Classical

Esa-Pekka Salonen

on 'distributing the death' in the awe-inspiring Ninth

All conductors doing Mahler's Ninth are in awe of the score to some degree. There is something so universal and powerful there – it makes you feel little at times. Both *Das Lied von der Erde* and the Ninth Symphony present a very specific challenge to a conductor, because Mahler himself never heard them.

His way of orchestrating was very practical. He consciously over-orchestrated, then in rehearsals he would thin the music out, crossing out unnecessary doublings. It's always easier and faster to take things out. He would then continue to tweak his scores from performance to performance, according to the specific requirements of different orchestras and venues. For Mahler, composition was a continuous process. There's very rarely a 'final score'. For a conductor of that calibre there was no finality – just a moment when the score had to be printed. In that sense, with the Ninth Symphony you are dealing with an essentially unfinished score.

The problems with the score are more subtle and less obvious than those in the score of *Das Lied* – think of the famous balance problems in the first song – but they are there. The mature Mahler style started to emerge in his Sixth Symphony and one of its characteristics was his desire to achieve maximum clarity and maximum transparency, by trying to place the harmonic structure so as to ensure every motivic element was completely and clearly audible. Unlike, say, Strauss or Debussy, there is no padding in the texture. There is a complete unity of harmony, melody, rhythm and texture. The Ninth Symphony doesn't automatically sound clear or transparent. In some of the string passages thematic and secondary lines collide within a very narrow register. I am absolutely clear in my mind that he would have changed that. There are also some wrong harmonies left in the score – some places where he might have made a mistake, especially in the first movement. How do I know? I can only guess, but based upon years of study and admiration and love of Mahler's music. In many places the conductor has a choice – to be totally true to the score or to clarify certain phrases. These are treacherous waters. I wouldn't dare to fiddle with instrumentation but internal balances are a different matter. It's a personal preference but I don't find chaos emotionally powerful.

Late Mahler was toying with the idea of atonality but very rarely are there chords that bear no relationship to tonality at all. There is a moment of deepest despair in the opening *Adagio* of the Tenth Symphony that stands totally outside major/minor modality. The main challenge with the Ninth Symphony is how to manage the overall shape of the piece – how to distribute the death, as it were. It must all sound inevitable. The *Scherzo* takes us into the vortex, with a benign Ländler turning into something totally different. It contains all the prototypes of a Mahler *scherzo* – it's the mother of all *scherzos*. This journey within just one movement is quite amazing. It contains some of Mahler's most sophisticated music but it's also uber-rustic and, in places, downright funny. It's a technical showcase, like a miniature concerto for orchestra.

The last page is one of the most amazing pages of score by anybody, by any standards. Every phrase has an incredible intensity. It's like a reverse biological evolution, with a musical phrase being dismantled, bit by bit. You start with sophistication, and go back to an amoeba, the very basic DNA of all music. This is the most basic figure in all music, the last signal being sent out before silence. What a very, very bold thing to do. When music is being decomposed, there is nothing left but silence. I believe the long retirement of Sibelius was the result of his own motivic process – after the stark simplicity of *Tapiola*, where else could he go?

Our new recording of the piece is a live recording, of a performance we gave after we had played the piece on tour in places such as the Concertgebouw and Cologne. I very much like the idea of recording this piece live. In fact, the idea of recording that finale in a studio doesn't feel right. So many of the most celebrated recordings of the piece – Bernstein, Karajan, Bruno Walter in 1938 – have been concert recordings. It's no accident. This is about death and there must be a sense of no return. It's your only shot. You just do it and live with the results. This is real life and death, not a video game.

> *With the Ninth you are dealing with an essentially unfinished score*

▶ Esa-Pekka Salonen's recording of Mahler's Symphony No 9 with the Philharmonia Orchestra is available from Signum

Esa-Pekka Salonen: sailing into treacherous waters

Riccardo Chailly

on Mahler's great symphonic torso and its famous completion

Das Lied von der Erde and the Ninth and Tenth symphonies are three late masterpieces of Mahler. In 1960 Deryck Cooke unveiled a masterpiece which was absolutely not known before. I have been conducting the Cooke version of this symphony for more than 25 years and I can say only good things about him. I think what counts is the value of the piece and the greatness of the music in his version. Mahler seems to have intended that the Tenth should be played straight through and Cooke recognised this is a mirror piece and, towards the end of the finale, there is that clever idea when the horns, in that desperate, high tessitura, recall the violas' theme from the very opening of the piece. The 'Purgatorio' is the centre, the 'Dante element', a treasure fully orchestrated by Mahler himself, surrounded by two *scherzos* of similar length and two outer *adagios* almost of the same length. Too often the first *Adagio* is done too slowly and I have been trying, in my most recent performances, to balance the two *adagios*.

Fortunately, the published score enables the conductor to see a reproduction of the original sketches of Mahler. You see how much Mahler there is there. Deryck Cooke only added the minimum necessary to perform the piece and there is no ego present there at all. The winning point is the simplicity of Cooke and how faithful he was to the sketches, without any exuberance or pretence of originality. Obviously Mahler would have done it differently, but then think of *Das Lied von der Erde*. If he had heard the first movement, how the balance runs the risk of murdering the tenor, knowing how hyper-critical he was of his own music, he would certainly have improved that as well. The one thing I do wish is that Faber Music, the British publishers, should print the orchestral material, as they printed the orchestral score. The piece is so difficult to play in any case, so the last thing the orchestra needs is to have difficulty reading the notes from handwritten material. This is one of the main reasons why there are still so few performances of this piece.

Unfortunately we also have to blame Alma for what she said and wrote, with the support of Bruno Walter, which influenced great Mahler figures such as Bernstein. When I conducted the piece in Berlin in the 1980s, Maestro Karajan asked me for a private chat. I had great reverence for him and arranged to see him at the Philharmonie at nine in the morning. He wanted to ask about the Tenth Symphony. I gave him my impressions and he asked me how difficult it is to conduct the second movement. I told him how impossibly complicated it is to play and to conduct, and told him I regarded it as being as technically difficult as the 'Danse sacrale' in *The Rite of Spring*. 'In that case, I had best not look into it,' he said. 'Why?' I asked. 'You are such a splendid Mahler interpreter, maestro.' He responded, 'Some things just come into your life too late.'

I have looked into other performing editions of the piece. They all have interesting ideas but I think they add too much to

Riccardo Chailly: values the simplicity of Deryck Cooke's edition

the torso of the original Mahler sketches. There is a tendency to overdo, which Mahler would not like. I have studied the way Mahler handled the scores of the Second and Fifth symphonies. As he revised those pieces, it was only ever a process of taking away, never a process of adding. He always slimmed down his works. That is why I prefer the 'spartanity' of Deryck Cooke's orchestration, which truly takes us to the heart of the piece. Mahler was moving, by himself, into the 12 tone system. In the first *Adagio* there is a vertical cluster of nine pitches altogether, like a horrified scream for symphony orchestra. Had he lived even five years longer, as he approached the 1920s, I believe, like Puccini in the sketches for the finale of *Turandot*, Mahler would have carried on in the direction of 12 tone. We know about Mahler's conversations with Schoenberg about the theory of *Klangfarben* as exemplified in the Six Orchestral Pieces. According to Alma, he was indifferent to this theory, but at the beginning of the First Symphony there is that marking, *Wie ein Naturlaut*, which almost amounts to the same thing. He simply was not impressed by theories and preferred to do things in his own way. He was a real conductor, very pragmatic and bored with having to explain everything, which conductors have to do on a daily basis, not only with their arms, but also with words!

Mahler was moving, by himself, into the 12 tone system.

▶ Riccardo Chailly's recording of Mahler's Symphony No 10 with the Berlin Radio Symphony Orchestra is available on Decca

PHOTOGRAPHY: SASHA GUSOV / DECCA

THE GRAMOPHONE COLLECTION

Mahler's Fourth Symphony

Naivety or knowingness? In February 2020, **David Gutman** explored the finest conductors' different takes on this fin de siècle masterpiece

I n the early 1950s the ever-sceptical *Record Guide* of Edward Sackville-West and Desmond Shawe-Taylor already understood that at his best Mahler had 'achieved a final precision in the expression of nostalgia for the low ceilings, the wavering nightlight, the fields and woods, the unambiguous affections, the stilled terrors and the sharp, fleeting raptures of childhood'. Unlike most Mahler symphonies, his *fin de siècle* Fourth did not take decades to secure a place in the repertoire. Its comparative brevity and relatively modest orchestration seem to have emboldened colleagues, acolytes and their disciples to parade their insights in concert and preserve them for posterity.

Today's discography contains few significant gaps. We can only guess how Henry Wood and his first wife dealt with the British premiere at the Proms on October 25, 1905 – but we *are* able to eavesdrop on the composer himself. On November 9 Mahler was in Leipzig to set down a strangely uneven piano reduction of the finale alone for M Welte & Sohne (Dal Segno, 6/04, Accentus, 8/13 et al). Blame the piano roll mechanism or the executant for the lumps and bumps. Or could it be that Mahler's 'funny walk' – the incessant 'change of pace' recalled by musicians who played under his direction in New York – fed into his performance style? There is a sense in which **Willem Mengelberg**, live in Amsterdam at the start of the Second World War, leads the whole work this way, letting the music tell a story for which the printed score is merely the starting point. Then again, how likely is it that Mahler, a frequent guest with Mengelberg's orchestra, ever heard his friend conduct

a finished performance of his music? Mahler's metronome marks as logged by Mengelberg are by no means identical to those he himself adopted in 1939. The different priorities of Bruno Walter, Mahler's own protégé, or Otto Klemperer, least sentimental of his aides, remind us of the pitfalls of retrospectively imputing authenticity, not to mention the elusive nature of the work itself.

Compositionally speaking, the finale came first, a seemingly unassuming setting of verse from the voluminous anthology of traditional German poems, *Des Knaben Wunderhorn* ('Youth's Magic Horn'). As early as February 1892 Mahler completed a setting for voice and piano of a child's naive evocation of celestial bliss to which he ascribed his own title, 'Das himmlische Leben' ('Heavenly life'). Orchestrated and performed, it remained unpublished, having been earmarked for inclusion in the Third Symphony. Later it became the goal of a new symphonic project, more explicitly journeying from complexity to simplicity, on which he worked between June 1899 and April 1901, mainly during his summer breaks. Making the song appear as the logical destination of three new symphonic movements was a challenging assignment for the composer, as it has been for his interpreters.

Mahler himself conducted the first performance in Munich on November 25, 1901. As ever the critics were bewildered. The last of his symphonic flirtations with Romantic nationalism also points the way to a texturally transparent, anti-representational art of the future. So is it an ode to youthful innocence in an increasingly industrialised world or

something more sceptical? Beethovenian archetypes abound. The slow movement seems to channel the wondrous quartet from Act 1 of *Fidelio*, one thread in the first movement is provided by a Beethoven piano concerto (No 4 in G for another No 4 in G), while Mahler's brief preamble feels indebted to the impish *Allegretto scherzando* of the Eighth Symphony. The jingling bells, evoking the jester's cap quite as much as an approaching sleigh, signal a unique synthesis of old and new. **Simon Rattle**, among the first to revel in the minutiae of discontinuity, makes the flutes and sleigh bells wholly independent of the ritardando of clarinets and first violins, an oil-and-vinegar effect no longer uncommon. Mengelberg has a different agenda, applying exaggerated *Gemütlichkeit* to the first three notes of the melody in the violins as if introducing a Viennese waltz. Others smooth things over and may not notice that the main tempo is intended to differ from that of the opening vamp. With many an equivocation to follow, the narrative drifts in and out of real time.

Listeners for whom the blue skies are threatened only fleetingly by storm clouds detect a return to the old Austro-German verities: a first movement with clear-cut themes developed and restated in sonata form, followed by a scherzo, slow movement and upbeat (albeit sung) finale. Mahler's sound world can retain generalised Schubertian warmth or usher in the new century with a more manicured sonic palette. And what to make of the squeaky-clean precision nowadays mysteriously associated with period practice? When the composer indicates a string glissando we cannot say whether these should be slightly enlarged portamentos or something more 'modern': long, even slides which call attention to themselves like fingernails on a blackboard rather than confirming the direction of travel.

Each movement brings its technical challenges. The second was inspired by Freund Hein, a Death-surrogate and alternative Pied Piper from German folklore. Here the leader is required to tune the violin a whole tone higher than usual, the uneasy *scordatura* conveying, for Norman Lebrecht, 'a migrant threat to sedate society'. Where an ensemble as a whole has reverted to gut strings it can make sense to give the depiction of Freund Hein a literally metallic core. The third movement, peculiarly affecting, is not all divine serenity, its 'accelerating' dancelike variations as difficult to pace as the emotive throwing open of the gates of Paradise is tough to pitch (intonationally

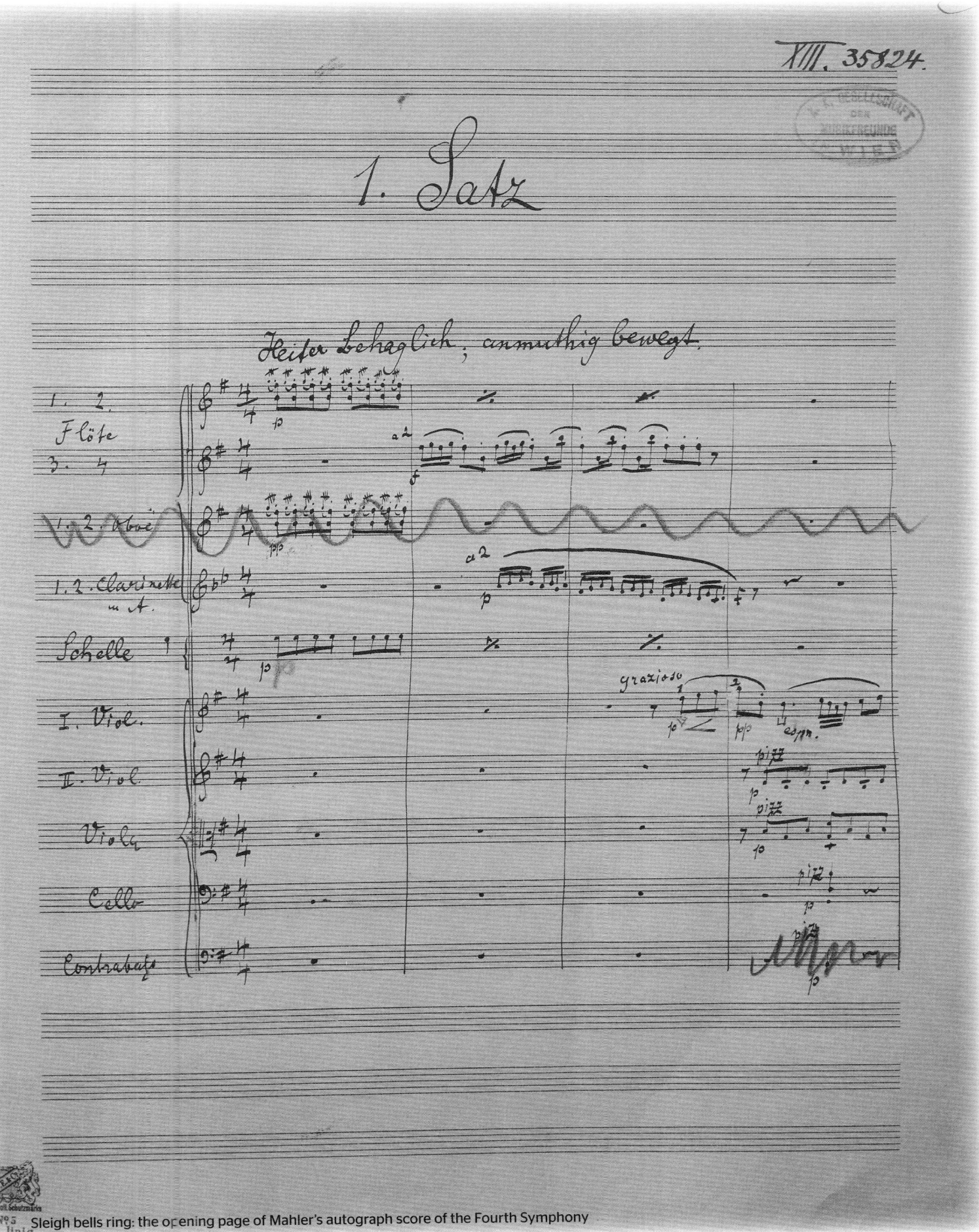

Sleigh bells ring: the opening page of Mahler's autograph score of the Fourth Symphony

The hut in which Mahler composed much of his Fourth Symphony

and interpretatively). Audiovisual formats parade other variables, from the unfathomable variety of sleigh bells and seating plans to the sartorial presentation of the soloist and her arrival on stage.

'Who have you cast for the soprano solo?' asked Mahler in 1904. 'She must be capable of singing with a naive, childlike expression, and with particularly good diction!' Solutions come in all shapes and sizes. **Leonard Bernstein**'s first, 1960 recording, curiously denied a separate release in the UK, was a breakthrough for Reri Grist, an unaffected artist just emerging from music theatre (expressly *West Side Story*). In preparing for his third version (DG, 8/88) Bernstein was seduced by the plainer sound of the boy treble. Those who consider the experiment doomed to failure should seek out Anton Nanut's contemporaneous Ljubljana account (Stradivari Classics). His remarkably assured boy soprano, strong and true (and uncredited on some reissues) is Max Emanuel Cencic, today a renowned countertenor. Back in 1968 Maurice Abravanel could count on a Vanguard

label stablemate, the polyglot Soviet-born Israeli soprano Netanya Davrath. As in Canteloube's *Chants d'Auvergne* so here her silvery, folk-like timbre is unsullied by excessive vibrato, while the breezy tempo is not far off Mahler's (even if that was designed for domestic consumption).

Canny indeed those with the foresight to preserve future stars in their early prime. Even in 1970 Margaret Price was not perhaps a 'natural' for childlike wonder yet her glorious, firm singing raises to another level what now seems a rather penny-plain traversal from **Jascha Horenstein**'s LPO. The young Kathleen Battle, almost too creamy, complements the *Sachertorte* of Lorin Maazel's Viennese reading. Juliane Banse copes admirably with impatience – Pierre Boulez in Cleveland (DG, 5/00) – and inertia – Giuseppe Sinopoli in Dresden (Profil, 8/08).

Close microphone placement can spoil the recipe. Sylvia McNair, vocally ideal, sounds constrained rather than intimate in Berlin with Bernard Haitink (Philips, 2/94). By contrast, Lisa Della Casa for Fritz Reiner (RCA, 8/60) reaches us as if

from the far side of an Alpine valley. Nor is she always in tune. Singers conventionally defined as mezzos, on paper unsuited to the task, have sometimes triumphed. Dodgiest are the celebrity sopranos doing mid- or late-career star turns. Fining down her voice only to be defeated by the German text is the unlikeliest of them all, the great Galina Vishnevskaya, with David Oistrakh on the podium in 1967 (Russian Revelation, 6/97).

The first Fourth, the earliest electrical recording of any (almost) complete Mahler symphony, was made in Japan in May 1930. Viscount Hidemaro Konoye and his New Symphony Orchestra (precursor of today's NHK Symphony Orchestra) were joined by soprano Eiko Kitazawa in Tokyo's Parlophone Studio. As transferred to CD (Denon, 6/88), this is a curio rather than a contender. Best known in the West for recording the *Horst Wessel Song* with the Berlin Philharmonic and declining to perform Britten's *Sinfonia da Requiem*, Konoye is understandably cautious. There's a major cut at the heart of the slow movement and the last three bars of the finale exceeded the capacity of the original 78rpm side.

In his widely distributed New York set **Bruno Walter** hurries those two movements along, apparently in keeping with an interpretation lighter and more linear than Mengelberg's. With an overall timing of 49'21" this is the shortest Mahler Fourth; the longest, clocking in at 65'05", is Wyn Morris's (Collins Classics, 11/89). That the limitations of the medium inhibited the message is supported by the recollections of Walter's soloist Dési Halban. Preserved in wiry sound, Walter's 1950 Salzburg Festival performance (53'55") goes deeper and benefits from the seductive presence of Irmgard Seefried. Ragged entries indicate that the music was none too familiar, yet at a time of political uncertainty and economic privation the audience was reportedly in tears at the end.

HISTORIC CHOICE
Vincent; Concertgebouw Orch / Mengelberg
Pristine Audio PASCO55

A conductor with god-like status before blotting his copybook in the Second World War, Mengelberg imposes seemingly

eccentric nuances on a timbrally distinctive band the composer knew well. The interpretation may or may not be modelled on Mahler's own.

CHILL-OUT CHOICE
Battle; VPO / Maazel
Sony Classical ⑩ 88985 38136-2

Maazel, at his most relaxed, lets the Vienna Philharmonic do its thing while soprano Kathleen Battle does hers. While some

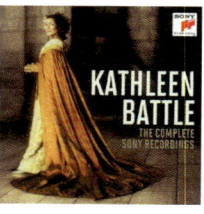

will deem the results insufficiently Grimm (*sic*), there's nothing transatlantic about the music-making and the exquisite details show that no one is coasting.

AUDIOVISUAL CHOICE
Kožená; Lucerne Fest Orch / Abbado
EuroArts DVD 205 7988

The audiovisual winner finds Abbado near the end of his career coaxing a performance

of chamber-like delicacy from the world's classiest citizen-of nowhere scratch band. The filming may not be perfect but the players actually smile and what a luxury to have some silence at the end!

Insofar as it existed, the Mahler tradition was strongest in Holland. Post-Mengelberg renditions by Paul van Kempen with Hilversum forces for Telefunken in 1950 and Edward van Beinum with the Concertgebouw Orchestra (Decca, 10/52) have been digitised by Pristine Audio. The Concertgebouw retains its distinctive sound, the first movement moving forwards at Mengelberg's vigorous basic tempo but without his hair-raising bar-by-bar rubato. Fresh openness distinguishes **Benjamin Britten**'s Aldeburgh Festival relay. The eager, lean-sounding LSO of 1961, measured in the slow movement, is frisky elsewhere. Technical mishaps demonstrate that this is live and unedited. John Barbirolli finds more shadow in a fallible BBC Symphony Orchestra broadcast from a behind-the-Iron-Curtain tour (BBC Legends, 4/99). Although Heather Harper has a more appropriate timbre than Britten's Joan Carlyle and unlike her never gets lost, she can't quite make us believe in Barbirolli's lethargic pacing.

Otto Klemperer, the last of Mahler's intimate colleagues to set down a studio rendition, is a different kind of heavyweight. Ungenial in the first movement, he convinces in the second with his ponderous characterisation of the Austrian-sounding Trio. Then again, his *Poco adagio* moves too fast for ineffable serenity. Winds are typically left unblended rather than coasting on a cushion of strings. We cannot know whether these traits were present in the 1912 Hamburg rendering with which he made his professional concert-hall debut. One unlikely admirer is Yevgeny Svetlanov (CdM, 3/97), persuaded to opt (against type) for the same kind of literalism. Klemperer's 1961 recording has tended to eclipse the Philharmonia's earlier effort under Paul Kletzki (Columbia, 7/58), where the principal horn is Dennis Brain and the soloist Emmy Loose. Klemperer has the more marketable Elisabeth Schwarzkopf, anything but artless.

By now **Leonard Bernstein** had entered the fray, redefining what 'Mahlerian' might mean for a new generation in the US: a roller-coaster ride in which schmaltz and irony are seen as essential components of the style rather than lapses of taste. The neurotic tone (and jumpier transitions) might be thought to run counter to the Fourth's classical temper, the slow movement touching rather than unduly relaxed. More satisfying is Bernstein's audiovisual account from Vienna, 1972; Edith Mathis evokes heaven with lovely tone and a twinkle in her eye which is distinct from self-conscious 'knowingness'.

Magdalena Kožená is fidgety and Claudio Abbado fragile in a 2009 Lucerne performance

Bernard Haitink had a special affection for this score, amassing as many as seven commercial recordings with various ensembles. Some of those could do with a bit more of the weightless élan of his earliest outing with what is still recognisably van Beinum's band (Philips, 10/68). In a fondly remembered Christmas Mahler broadcast from 1982, Haitink encourages the Amsterdam players to give of their best and is notably well served by soloist Maria Ewing, every aspect of whose presentation rings true. The film stock has faded but how fascinating to see as

well as hear **Klaus Tennstedt** in 1977. His marionette-like stance is Furtwänglerish, the music's unfolding more obviously German even when the orchestra is the Boston Symphony. Lucia Popp graces his audio-only alternative (EMI, 4/83). **George Szell**'s Cleveland version, scrupulously prepared and long top-rated, has comparable Teutonic density.

With Mahler becoming mainstream, non-specialist conductors were encouraged to undertake one-off LPs or even complete cycles. Those pining for saturated string sonority can turn to Herbert von Karajan's

SELECTED DISCOGRAPHY

RECORDING DATE / ARTISTS	RECORD COMPANY (REVIEW DATE)
1939 Jo Vincent; Concertgebouw Orch / **Mengelberg**	Philips ⟶ 426 108-2 (4/86ᴿ); Pristine Audio PASC055
1945 Dési Halban; New York PO / **Walter**	Naxos 8 110876; Sony Classical ⑦ 88691 92010-2 (9/46ᴿ, 7/73ᴿ)
1950 Irmgard Seefried; VPO / **Walter**	Orfeo C818 101B
1960 Reri Grist; New York PO / **Bernstein**	Sony Classical ⑫ 88697 94333-2 (10/71ᴿ)
1961 Elisabeth Schwarzkopf; Philh Orch / **Klemperer**	EMI/Warner Classics ⑥ 248398-2 (7/62ᴿ)
1961 Joan Carlyle; LSO / **Britten**	ICA Classics (20 discs) ICAB5141 (4/99ᴿ)
1965 Judith Raskin; Cleveland Orch / **Szell**	Sony Classical (106 discs) 88985 47185-2 (8/67ᴿ, 11/18)
1968 Elsie Morison; Bavarian RSO / **Kubelík**	DG ⑩ + ☒ 483 5656GM11 (12/68ᴿ, 8/75ᴿ)
1968 Netanya Davrath; Utah SO / **Abravanel**	Vanguard ATMCD1212; Musical Concepts ⑩ MC182
1970 Margaret Price; LPO / **Horenstein**	EMI/Warner Classics ⑯ 608985-2 (5/71ᴿ, 7/84ᴿ)
1972 Edith Mathis; VPO / **Bernstein**	DG ② DVD 073 4090GH2; ⑨ DVD 073 4088GH9 (2/06)
1977 Phyllis Bryn-Julson; Boston SO / **Tennstedt**	ICA Classics DVD ICAD5072
1982 Maria Ewing; Concertgebouw Orch / **Haitink**	Arthaus DVD 109 108; ☒ 109 109
1983 Kathleen Battle; VPO / **Maazel**	Sony Classical ⑩ 88985 38136-2 (3/85ᴿ, 1/86ᴿ)
1988 Christine Whittlesey; SWR SO / **Gielen**	SWR Music ⑰ + DVD SWR19042CD (6/18)
1997 Amanda Roocroft; CBSO / **Rattle**	Warner Classics ⑫ 9029 58691-7 (6/98ᴿ)
2003 Laura Claycomb; San Francisco SO / **Tilson Thomas**	SFS Media 🔊 SFS0004 (7/04); ⑰ 🔊 SFS0039
2005 Anu Komsi; Stuttgart RSO / **Norrington**	SWR Music SWR19524CD (10/06ᴿ)
2008 Miah Persson; Budapest Fest Orch / **I Fischer**	Channel Classics 🔊 CCSSA26109 (4/09)
2009 Magdalena Kožená; Lucerne Fest Orch / **Abbado**	EuroArts DVD 205 7988; ☒ 205 7984 (2/11)
2012 Christina Landshamer; Leipzig Gewandhaus Orch / **Chailly**	Accentus DVD ACC20257; ☒ ACC10257 (8/13)
2016 Sofia Fomina; LPO / **Jurowski**	LPO LPO0113 (9/19)
2016 Hanna-Elisabeth Müller; Düsseldorf SO / **A Fischer**	AVI-Music AVI8553378 (1/17)

GRAMOPHONE

CHOOSE YOUR PACKAGE

SUBSCRIBE TODAY

Never miss an issue of the world's most authoritative voice on classical music, with five great subscription options to choose from.

THE COMPLETE PACKAGE

GRAMOPHONE
THE CLUB

BEST VALUE

Our premium subscription option is a must-have for every classical music enthusiast. Combining all our subscription packages into one, joining The *Gramophone* Club is the most comprehensive and cost-effective way to enjoy *Gramophone*.

▶ 13 new print and digital issues during the year

▶ Read every issue of *Gramophone* since 1923

▶ Access to 50,000 recording reviews

From £11.45 / every month*

THE DIGITAL PACKAGE

GRAMOPHONE
DIGITAL CLUB

The complete digital subscription. Perfect for when you're on the move, the Digital Club gives you full access to every edition since 1923 and 50,000 recording reviews.

From £9.20 / every month*

OTHER SUBSCRIPTION PACAKAGES

GRAMOPHONE **PRINT**	GRAMOPHONE **DIGITAL**	GRAMOPHONE **REVIEWS**
Receive 13 new print editions during the year, delivered straight to your door.	13 new digital editions during the year, plus every issue since 1923.	Searchable database of 50,000 expert recording reviews
From £6.87 / every month*	**From £6.87 / every month***	**From £6.87 / every month***

Three easy ways to subscribe

 magsubscriptions.com/gramophone   +44 (0)1722 716997   @ subscriptions@markallengroup.com

No weak links: Miah Persson with the Budapest Festival Orchestra under Iván Fischer

first Mahler symphony recording (DG, 11/79). André Previn's sole Mahler disc (EMI, 9/79), highly regarded by some despite a wayward first movement, has more excitable (Pittsburgh) horns and brass. Likewise Georg Solti's very present Chicagoans (Decca, 7/84). James Levine (RCA, 10/75), Franz Welser-Möst (EMI, 12/88) and Colin Davis (RCA, 7/96) excel in profound and variously drawn-out readings of the slow movement.

Lorin Maazel managed three recordings, the finest arriving during an otherwise lacklustre 1980s cycle. Devotees of the Vienna Philharmonic appreciate the wistful style, the slowly unspooling phrases. Even his sleigh bells sound mellow. The Scherzo is just unsettling enough. Maazel offers nothing galvanic, nothing remotely casual either. Close to him in mood is Michael Tilson Thomas in San Francisco, where superb orchestral playing is flattered by sound recording of hitherto unmatched sophistication. From the Mengelberg-style opening, MTT inhabits a dreamworld one is reluctant to leave. Does it matter that the refined torpor is almost certainly remote from anything Mahler intended, beauty standing in for truth?

The boom continues unabated. Valery Gergiev has releases targeting three discrete constituencies (LSO, 5/10; C Major, 8/11; Münchner Philharmoniker, 11/17). None offers the bucolic poetry of Rafael Kubelík's Bavarian Radio forces in 1968. A Bohemian composer-conductor more lightly

Germanised than Mahler himself, Kubelík first heard the Symphony under Alexander Zemlinsky in Prague in the early 1930s and directs it in almost chamber-like fashion. The breezy, unaffected quality which doesn't quite pass muster in Mahler's more gargantuan scores succeeds here. Insofar as Kubelík has heirs, they are Hungarian-born. Working in Düsseldorf, Adám Fischer nonetheless preserves that open-air feeling, more self-conscious in the moulding of detail as might be expected by 2016, still very persuasive. Younger brother Iván Fischer, whose expressive reach and dynamic range are wider, has the advantage of the Budapest Festival Orchestra and the ideal soprano for his zesty yet easeful finale. With Miah Persson invoking St Martha, it's as if we're transported to a small village church (fig 10), the organ made tangible in the exquisite treatment of the accompanying instrumental texture. Arriving at St Ursula's laugh (fig 14), her descending glissando is so perfectly matched with that of the first violins that it takes the breath away. There are no weak links and the surround sound will delight audiophiles.

Other contemporary options include an 'authenticist' lobby whose antipathy to string vibrato brings a certain glassiness to sustained music. Philippe Herreweghe (PHI, 2/11) is less doctrinaire in this respect than Roger Norrington, who deploys his modern instruments with a close-miked brightness complemented by Anu Komsi's

detailed, pre-school characterisation. Of the 'modernists', Michael Gielen betters Boulez, albeit with a weaker soloist.

Standing slightly apart are Riccardo Chailly and Claudio Abbado. Chailly tapped into Mengelberg's local legacy for his Mahler series with the now 'Royal' Concertgebouw (Decca, 4/00). More recently he has presented a tautened rethink in sound and vision, the best recorded and packaged in its class. In Leipzig everything is bright and immediate. Christina Landshamer delivers her child's-eye view of the afterlife in a glamorous grown-up's turquoise frock. Abbado is a subtler, silkier musician whose four versions chart his quest for collegial ways to make music. What sounds like choppiness in Vienna, with Frederica von Stade only theoretically miscast (DG, 6/78), feels appropriately agile with the Gustav Mahler Jugendorchester in 2006 (EuroArts) and hyper-sensitive in Lucerne in 2009. Some will avert their eyes from the fidgety antics of Magdalena Kožená and the fragility of the ailing maestro, conducting without a stick (save when rehearsal footage is ineptly spliced in). The hall is on the dry side.

Dozens of major recordings from Abbado in Berlin to Zinman in Zurich haven't had a mention (and no one makes the finale's initial muted cellos sound more like cattle lowing than Zinman). The evidence nonetheless suggests that rising playing standards don't necessarily guarantee the twilit atmospherics – which is where we came in. If you've read this far you'll be looking for something beyond the sheer competence of Vladimir Jurowski and his peers in a library choice, that special spark which Iván Fischer so deftly delivers. Abbado may magic more instantaneous rapture at the start of the slow movement but no 21st-century rival so skilfully squares the circle of neoclassical modernity and old-world charm. Fischer is at once crystalline and 'retro', recalibrating Mengelberg's interventionism for our own time. **G**

LIBRARY CHOICE

Persson; Budapest Festival Orch / I Fischer
Channel Classics CCSSA26109
Though every detail is burnished into enchantment, Fischer manages to avoid a stage-managed effect. The slow music never lacks profundity, nor does the

line flag when the argument needs to press on. Perfect singing, perfect playing, spontaneous-sounding rubato and state-of-the-art sound.

THE GRAMOPHONE COLLECTION

Supersize Mahler

Mahler's Eighth Symphony is the calling-card for all orchestras with ambition: but which ones should you welcome in? This was the challenge **Ken Smith** set himself in December 2008

As soon as I got the invitation I immediately called my wife to tell her why I'd be gone for the rest of the week. 'The Macau International Music Festival just asked me to sing in the chorus of Mahler's Eighth,' I explained. 'Seems they did a head-count the other night and came up with only nine hundred and ninety-nine.' Before she could figure out whether or not I was serious, I was already out the door. About Mahler's infamous *Symphony of a Thousand*, I was very serious indeed. I don't often feel the need to explore a piece from the inside, but this was a special case. Mahler's Eighth Symphony has long been regarded as the biggest love letter in musical history ('Every note addressed to you', Mahler confessed to his wife, Alma), the most successful premiere of the 20th century (the initial Munich performances in 1910 being the composer's first unqualified success), and the most reliable attention-getter in the repertoire ever since. The Philadelphia Orchestra's US premiere in 1916 turned that institution from a financial drain to a civic asset. Nearly half a century later, Leonard Bernstein and the New York Philharmonic celebrated the opening of Lincoln Center by performing the first movement. Now, whenever an orchestra, city or country wants to announce that it's ready to be taken seriously, you can guess what's on the programme.

As a symphony, though, the piece's standing has been less secure. Scored for huge orchestra, offstage brass section, organ, double chorus, boys' choir and eight soloists, the piece could easily be termed a dramatic cantata or a secular oratorio (the composer poetically called it his Mass).

But Mahler was an established symphonist who frequently used words to convey ideas, often writing music before a specific text was involved. Combined with the fact that the first movement incorporates sonata-allegro form, that generally puts the piece in the symphony category.

That uneasy definition, though, still haunts even successful performances. As Mahler cycles began to proliferate, conductors who had provided memorable Second Symphonies or insightful Sevenths often fell noticeably short in the Eighth. More than any other piece, the Eighth Symphony requires a traffic cop – not only in directing the forces on stage, but in connecting the ideas and inner musical

Mahler's Eighth could easily be termed a dramatic cantata or a secular oratorio

relationships in the score. A depressing number of fine orchestral performances have been dampered by the chorus, or by soloists not well integrated into the musical and emotional texture (though occasionally the reverse has been true). But many conductors, even after getting their musical forces into place, miss Mahler's delicate duality, whereby a boisterous, polyphonic 'Veni, Creator Spiritus' is answered by the more freely homophonic scene from Goethe's *Faust* revelling in German Romanticism. The Latin Pentecost hymn must eventually reconcile with the idea of humanist salvation through the Eternal Feminine, but most performances emphasise those contrasts either too much or too little.

As my stack of Mahler Eighths doubled in the past few years, it became apparent that it was finally time to re-evaluate the piece. Rehearsing in the chorus was the easy part; how does one navigate nearly 30 recordings? First, there's industry history to consider, which sets archival live performances apart from studio efforts before returning to live recordings.

Then there's the composer's history. A few years ago it became fashionable for those seeking 'the real Mahler' to focus first on ensembles that Mahler himself conducted, namely the Concertgebouw Orchestra and the Philharmonics of Vienna and New York. Given the nature of the Eighth Symphony, that seemed a pretty good place to start.

THE NEW WORLD
After initiating the piece in 1906 and before conducting its Munich premiere in 1910, Mahler had served as principal conductor at the Metropolitan Opera and completed his first season as music director of the New York Philharmonic. One could easily overemphasise the effect of America on his music-making; Mahler himself derided the Munich concert producer's 'Barnum and Bailey' marketing strategy (although *Symphony of a Thousand* was in fact a reasonably accurate accounting of the personnel involved: 858 singers and 171 instrumentalists). But other observers in Munich noted the piece's 'American' dimensions, and no doubt that sense of raw spaciousness did shape the piece's eventual realisation. Encountering Niagara Falls for the first time, Mahler had exclaimed, '*Fortissimo*, at last!'

Coming back to my 1971 Decca recording with the Chicago Symphony

The composer conducts: Mahler rehearses the Symphony of a Thousand prior to its 1910 Munich world premiere

Orchestra and combined Vienna State Opera Chorus, Singverein and Vienna Boys Choir, I find that **Georg Solti** is still the reigning champion of the 'shock-and-awe' school. In terms of sheer orchestra brilliance there's simply no better ensemble captured more fully on record. Right from the opening organ blast, which was added later in the studio, Solti wields such command that no one element overshadows. A better cast of soloists has still never been assembled (even if others have sung with a better sense of ensemble), and the main forces complement each other perfectly, as if the chorus singing in Mahler's mother tongue tempers the instrumentalist playing in his orchestral father tongue.

The downside of all this is that in his zeal to find the drama, Solti often misses the poetry. Operatic intensity comes at the sacrifice of symphonic subtlety. Detractors have claimed that the sound is more Solti than Mahler – and there are several recordings that are arguably more musical – but still, as far as phrasing and control are concerned, no other performance builds, sustains and releases tension quite like this one. Solti

is still the standard with which to compare all the others.

That didn't bode well for **Robert Shaw**. Of all the conductors who made their mark with the piece, Shaw had the best grasp of the choral side of the equation. Given the size of his forces, there's a surprising level of precision and clarity. The young Deborah Voigt and Heidi Grant stand out among the soloists. And although Shaw's conception is more oratorio than opera, there's a bit of déjà vu hearing his pacing, as this recording is only about 10 seconds shorter than Solti's. Unfortunately, the comparisons end there. The Atlanta Symphony Orchestra is simply not the Chicago. It's enough to bring out the military strategist in me: if Solti could insert an organ, why couldn't someone airlift the Atlanta Symphony Chorus into, say, the Vienna Philharmonic? This is one case where I say with regret that the recording quality captures the orchestra perfectly, warts and all.

Putting Solti up against **Leonard Bernstein**, the most eminent of American Mahlerians, the Eighth Symphony is hardly a fair comparison, as the piece shows Solti at his best and Bernstein at

his worst. Bernstein's first recorded effort, a 1962 live recording of the 'Veni, Creator Spiritus' from the Lincoln Center opening concert, embodies a great sense of occasion, coming only two years after Bernstein had presided over the Mahler centenary festival at the New York Philharmonic. But without the contrasts in the second movement, nearly 24 minutes of breathless excitement seems a bit one-sided.

A few years later, as part of the first complete Mahler cycle in stereo, Bernstein's 1966 performances with the London Symphony Orchestra essentially ushered in the modern era of studio Mahler Eights (including the idea of recording of the organ off-site). This time, though, Bernstein's breathlessness often borders on recklessness, with a few tempi seemingly appearing for momentary effect rather than illuminating the piece. Not only does the chorus – a mix of professional and avocational British singers – lack Solti or Shaw's level of clarity, but Bernstein lacks his usual sureness of touch with Mahler. The recording quality, even in Sony's much-hyped transfer, is barely comparable.

The third time could have been the charm, as Bernstein's later Mahler cycle on the whole took a broader, more thoughtful approach. But Bernstein's plans for a New York Mahler Eighth were left unfulfilled at the conductor's death, leaving Deutsche Grammophon to fill the collection with a live recording of Bernstein and the Vienna Philharmonic from the 1975 Salzburg Festival – a noticeably weak link in the cycle. A more intriguing alternative, recently released on DVD, is the video recording of Bernstein's performance with the VPO later that year. Director Humphrey Burton does make the on-camera rounds of key vocalists and instrumentalist during their showcase moments, but this is mostly Bernstein's show.

Riccardo Chailly: offers plenty of interpretative weight in his recording

THE ARCHIVE

The New York Philharmonic sometimes wears its 'unbroken Mahler tradition' a little too smugly – especially compared with the Vienna Philharmonic, where Mahler was unknown to many members after the Second World War. Even in America, New York has competitors, with Stokowski having championed the Eighth Symphony in Philadelphia two years before the piece was performed in Vienna. But no other orchestra in the world compares in terms of documenting that history, or – at least until the orchestra began neglecting its Special Edition archival recordings – in keeping its past back in the public ear.

The strangest omission in the Philharmonic's 1998 12-CD, 500-page Mahler compendium was any contribution by Bernstein. The most notable inclusion was a 1950 broadcast of the Eighth Symphony conducted by **Leopold Stokowski**, who had attended the piece's 1910 Munich premiere under

Mahler and used this occasion to mark his last appearance with the Philharmonic. Here, by any standards, is true musical authority, the music flowing of its own accord with vocal and instrumental phrasing perfectly matched. Sonically, however, it remains an archival document. The transfer is head and shoulders above previous pirate releases, but it in no way challenges modern recordings.

It does, however, go head to head fairly evenly with **Jascha Horenstein**'s 1959 live performance with the London Symphony Orchestra at the Royal Albert Hall, which also came out in 1998 on BBC Legends. Unlike New York, London had heard the Eighth Symphony only three times before; unlike Stokowski, Horenstein had never before conducted the piece. Still, Horenstein's performance all but ignited Britain's Mahler revival. The reading is broader, less impulsive than Bernstein's, made

with more or less the same musicians seven years later. Perhaps allowing for the acoustics of the hall, Horenstein takes the opening rather slowly. But rather than alternating between gas and brakes, Horenstein finds a rather comfortable middle speed that can ease or advance with minimal effort, making the music's dramatic effects – and the realisation that many of the ideas developed in the second movement had already been introduced in the first – emerge from the score rather than the podium. This is not the most beautiful playing by a long shot; several flubs would've been deleted in the studio, and the audience noise is equally distracting. But if you can listen past those imperfections the recording does offer a superb sense both of the piece and arguably its most perfect venue.

Stokowski and Horenstein both fare better than **Dimitri Mitropoulos**'s live performance with the Vienna Philharmonic at the 1960 Salzburg Festival. The sound is generally clear, though exceedingly one-dimensional. Musically, Mitropoulos starts out even slower than Horenstein, but without the flexibility, nearly allowing the first movement to crumble beneath its majesty. In the second movement, that grandeur is much better placed; the performance works well as opera, in fact, but ultimately fails as a symphony, with the soloists remaining in their own realm rather than emerging from the orchestral texture. As for the rest of the forces, I'm not sure which is more frustrating: to realise that these are the same choruses that Solti used much more effectively a decade later, or to hear the out-of-tune brass (admittedly without the benefit of a

---

BUDGET CHOICE

Chicago SO / Georg Solti
Decca 4757521DOR

Solti's high-octane recording defined the work for a generation, and even today remains the one to beat. With super-budget

label Naxos spreading their recording over two discs, there's really no other choice here.

HISTORICAL CHOICE

LSO / Jascha Horenstein
BBC Legends ② BBCL4001-7

Though he never conducted the work before this concert, Jascha Horenstein and 750 musicians and singers on stage at the Royal

Albert Hall ignited Britain's Mahler revival in a single stroke.

DVDCHOICE

VPO / Leonard Bernstein
DG ② DVD 073 4091GH2

When Bernstein died before finishing his second Mahler cycle, this became his final statement on the Eighth. This superb performance hints at what these forces could have accomplished under more pristine studio conditions.

PHOTOGRAPHY: MARCO BORGGREVE / DECCA

second take) and realise this is not the Chicago Symphony.

THE OLD WORLD

Inspiration from America notwithstanding, when Mahler called the Eighth Symphony 'a gift to the entire nation' he wasn't speaking to the ladies on the New York Philharmonic committee. This is a piece where the inherent conflicts in the first and second sections – between language and culture, historical period and general sentiments – reflect an undeniably European sensibility in an era of volatile transition. European conductors and musicians usually grasp that milieu intuitively, although that doesn't always guarantee superb results.

Holding my initial principle of Mahler conductivity, I reached for my only remaining recording of his key musical workshop: the Vienna Philharmonic. **Lorin Maazel**'s 1989 account for Sony was definitely a white-tie affair, with a superb roster of soloists and top-notch choral line-up. It's immediately obvious that both singers and musicians are so attuned to Mahler's music that they could perform it in their sleep. Before long, it sounds as if they're doing precisely that, so little sense of purpose does the performance exude. From moment to moment, there's some lovely, idiomatic playing, but there's no clear sense of direction that sustains interest for the duration of the piece. This was a low point only until I started playing **Bernhard Haitink**'s 1971 Concertgebouw recording for Phillips, which may well stand as the dullest contribution from a major orchestra in the catalogue. Perhaps this was a response to Solti's bombast of the same period, but Haitink's laid-back approach does no service to the music. Nor is the choral singing terribly distinguished. The women soloists so greatly overshadow the men that a true ensemble never has a chance to develop. A recent SACD release on Pentatone has made the overall sound considerably crisper, but does nothing to help the performance.

Riccardo Chailly takes exactly the opposite approach throwing plenty of interpretative weight into the Concertgebouw's sound in his 2000 release on Decca. Objectively, this is a remarkable recording: strong orchestral playing, a graspable musical flow, and a gathering of vocal soloists that supremely understands the concept of ensemble. The only performance drawback is that the Prague Philharmonic Choir and the

SELECTED DISCOGRAPHY

RECORDING INFORMATION DATE / ARTISTS /	RECORD COMPANY (REVIEW DATE)
1950 NYPO / **Stokowski**	New York Philharmonic ⑫; Music & Arts ② CD280
1959 LSO / **Horenstein**	BBC Legends BBCL4001-7 (12/98)
1960 VPO / **Mitropoulos**	Orfeo ② C519 992B (4/00)
1962 NYPO / **Bernstein** (Pt 1 only)	Sony ② SM2K63159
1966 LSO / **Bernstein**	Sony ② 517493-2
1970 Bavarian Rad SO / **Kubelík**	DG 447 529-2GGA (2/96); ⑩ 463 738-2GB10
1971 Concertgebouw / **Haitink**	Philips ⑩ 442 050-2PB10 (11/94); Pentatone 🔊 PTC5186 166 (1/07)
1971 Chicago SO / **Solti**	Decca 475 7521DOR (5/96); ⑩ 430 804-2DC10
1975 VPO / **Bernstein**	DG ⑯ 459 080-2GX16 (10/91)
1975 VPO / **Bernstein**	DG **DVD** 073 4091GH2; ⑨ **DVD** 073 4088GH9 (2/06)
1981 Frankfurt Op Orch / **Gielen**	Sony SBK48281
1986 Frankfurt Rad SO / **Inbal**	Denon ② CO1564/5 (2/88)
1986 LPO / **Tennstedt**	EMI ② 361572-2 (3/87; 5/87); ② **DVD** 367743-9
1989 VPO / **Maazel**	Sony ② SM2K60307 (9/90)
1991 Cologne Rad SO / **Bertini**	EMI ⑪ 340238-2 (6/06)
1991 Atlanta SO / **Shaw**	Telarc Ⓜ CD80267 (1/92)
1991 Sofia PO / **Tabakov**	Capriccio ⑮ 49 043 (3/97)
1994 BPO / **Abbado**	DG ② 445 843-2GH2 (6/95); ⑫ 447 023-2GX12 (12/95)
1994 Gothenburg SO / **N Järvi**	BIS BIS-CD700
1994 Netherlands Rad PO / **de Waart**	RCA ⑭ 74321 27601-2 (1/96)
1996 Bavarian Rad SO / **C Davis**	RCA ② 🔊 82876 62864-2 (6/97R)
1998 SWR SO / **Gielen**	Hänssler Classic ② CD93 015 (1/03); ⑬ CD93 130
2000 Concertgebouw / **Chailly**	Decca ② 467 314-2DH (4/01)
2004 CBSO / **Rattle**	EMI 557945-2 (4/05)
2005 DSO Berlin / **Nagano** /	Harmonia Mundi ② HMC90 1858/9; 🔊 HMC80 1858/9 (3/05)
2005 Warsaw Nat PO / **Wit** /	Naxos ② 8 550533/4 (9/06)
2007 Staatskapelle Berlin / **Boulez** /	DG ② 477 6597GH2 (A/07)

Netherlands Radio Choir never quite agree in articulation, disturbing the moments requiring utmost clarity. A more significant obstacle is Chailly's interpretation, which often seems a reaction to Mahler rather than Mahler's score. There are some surprises here – a subtler opening that does not take the audience by force, a highly mystical 'Faust' movement – but not all are equally convincing. Still, it's exceedingly hard to believe this is the same orchestra that Haitink conducted 30 years before.

From the same neighbourhood, broadly speaking, comes **Edo de Waart**'s 1994 performance with the Netherlands Radio Philharmonic for RCA Victor, which falls almost exactly between the blandness of Haitink and the idiosyncrasies of Chailly. The sound is comfortably warm and spacious, showcasing the second movement very nicely. The choruses are far superior to Chailly's, and de Waart achieves a comparable freedom in the sound without totally imposing or removing his own personality. Ultimately, though, de Waart's subtleties are less memorable than Chailly's quirks.

Having covered Mahler's various turfs with mixed results, I decided to get as far away as possible. **Emil Tabakov**'s 1991 version with the Sofia Philharmonic for

Capriccio is the kind of recording you keep listening to, hoping it gets better. Alas, it never does. The chorus overpowers the orchestra in the first section, then seems miles away in the second. Playing is spotty, the miking amateurish at best. I then turned to **Antoni Wit**'s 2005 account with the Warsaw National Philharmonic for Naxos, which was musically solid without being showy. Mastering both the broad and small strokes, Wit sets comfortable tempi while coaxing a rare level of subtlety from his players. Choruses are clean and precise; soloists well balanced and integrated into the orchestral texture. My only complaint is an overly resonant acoustic, but Wit generally finds ways to make it work, mostly by stretching the tempi. After the Warsaw, which ran 81 minutes, **Neeme Järvi**'s 1994 performance with the Gothenburg Symphony on BIS clocks in at 70 minutes. Strangely, the piece never feels hurried, and the performance comes together seamlessly, which makes me question anyone who cites tempo as a primary indicator of good Mahler.

Klaus Tennstedt's 1986 account with the London Philharmonic Orchestra and Choir is generally beloved by the anti-Solti camp, and indeed his approach stands in great contrast. Where Solti is

extroverted, Tennstedt is introspective; where Solti's soloists and chorus command attention on their own, Tennstedt's vocal forces emerge gradually from within the symphonic texture. The concept fully respects the integrity of the piece as a symphony, but in practice the organ and chorus end up sounding fairly anaemic, like amplifying a piano at the expense of the violin in a sonata. Tennstedt, though, is utterly at home, and the clarity of ideas in this 1987 *Gramophone* Award-winner still holds up.

Simon Rattle's 2004 live recording with the CBSO for EMI brings to mind elements of both Solti and Shaw – as if Solti were encountering an orchestra more provincial than Chicago, or Atlanta was facing a conductor not so out of his depth. On his own terms, Rattle brings Solti-like attention to the piece, but instead of focusing energies on shaping phrases for dramatic effect, Rattle illuminates the inner details that often pass unnoticed. In the end, sober commitment wins over emotional intensity. The recording, though, lacks Decca or Telarc quality: soloists (who are on a par with Shaw's rather than Solti's) have a bit too much prominence, the chorus not quite enough.

My pile of German orchestral recordings started looking less formidable the more I started listening. **Eliahu Inbal**'s 1986 studio effort with the Frankfurt Radio Symphony for Denon was fine interpretatively, but the playing lacked control and discipline. **Rafael Kubelík**'s account with the Bavarian Radio Symphony Orchestra for DG, almost exactly contemporaneous with Solti, was perhaps the original anti-Solti in approach and has probably suffered as a result. A bigger problem, though, is the sloppy winds and brass and a mismatched line-up of soloists. **Colin Davis** has a different vocalist problem in his 1996 recording with that orchestra for RCA Victor: a superb symphonic choral approach is nearly derailed by a team of operatic soloists who seem to be performing an entirely different work.

A German recording fully worthy of attention is **Claudio Abbado**'s 1994 performance with the Berlin Philharmonic for DG, the breadth of which contrasts with Solti's single-minded momentum. Not that Abbado doesn't move the piece, he just does so

Claudio Abbado: conducts the symphony on Mahler's terms

on Mahler's terms rather than dictating from the podium. The soloists are good but misbalanced (stand-outs this time are the men, including Bryn Terfel and Peter Seiffert); the chorus neither weak nor dominating. The real star, however, is the orchestra, which plays with a deep sense of the composer's idiom that few in the world can match.

A musical surprise was **Gary Bertini**'s live Tokyo performance of the Eighth Symphony with the Cologne Radio Orchestra and Chorus, originally released on EMI in 1991. Later included as part of EMI's eminently affordable Bertini Mahler cycle a couple of years ago, it was the highlight of the collection and remains consistently illuminating. Rarely does a tempo seem out of place, nor does the orchestra ever fall short technically or musically. Alan Titus is the stand-out in a superb cast of singers.

Two recordings, now, by **Michael Gielen**: first, his 1981 live recording by Opernhaus und Museumorchester Frankfurt. Gielen's coolly analytical approach, neither emotionally charged not mystically exalted, is balanced by a palpably energetic performance – not lively enough to make this a primary choice, but at Sony's bargain price maybe a second or third. His 1998 recording with the SWR Symphony Orchestra of Baden-Baden and Freiburg, however, is another world entirely. Not that he's completely forsaken his obsession with counterpoint and thematic development, but this time there's more leeway for the heart – and the ears – in making beautiful sound for its own sake. Hänssler has not

only captured the sound beautifully, but in pairing it with Schoenberg's *Jacob's Ladder* on its 2002 release, the label has nearly assured that Gielen achieves the Eighth Symphony's sense of transcendence practically from its opening down-beat.

Kent Nagano's 2005 release with the Deutsches Symphonie-Orchester Berlin on Harmonia Mundi is yet another anti-Solti: where Solti pushes forward, Nagano dwells. Where others hammer us into submission, Nagano charms. Where others find transcendence in reaching their destination, Nagano focuses on the mystery and sensuality of the journey. The dangers are obvious, and Nagano's major problem is keeping momentum. Although most of the elements are superbly in place and brilliantly recorded – the orchestra shimmering, a chorus precise yet atmospheric, an organ that doesn't seem like an afterthought – after some 88 minutes everyone seems to forget where they're going.

I had already been contemplating a dream performance of Mahler's Eighth, one that combines the strengths of other recordings while downplaying their weaknesses (my own anti-Solti, if you will), when I encountered **Pierre Boulez**'s recording with the Berlin Staatskapelle last year for DG. Finally, we have the analytical rigour of Gielen balanced with Nagano's mystical streak, a true symphonic tenure worthy of a Tennstedt with the attention to detail worthy of a Rattle. Instead of the Grand Gesture, we get a steady stream of little gestures, all of which add up to a clear – and surprisingly warm – portrait that finesses any inconsistencies in the score rather than bulldozing through them. Does it finally replace Solti? Not really, but it deserves to sit on the shelf alongside it. **G**

TOP RECOMMENDATION
Staatskapelle Berlin / Pierre Boulez
DG ② 121477 6597GH2

A recent entry in the Mahler Eighth field, Boulez shoots straight to the top with an account that, without undue dramatics, brings out the excitement inherent in the score and makes sense of an often unwieldy piece.

Discover
a world of
music

With magazine subscriptions –
whatever your musical passion

Why subscribe?

Each of our authoritative titles bring you:

- In-depth features and news exploring your favourite music
- Previews and concert listings for live performances around the globe
- Exceptional new recordings reviewed by our expert critics
- Interviews with the world's finest performers and artists

Start your subscription today

GRAMOPHONE

The world's best classical
music reviews

INTERNATIONAL PIANO

Expert advice for every
piano enthusiast

OPERA NOW

The opera lover's
essential guide

CHOIR & ORGAN

Two worlds of music,
one magazine

JAZZWISE

The UK's biggest selling
jazz magazine

SONGLINES

The best music from
around the world

THE GRAMOPHONE COLLECTION

Mahler's last love letter

On discovering Alma's betrayal, Mahler's outpouring of emotion found voice in his unfinished **Tenth Symphony**. The quest to complete it has led to multiple recordings – **David Gutman** set out to explore them in December 2010, the year we marked the composer's 150th anniversary

Now that Gustav Mahler looms over musical life much as Beethoven and Wagner once must have done, it is difficult to credit the neglect following his premature death. For almost 50 years Mahler has seemed special, not just because of the breadth and power of his output, but also because of his place in popular imagination as a man at the junction of two centuries and two eras – the Romantic and the modern. In retrospect he is seen to have stamped his emblematic personality on a formative epoch in Western art and science: the Einstein, or rather Freud, of music. For good or ill he is a composer frequently discussed in non-musical terms. And

outcome is love- and life-affirming. Here encapsulated is our contemporary longing for meaningful narrative and an ameliorative end, a pilgrimage from death to life, the catharsis once only identified with religious faith. For Paul Griffiths, 'Mahler unsettles this prospect, in that bridges in his journeys may be traversed by means of kitsch and arrivals may still be tinged with doubt, but this only heightens his relevance to listeners in a later world.' The Tenth was always going to be a special case but how special remains a matter for dispute. While Mahler and Sibelius are sometimes viewed as antipodes, the latter seeking profound logic and inner connections, the former 'embracing the world',

the intermezzo-like third movement, or 'Purgatorio'. A cleaner text was issued in 1964 and many who reject a five-movement Tenth have accepted Erwin Ratz's critical edition of the *Adagio* as holy writ. Yet given that Mahler reworked the first two movements of his Ninth after completing the orchestral draft, the definitive status of this *Adagio*, with a mere seven tempo markings, remains doubtful, its form provisional, its sound world implausibly stark. The balance of the argument begins to shift.

For the musicologist Robin Holloway, usually a Mahler sceptic, the point about the Tenth and its palindromic five-movement scheme of *Adagio*, first *Scherzo* (half march, half ländler), 'Purgatorio' (deceptively slight, motivically rich), second *Scherzo* and finale, is that it makes a coherent, formal, expressive entity greater than the sum of its parts. Impossible to know quite how it would have sounded when, like Beethoven and Sibelius, Mahler gives each of his symphonies a freshly imagined sound world. Still, for many, just hearing the finale's eloquent flute solo justifies the various realisations. The 'intolerant and intolerable Alma Mahler of the huge violet handwriting' (BBC producer Leo Black's description) having finally rescinded her ban on Deryck Cooke's nascent performing version, the work was first given publicly on August 13, 1964, at the Proms, Berthold Goldschmidt conducting the London Symphony Orchestra. From that moment the Tenth was restored to life as a totality as well as a torso.

Mahler was an inveterate tinkerer whose symphonies achieved their final forms (if they did) only after superhuman Beethovenian toil

details of biography do matter. Part of our fascination with Mahler's unfinished Tenth Symphony lies in the way its emotive force is apparently attributable to the discovery of his wife's affair with the architect Walter Gropius, provoking a rip in the fabric of diatonic harmony which today has much the same iconic significance as the gaping mouth of Munch's *The Scream*. The argument twice explodes into a dissonant pile-up which Boris Tishchenko calls 'the most terrifying chord in the history of music'. Heartfelt exclamations addressed directly to Alma, the artistic community's emblematic femme fatale, litter the manuscript – 'für dich leben! für dich sterben!' (To live for you! To die for you!) – yet the

both were inveterate tinkerers whose symphonies achieved their final forms (if they did) only after superhuman Beethovenian toil. Had Mahler heard the Ninth in performance, he would have revised much, as was his practice. Curiously we absorb performances of the *Rückert-Lieder* scarcely noticing that 'Liebst du um Schönheit' was orchestrated by Max Puttmann, an employee of its publisher. Listen again and see if it affects your personal take on the morality of 'completing' the Tenth. In the 1950s both Hermann Scherchen and Charles F Adler recorded its *Adagio*, presumably relying on a printed score that embraced the interventions of Ernst Krenek, Alexander Zemlinsky et al. George Szell was the first to include

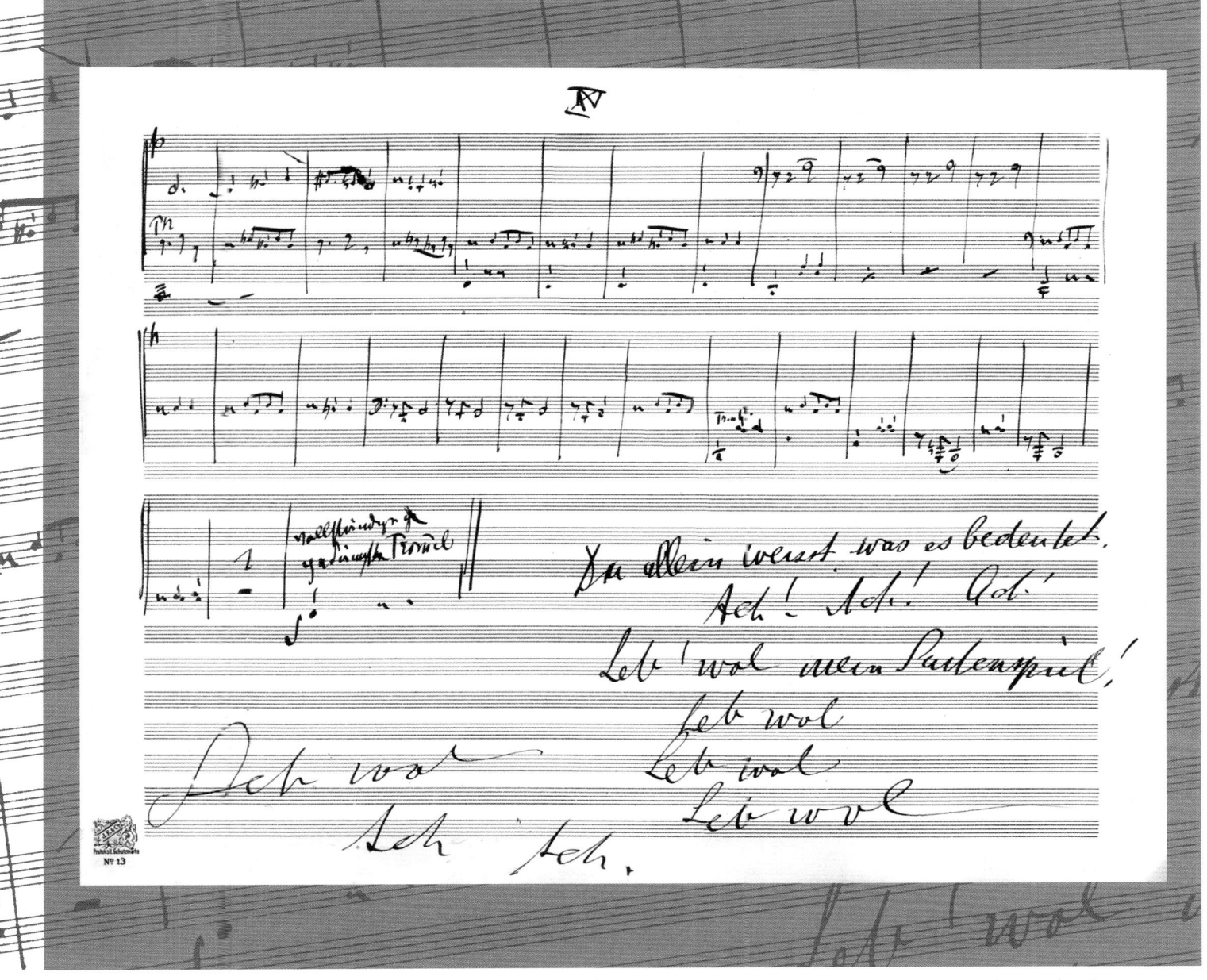

Heartfelt exclamations to Alma litter Mahler's Tenth Symphony. His inscription here, at the end of the fourth movement, can be translated thus: 'You alone know what it means. Oh! Oh! Oh! Farewell my lyre! Farewell, farewell. Farewell'

Today the work exists in a variety of editions and arrangements leaving behind the intellectual circumspection of Cooke and his collaborators, who aimed only to provide a performing version of a more-or-less detailed sketch. Andrew Litton makes the case for Clinton Carpenter's more maximalist, speculative approach with disarming frankness: if you have the audacity to complete a work by a great genius, you might as well 'go for it'. I am not persuaded but readers will have their own ideas. And we can immediately rule out two recordings. The commercial cachet of 'Mahler 10' is confirmed by two distinctly weird additions to its discography. A portmanteau piano reduction of the Cooke score is peddled, capably enough, by Christopher White on

Divine Art, but the project seems like a throwback to the days when the only way to experience new music was to hack through it on the parlour piano. More disturbingly, DG's recent offering entitled 'Recomposed By Matthew Herbert: Mahler Symphony X' is little more than a remix of Giuseppe Sinopoli's 1987 recording of the *Adagio* alone. Whatever your take on the playful ephemerality of 'pop', there is an irony in its reprocessing games being played out with this of all pieces. The 'sampling wizard' deconstructs Mahler's goal-directed argument into ambient soup. The experiment begins with rural atmospherics, an unfocused memory of that climactic chord and the work's opening idea as re-recorded by a solo viola player at Mahler's graveside.

Later we are given the music as from beyond the grave. The proceedings end with the sound of a door, or coffin lid, closing.

The more conventional realisations of what is, or should be, a horizontally uninterrupted argument present less radical incongruities. Those featured on disc are by US insurance man Carpenter, who began his endeavours as early as 1949, a cleaned-up version of the score by UK civil servant Joseph Wheeler, the various Cooke performing versions prepared with the assistance of Goldschmidt and Colin and David Matthews, Remo Mazzetti's editions unveiled in 1989 and 1999, and two alternatives premiered in 2001, one by the distinguished conductor and arranger

Rudolf Barshai, the other by Giuseppe Mazzuca and Nicola Samale, best known for 'completing' the finale of Bruckner's Ninth Symphony.

The opening seconds of the Tenth's finale demonstrate the sway of anecdote and how far the symphony is a 'work in progress' in which the maestro has the right to innovate. We know that on February 16, 1908, Mahler witnessed the funeral procession of Charles W Kruger, a deputy chief of New York's Fire Department – but not how (or even whether) this incident should be reflected directly in sound. Passing seamlessly from the fourth to the fifth movement by excluding one of the indicated drum strokes has made such

Eugene Ormandy undertook the American premiere and first commercial recording. Not chiefly remembered as a Mahler specialist today (he had set down a pioneering *Resurrection* Symphony in Minneapolis some 30 years earlier), and despite the compression of CBS/Columbia sound engineering, one gets a sense of the tonal luxuriance and urgent if generalised interpretative thrust of his classic Philadelphia partnership. With the help of teenage Mahler fanatics Colin and David Matthews, Cooke subsequently obtained more pointed orchestral sonorities with a larger contingent of woodwind, superseding certain features heard here and in Jean Martinon's Chicago taping which

retouchings have been taken up by colleagues, including the elision of the fourth and fifth movements, the use of bass clarinet rather than bassoon for Cooke's pastiche counterpoint from bar 162 of the *Adagio* and the notion that some percussive underpinning is implied by the return of the wrenching, nine-note dissonance.

At the start of the 1980s, **James Levine's** mooted Mahler symphony cycle for RCA looked like being the first to include a five-movement Tenth but the headline news was made by the arrival of a little-known Brit, the young **Simon Rattle**, whose blazing conviction and emotional clout made one forget scholarly debate. Tempi are broader than Ormandy's, tauter than Levine's, with some of Sanderling's textual novelties incorporated alongside a more visceral style of projection and a freer use of rubato. While the Bournemouth orchestra does not play with svelte assurance – its violas strain at the outset, there are problems of coordination in the difficult second *Scherzo* and the finale's recrudescence of that nine-pitch cluster seems underpowered even with added percussion – this is music-making of extraordinary fervour. Sir Simon's return to the work in Berlin, by which time he had performed it nearly 100 times, more than anyone, was a famous triumph, boasting technical standards so exalted that some discerned expressive reticence in the clinical precision. We were unused to hearing the opening viola line immaculately tuned with every accent clearly defined. The subtlety of the orchestral response allows more scope for special effects, such as the achingly beautiful treatment of the episode marked *a tempo aber sehr ruhig* in the second *Scherzo*. The finale, if anything, is finer still, the Berlin flautist floating his tone yet more poignantly in the principal theme while an older, wiser, albeit more self-conscious maestro

'Here encapsulated is our contemporary longing for meaningful narrative and an ameliorative end, a pilgrimage from death to life, the catharsis once only identified with religious faith'

sense in performance that unsuspecting listeners might attribute an editing fault to those who stick by what the composer actually drafted. Kurt Sanderling was the first to make the change. Sir Simon Rattle followed and, in Bournemouth, he makes the drum strokes as earth-shattering as possible. Riccardo Chailly is more restrained (searching for the kind of sound that might have been heard from the Mahlers' 11th-floor window, he now, in concert, prefaces the main beats with extra grace notes as in a tattoo). Litton/Carpenter goes for muffled thuds. Barshai retains the minatory thwacks but accompanies them with distant, low-frequency rumbling. Robert Olson/Wheeler and Martin Sieghart/S&M prefer something drier, giving the intervening ascending figures to vaguely Sibelian low strings, variously paced, rather than Cooke's Wagnerian tuba. Litton/Carpenter and Mazzetti do likewise. Barshai follows Cooke. And so it continues …

has enjoyed more limited circulation. **Wyn Morris's** 1972 set, originally a Philips issue, lacks Ormandy's technical assurance: neither *Scherzo*, the second the biggest beneficiary of the revamped scoring, really takes off. However, the greater weight given to the outer movements reveals a conception of rare emotive power, everything deeply felt if at times messily executed.

Based in East Germany, **Kurt Sanderling** studied the (second) Cooke score for over a year, perhaps seeking a way to hold everything together in classical balance without neglecting the more disruptive elements of Mahler's invention; he also exchanged ideas with project veteran Berthold Goldschmidt. The result is a balder reading, with faster speeds and fewer subtle inflections than Morris attempts. With the two main tempi of the opening movement carefully delineated, its progress feels neither over-pressed nor droopy, and many of Sanderling's own

HISTORIC CHOICE
Berlin Symphony Orchestra / Kurt Sanderling
Berlin Classics 0094422BC

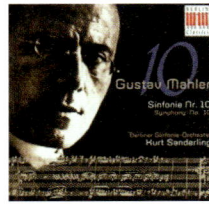

Kurt Sanderling was a key figure in the Tenth's reception history, the one Old World, Old School maestro to engage with the Cooke edition when it was still a rarity. His recording, not quite state-of-the-art, is less familiar than it deserves to be.

THE MAVERICK
Junge Deutsche Philharmonie / Barshai
Brilliant Classics 92205

The filling-in-the-blanks approach is most successfully advocated by Rudolf Barshai, whose imaginative realisation is offered at

bargain price. And there's superb playing from the Junge Deutsche Philharmonie, too, captured live in concert the day after 9/11.

A TENTH TO LIVE WITH
Berlin Radio Symphony Orchestra / Chailly
Decca 466 955-2DH; 475 6686DX12

Riccardo Chailly has been a consistently effective champion of the Cooke score. He has changed his mind on details but

his 1986 recording remains wholly recommendable, a forthright, mainstream reading presented in the bold sonics associated with this record label.

The betrayal of 'femme fatale' Alma Mahler provoked a 'rip in the fabric of diatonic harmony'

gets a real triple *piano* for the entry of the strings. Reinforcing the return of that expressionistic chord with the low rumble of drums underpins rather than obscures the harmony.

Riccardo Chailly's 1986 recording has different merits, as Michael Kennedy suggested in his original *Gramophone* review: 'Chailly accepts the Tenth as a fait accompli. For him, it exists, there are no points to prove.' Whatever the issues of deciphering handwritten orchestral material, conductor, orchestra and sound team secure a technically comfortable, tonally refulgent reading, of a piece with what we know of the maestro's subsequent Mahler conducting. Part of its collectability for admirers of Mahler ed Cooke will be the departures from Sir Simon's solutions, following the score published in 1976 as opposed to the 1989 revision of it. Where Rattle enlivens the first *Scherzo's* denouement with a cymbal clash, Chailly here is being literal, the effect not restored until the 1989 edition. Nor is he among those who underwrite the dissonant 'breakdown' chords with added percussion.

Eliahu Inbal in 1992 is softer-grained, the 'Purgatorio' sounding fresh and Bohemian rather than the stuff of nightmares. The biggest surprise comes at the very end with the upward thrust of the heart-wrenching sigh (where Mahler inscribes his wife's name as a last gesture of love). The violins' ecstatic vault through nearly two octaves is here rendered as a long slide swelling from *pianissimo* to *fortissimo*. But then an exaggerated *glissando* features in several distinguished accounts, including one from Mark Wigglesworth and the BBC National Orchestra of Wales and, more surprisingly, that of Michael Gielen.

From the mid-1990s a paradox. Just as Cooke's performing version appeared to achieve near-universal acceptance in the concert hall and on disc, so the work's growing popularity prompted a revival of interest in the alternatives. The first widely available commercial recording to use a radically different text was **Leonard Slatkin's** account of Remo Mazzetti's edition, since revised and re-recorded by **Jesús López-Cobos**. Conflating the 'best' aspects of the existing realisations, Mazzetti's jerky swatches of colour seem intuitive as much as research-driven. The wider dissemination of rival editions can be a useful reality check. But it is also legitimate to ask what we are trying to achieve by obscuring the fragmentary character of what Mahler left us. Mazzetti's may sound less like a 'performing version' and more like a finished piece, but that does not make for 'authenticity'. Like all the more interventionist editors he has a fondness for drum rolls, typically prefacing significant peaks. Mahler himself allocated the finale's ethereal 'big tune' to flute so why give the tail end of it to clarinet and then oboe?

The Carpenter edition first set down by Harold Farberman and the Philharmonia Hungarica but more widely heard in **Andrew Litton's** expert Delos production is 'fatter', interpolating the thicker contrapuntal textures supposedly characteristic of Mahler's symphonic writing. **Robert Olson's** account of the Wheeler realisation which he and Mazzetti helped correct is rather different, balder even than Cooke's in its determination to avoid the big-boned style that Mahler himself abandoned with *Das Lied von der Erde*. Still, Wheeler could be inelegant, reluctant to make 'corrections'. Is it Olson's restrained interpretative manner or Wheeler's indications that make the final pages drag?

Martin Sieghart's pacing is deliberate throughout, which may or may not be a feature of the Samale and Mazzuca score from which he works. The band is well rehearsed but plain of timbre; most striking is the extreme lucidity of Exton's sonics. The editors place the emotive climax of the finale slightly later than Cooke does – a legitimate tactic – but why sentimentalise its impact with a thickened accompanying texture? And why so much percussion?

Rudolf Barshai offers by far the most carefully conceived, best executed of

SELECTED DISCOGRAPHY

Date / Artists		Record company (review date)
1965	Philadelphia Orch / **Ormandy** (ed Cooke I)	Sony 82876 78742-2 (6/66R)
1972	New Philh Orch / **Morris** (ed Cooke I)	Scribendum ② SC010 (3/74R)
1979	Berlin SO / **K Sanderling** (ed Cooke I)	Berlin Classics ⑭ 094422BC (9/01)
1980	Philadelphia Orch / **Levine** (ed Cooke II)	RCA RD84553 (7/81R, 6/86)
1980	Bournemouth SO / **Rattle** (ed Cooke II)	Warner Classics 50021-2 (12/80R)
1986	Berlin Rad SO / **Chailly** (ed Cooke II)	Decca 466 955-2DH (3/88R, 12/00); ⑫ 475 6686DX12
1992	Frankfurt Rad SO / **Inbal** (ed Cooke I)	Denon CO75129 (4/93)
1994	St Louis SO / **Slatkin** (ed Mazzetti I)	RCA 09026 68190-2 (4/96)
1999	BPO / **Rattle** (ed Cooke III)	EMI 556972-2 (5/00); 503420-2
2000	Cincinnati SO / **López-Cobos** (ed Mazzetti II)	Telarc CD80565
2000	Polish Nat Rad SO / **Olson** (ed Wheeler IV)	Naxos 8 554811/12
2001	Junge Deutsche Philh / **Barshai** (ed Barshai)	Brilliant Classics 92205
2001	Dallas SO / **Litton** (ed Carpenter)	Delos DE3295 (4/03)
2005	SWR SO / **Gielen** (ed Cooke III)	Hänssler Classic CD93 124 (1/06)
2007	VPO / **Harding** (ed Cooke III)	DG 477 7347GH (7/08)
2007	BBC PO / **Noseda** (ed Cooke III)	Chandos CHAN10456 (3/08)
2007	Arnhem PO / **Sieghart** (ed Samale/Mazzuca)	Exton ② ⑨ EXCL00013

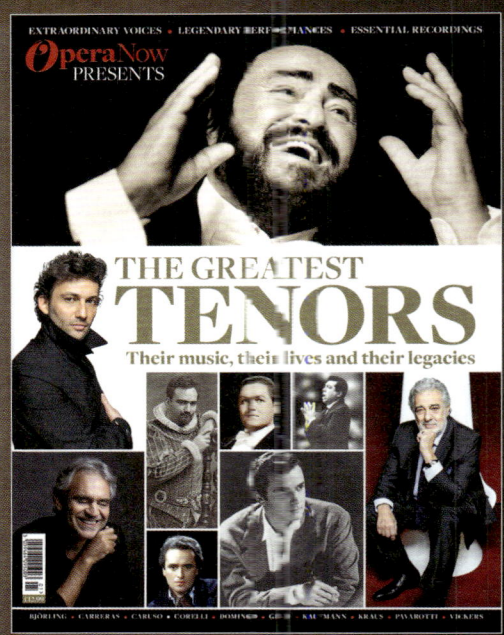

Simon Rattle's recording brought blazing conviction and emotional clout to Mahler's Tenth

post-Cooke options. String lines are moulded with exquisite care but puzzling is his capricious selection of noise-makers – castanets, triangles vibraphones and glockenspiels – in a 'Turkish' treatment of the first *Scherzo*. Guitar obtrudes during the Trio. Otherwise no great shocks, except perhaps the superb playing of the Junge Deutsche Philharmonie. The great crises of movements one and five are powerfully realised, the 'Purgatorio' deliberate and dark, the fourth movement's disturbing disruptedness convincing. The symphony's valedictory close is more richly scored than by Cooke but, unlike the work of other second-guessers, it avoids sounding like a Nino Rota pastiche.

Barshai's interpretation has a high seriousness whatever the eccentricities of his realisation; so, too, has **Michael Gielen's**. Gielen, a late convert to Cooke, believes that the intellectually honest response to the conundrum of the Tenth is to lay bare its gaunt, unfinished state, exposing even parts of the *Adagio* as the harmonic frame over which Mahler would have stretched more complex contrapuntal detail. No inexorable meditation, the movement becomes rather an unfinished dialogue between arrest and movement. The

orchestral sound, lean and light, has some exceptionally hushed playing from the strings and much exquisite detail. The finale's great flute melody is almost plain as well as pure, the focus on the strings' delicately nuanced response. Gielen has a way of foregrounding emotive detail before retreating to expository Klemperer-like stoicism. Like Chailly, he will not spoil you for more personalised interpretations.

The Vienna Philharmonic had not played Cooke's realisation until **Daniel Harding** introduced it in 2004. While orchestral timbre is striking, showcasing glorious horns and the burnished unanimity of high-lying strings, the inflections seem more authentically Viennese than idiomatically Mahlerian. **Gianandrea Noseda** has similar problems eliciting a properly neurasthenic edge in Manchester. The flute solo is eloquent enough – until you hear from team Rattle in Berlin. David Matthews's booklet-notes, as so often unmitigated gain, help make the Chandos package worthwhile.

Listening to these recordings it has not always been possible to distinguish misreadings perpetrated by individual instrumentalists from the interventions

of quixotic editors. Post-Cooke arrangers have rarely gone back to manuscript sources – much easier to copy from existing precedents when what endures in Mahler's hand has the quality of an aide-memoire with missed accidentals and dodgy clefs. Readers wishing to explore these issues in more depth should seek out the writings of Frans Bouwman, his goal nothing less than a chronologically ordered urtext of all surviving source material. There can be no one way to deliver a statement Mahler himself never voiced. To have a Mahler Tenth – almost any Mahler Tenth – adds a vital human and musical experience to our lives. **ⓖ**

THE TOP CHOICE

Berlin Philharmonic Orchestra / Rattle
Warner Classics 556972-2; 503420-2

Sir Simon Rattle has done more than anyone to establish the draft of the Tenth as a viable repertoire staple. The rougher edges  of his Bournemouth account have become part of the intended expressive effect, but the Berliners' greater finesse ultimately wins the palm.

THE GRAMOPHONE COLLECTION

Mahler's most personal love song

When Mahler presented 'Liebst du um Schönheit' as a gift to his new wife Alma, it became the fifth and last of the **Rückert-Lieder** – a collection of songs based on Friedrich Rückert's poems. In January 2013 **Richard Wigmore** listened to the many recordings and attempted to choose the ultimate version

As Mörike was to Wolf, and Heine to Schumann, so Friedrich Rückert (1788-1866) – poet, philologist, orientalist – was to Mahler. The composer identified profoundly with the directness and refined sensibility of his verses, declaring that 'after *Des Knaben Wunderhorn* I could not compose anything but Rückert – this is lyric poetry from the source, all else is lyric poetry of a derivative kind'. Apart from the earliest, 'Um Mitternacht' ('At midnight'), all the so-called *Rückert-Lieder* were written in the idyllic lakeside setting of Maiernigg in Carinthia, where Mahler had built a summer villa as a refuge from the habitual turbulence of the Viennese opera season. Four of the songs were completed, in both piano and orchestral versions, by August 1901. A fifth, 'Liebst du um Schönheit' ('If you love for beauty's sake'), followed a year later, as a gift to his new bride, Alma Schindler. It is Mahler's sole overt love song, and the only one of the *Rückert-Lieder* he never orchestrated – doubtless because of its intensely personal significance. When a plausibly Mahlerian orchestral version by the Leipzig musician-cum-critic Max Puttmann appeared in 1916, Alma, predictably, protested.

In their orchestral guise, four of the *Rückert-Lieder* were premiered at a sold-out concert in Vienna that many Lieder lovers might be tempted to nominate as the greatest ever showcase of new songs: a 'Lieder recital with orchestra' – itself a revolutionary concept – in January 1905 that also included the premieres of the *Kindertotenlieder* and settings from *Des Knaben Wunderhorn*.

Crucially, Mahler chose the small Brahmssaal of the Musikverein so that the songs could be performed 'in the manner of chamber music', in an apt acoustic.

There is no hint in the *Rückert-Lieder* of Mahler as purveyor of orchestral gigantism. Except for the brooding, starkly scored 'Um Mitternacht' (wind and brass, without strings), these are his most lyrical songs. Mahler matches their subjective intimacy with orchestration of vocal eloquence, at once intricate and exquisitely delicate: in the gossamer textures (no cellos or basses) of 'Ich atmet' einen linden Duft!' ('I breathed a gentle fragrance!') that prefigure the ravishing chinoiserie of *Das Lied von der Erde*; or the veiled, plangent contrapuntal weave of cor anglais, clarinets, horns and muted strings in 'Ich bin der Welt abhanden gekommen' ('I have lost touch with the world'), on the familiar Romantic theme of withdrawal into a secluded world of love, art and nature.

For economic reasons, concert-goers hear the *Rückert-Lieder* far more often with piano than with orchestra. Yet like the *Wunderhorn* songs and the *Kindertotenlieder*, their conception is essentially orchestral. Once experienced, it is hard to forgo the keening cor anglais in 'Ich bin der Welt abhanden gekommen', the mournful clarinets, oboe d'amore and nocturnal horns – and the final symphonic blaze – of

'Um Mitternacht', or the *con sordino* murmurings of 'Ich atmet' einen linden Duft!'. However sympathetic the performers, the piano versions tend to stand in relation to the orchestral as a pen-and-ink sketch does to a painting. So although recorded performances of the *Rückert-Lieder* are divided evenly between keyboard and orchestra, I shall concentrate primarily on the orchestral versions, taking in the pick of the keyboard-accompanied recordings en route. My self-imposed rule is that discs must include at least the four songs that Mahler orchestrated himself, which means no more than a rueful glance at Kathleen Ferrier's intensely felt 1952

However sympathetic the performers, the piano versions tend to stand in relation to the orchestral as a pen-and-ink sketch does to a painting

performance of three songs with Bruno Walter and the VPO (Alto ALC1120).

Although Mahler's two chosen soloists at the pioneering 1905 *Lieder-Abend mit Orchester* were baritones, most recordings feature mezzo-sopranos, the voice type we now think of as quintessentially Mahlerian. The published edition opens with the scherzo of the set. 'Blicke mir nicht in die Lieder' ('Do not look into my songs' – Mahler hated anyone prying into his unfinished works), followed by 'Ich atmet' einen linden Duft!'. Then come the longest, most profound songs, 'Ich bin der Welt abhanden gekommen' and 'Um Mitternacht', with 'Liebst du um Schönheit' as a radiant envoi. This ordering can work in performance, though many singers prefer to end with

Musical gift: Mahler's Rückert settings culminated in a wedding present for his wife Alma

'bound' legato, a *sine qua non* in these songs. The lumpy opening phrase of 'Ich bin der Welt abhanden gekommen' alone makes this a non-starter.

Dietrich Henschel has his bright, high baritone under far better control, while the luminous textures of a slimmed-down Hallé Orchestra under Kent Nagano are surely close to Mahler's ideal. He is tenderly confiding in 'Ich atmet' einen linden Duft!'; and he vividly catches both the existential questioning at the opening of 'Um Mitternacht' (where the oboe d'amore and clarinet slides give full value to Mahler's eerie night-bird calls) and the triumphant affirmation of faith at the end.

With incisive diction and a free-ringing top register, Henschel holds his own without strain against Mahler's brass chorale. Only 'Ich bin der Welt abhanden gekommen' slightly disappoints. Ushered in by one of the most eloquent of cor anglais soloists, it's beautifully paced, with an ardently flowing middle section. But with a hint of tension in the tone, Henschel misses the ultimate Mahlerian *Innigkeit*.

At his peak in 1963, **Dietrich Fischer-Dieskau** distils an otherworldly spirituality in this song, inspired by the sentient, deep-toned playing of the Berlin Philharmonic under Karl Böhm. Fischer-Dieskau sees everything and exaggerates nothing. 'Blicke mir nicht in die Lieder' is gently whimsical, 'Um Mitternacht' predictably magnificent, whether in the hushed, fearful opening, the lamenting quality of tone at the disconsolate 'Es hat kein Lichtgedanken mir Trost gebracht', or the final affirmation, warm and noble, without bombast. His responses to text and harmonic flux are specific, never generalised. Only 'Ich atmet' einen linden Duft!' is controversial. Fischer-Dieskau's caressing *mezza voce* is matched by playing of exquisite delicacy – 'very tender and inward', indeed. But can Mahler have intended the song to unfold at this trance-like tempo?

Caught live with the VPO under Zubin Mehta at the 1967 Salzburg Festival, **Fischer-Dieskau** takes 'Ich atmet' einen linden Duft!' more flowingly, though the pinched, nasal tone of the Vienna oboe at this period is a taste I've never acquired. Unlike the Böhm recording, the baritone here includes 'Liebst du um Schönheit', sung ardently if with slightly queasy *rubato*. Fischer-Dieskau completists will want this, though apart from the extra song,

the two 'big' songs, or to separate them with 'Liebst du um Schönheit'.

Whatever their chosen order, any singer tackling the *Rückert-Lieder* must be attuned to their tenderness and intimacy, while conductors need an acute feeling for instrumental balance and pacing, not

least in 'Um Mitternacht', with its many shifts of metre and tempo.

On a Naxos recording, **Cord Garben** draws some sensitive playing from the Hanover Radio Philharmonic. But baritone **Hidenori Komatsu** is unsubtle, often too loud, and lacks a true,

I see no reason for preferring it to his BPO studio recording. 'Ich bin der Welt abhanden gekommen' is still ineffably moving (I hope they throttled the cougher in the orchestral coda). But in 'Blicke mir nicht in die Lieder' and 'Um Mitternacht' he now sounds over-strenuous, jabbing unsuspecting consonants. The orchestra suffers in the recorded balance.

KEYBOARD EXCURSION

Fischer-Dieskau is even more prone to exaggeration in his 1978 recording of all five *Rückert-Lieder* in their piano versions. Though the nap on his tone has begun to wear, his breath control remains miraculous, effortlessly encompassing phrases that most singers break into two. He now finds new shades of desolation and tenderness in 'Um Mitternacht', abetted by Daniel Barenboim's vividly 'orchestrated' accompaniment. It is the three lighter songs that provoke misgivings. All receive the full F-D treatment. 'Ich atmet' einen linden Duft!', so magical in the Böhm recording, now shows bulges in the line. 'Blicke mir nicht in die Lieder' is neurotically fussy, while the sudden explosions on 'Sonne' and 'Meerfrau' in 'Liebst du um Schönheit' sound hectoring rather than ecstatic.

For all Fischer-Dieskau's probing mastery, the most satisfying versions with piano come from three younger baritones, all favouring mobile tempos. **Roman Trekel**, with Burkhard Kehring, uses his firm, dark resonance and incisive diction to magnificent effect in 'Um Mitternacht', and shapes 'Ich atmet' einen linden Duft!' with caressing tenderness. The timbre of his voice makes 'Ich bin der Welt abhanden gekommen' more elegiac than usual, marred here and there by a touch of flatness.

Stephan Genz is even more touching. If he lacks the ideal weight for the climax of 'Um Mitternacht', his gentle, companionable baritone and verbal sensitivity give consistent pleasure. Genz sings 'Blicke mir nicht in die Lieder'

Summer respite: Mahler enjoys a walk at his country villa in Maiernigg, Carinthia, in 1905

lightly, confidentially, with a smile in the tone, matched by the delicacy and point of Roger Vignoles's accompaniment. 'Liebst du um Schönheit' is flowing and simple, in extreme contrast to Fischer-Dieskau; and with seamless *legato* and perfect control of soft dynamics, he gives a mesmeric performance of 'Ich bin der Welt abhanden gekommen'.

Equally rapt and inward here is **Christian Gerhaher** in symbiotic partnership with Gerold Huber, who finds an ideal ebb and flow for the song's keyboard interludes. With his minute yet unexaggerated verbal response, Gerhaher charts each shade of spiritual desolation in 'Um Mitternacht' – placed as the recital's centrepiece – and uses the robust core of his baritone for a ringing final affirmation of faith. He and Huber catch the fun as well as the pungency of 'Blicke mir nicht in die Lieder'. Overall,

THE BARITONE CHOICE
Fischer-Dieskau; BPO / Böhm
DG

Some will regret the omission of 'Liebst du um Schönheit' from this recording, but Fischer-Dieskau combines beauty of tone, Mahlerian understanding and a spiritual quality.

THE MODERN CHOICE
Kožená; BPO/ Rattle
DG

In partnership with Rattle and the Berlin Philharmonic, Magdalena Kožená sings with youthful vocal radiance and an individual response to text and verbal music.

THE PIANO CHOICE
Hunt Lieberson; Vignoles
Wigmore Hall Live

From a trancelike 'Ich atmet' einen linden Duft!' to a serene 'Ich bin der Welt abhanden gekommen', the mezzo-soprano Hunt Lieberson's performances are lit with an inner glow.

Gerhaher is as touching and dramatically involved as Genz, but even wider-ranging in tone colour and expression.

Among a handful of versions with mezzo and piano, **Marie-Nicole Lemieux** – so often memorable in Handel and Vivaldi – sings here with a monochrome severity. The more communicative **Ann Murray** is lucidly partnered by Malcolm Martineau. 'Ich atmet' einen linden Duft!' and 'Liebst du um Schönheit', the final 'dich lieb' ich immerdar' blissfully savoured, are especially lovely; and her slightly strained tone at *mezzo-forte* and above somehow enhances the agonised questioning in 'Um Mitternacht'.

Even more moving is **Lorraine Hunt Lieberson**, with Roger Vignoles,

Like Verdi, Mahler was famed for choosing singers – sometimes controversially – for their expressive power rather than vocal beauty

recorded before a digitally silenced Wigmore Hall audience. She brought an almost unbearable emotional vulnerability to everything she sang. It is impossible to banish awareness of her premature death when listening to 'Ich bin der Welt abhanden gekommen', in which she distils an unearthly mix of poignancy and spiritual serenity. No one else quite matches her spontaneous yet contained passion in 'Liebst du um Schönheit'; and she vindicates her measured tempos in 'Um Mitternacht' (holding back where Mahler prescribes 'flowing'), with her haunting concentration, making the song a starkly intimate confession of the soul.

MEZZO AND ORCHESTRA

Like Verdi, Mahler was famed for choosing singers – sometimes controversially – for their expressive power rather than vocal beauty. No mezzo in the *Rückert-Lieder* has a richer or more vibrant voice than **Marilyn Horne**, but she never remotely suggests a true Mahlerian inwardness. She makes a meal of 'Liebst du um Schönheit', and, fatally, can't resist opening up on the high phrases in 'Ich bin der Welt abhanden gekommen'. Her determinedly sung 'Blicke mir nicht in die Lieder' might be summed up as 'Don't mess with me'. **Barnardette Greevy**'s warm contralto tones had lost their bloom by the time she recorded the songs in 1994. There are touching things here, including a gently musing 'Ich atmet' einen linden Duft!', but too much that is effortful.

Recorded at a concert with the San Francisco SO, **Susan Graham** combines

a rounded beauty of tone with a vivid sense of character: say, in her excitable 'Blicke mir nicht in die Lieder' – 'very lively', as Mahler demands – or the sensuous reverie of 'Ich atmet' einen linden Duft!'. She is impressive, too, in the spiritual drama of 'Um Mitternacht', where Michael Tilson Thomas skilfully negotiates the tricky gear shifts. But 'Ich bin der Welt abhanden gekommen' is too forthright and too indulgent, with singer and conductor taking Mahler's *zurückhaltend* ('held back') as a cue for ceaseless ritardandi, even when he specifies 'flowing'.

With a cooler, less creamy tone, **Katarina Karnéus** is more *innig* here. But her ultra-slow speed – necessitating a break in the opening phrase – suggests a soul weighted with sorrow rather than a blissful withdrawal from the world. A few raw top notes apart, Karnéus judges the three lighter songs nicely, not least a playful 'Blicke mir nicht in die Lieder', enhanced by the transparent chamber sonorities that Susanna Mälkki conjures from the Gothenburg Symphony Orchestra. Singer, woodwind and horns combine in anxious, intimate colloquy in 'Um Mitternacht'. With the turn to the major key at the words 'I cast my mind outwards, beyond the dark barriers',

Karnéus and the players respond to Mahler's indication *zart* – tender, delicate – where many singers just get louder.

Christine Schäfer, the sole soprano in this survey, gives performances that will fascinate or repel, according to taste. Her voice is not always ideally steady, and high notes can glare. Mahler's veiled colourings are inevitably brightened when songs are transposed upwards. In 'Ich atmet einen linden Duft!', oboe and first horn are replaced by flute and clarinet: easier to play smoothly in *alt*, but compromising Mahler's orchestral palette. Schäfer sparkles in the opening 'Blicke mir nicht in die Lieder'. 'Um Mitternacht' is neurotic, disturbed, as if soprano and conductor Christoph Eschenbach are already eyeing the Expressionism of Schoenberg's *Erwartung*. But I found both 'Liebst du um Schönheit' and 'Ich bin der Welt abhanden gekommen' well-nigh unbearable, the former inflated into a *Tristan*-esque wallow, the latter drawn out yet anything but *ruhig*.

A relief, then, to turn to two Mahler singers of an older generation. **Christa Ludwig**'s velvet mezzo and sumptuous legato are movingly heard in 'Ich bin der Welt abhanden gekommen', placed first. 'Um Mitternacht' has a sombre, hieratic majesty – the antithesis of Schäfer. From the opening cor anglais solo, Herbert von Karajan coaxes playing of

SELECTED DISCOGRAPHY

RECORDING DATE / ARTISTS	RECORD COMPANY (REVIEW DATE)
1963 **Fischer-Dieskau**; BPO / **Böhm**	DG 477 5556GM3
1967 **Fischer-Dieskau**; VPO / **Mehta**	Orfeo C336 931B
1969 **Baker**; New Philh Orch / **Barbirolli**	EMI 566981-2 (2/68R; 7/99); 208087-2; 457767-2; 608985-2
1974 **Ludwig**; BPO / **Karajan**	DG 457 716-2GOR2 (12/98); 453 0402GTA2; 469 304-2GP2
1978 **Fischer-Dieskau**; Barenboim pf	EMI/Warner Classics 567556-2; 476780-2; 456352-2
1978 **Horne**; Los Angeles PO / **Mehta**	Decca Eloquence 442 8287; Decca 478 0165DC11
1993 **Von Otter**; North German Rad SO / **Gardiner**	DG 439 928-2GH
1994 **Greevy**; Ireland Nat SO / **Furst**	Naxos 8 554156
1995 **Komatsu**; Hanover Rad PO / **Garben**	Naxos 8 554164
1988/89 **Fassbaender**; Deutsches SO Berlin / **Chailly**	Decca 473 725-2DF2
1998 **Hunt Lieberson**; Vignoles p	Wigmore Hall Live 0013 (6/07)
2000 **Lemieux**; Blumenthal pf	Cypres CYP8605
2001 **Henschel**; Hallé Orch / **Nagano**	Apex 2564 67538-9
2003 **Genz**; Vignoles pf	Hyperion CDA67392
2004 **Trekel**; Kehring pf	Berlin Classics 0017472BC
2005 **Murray**; Martineau pf	Avie AV2077 (2/06)
2008 **Schäfer**; Deutsches SO Berlin / **Eschenbach**	Capriccio CAP5026 (11/10)
2009 **Gerhaher**; Huber pf	RCA Red Seal 88697 56773-2
2010 **Graham**; San Francisco SO / **Tilson Thomas**	Avie/SFS Media 82193 60036-2 (11/10)
2010 **Karnéus**; Gothenburg SO / **Mälkki**	BIS BIS-SACD1600 (10/11)
2010 **Kožená**; Lucerne Fest Orch / **Abbado**	EuroArts 205 7988 (2/11); 205 7984
2011 **Kožená**; BPO / **Rattle**	DG 479 0065GH (7/12)

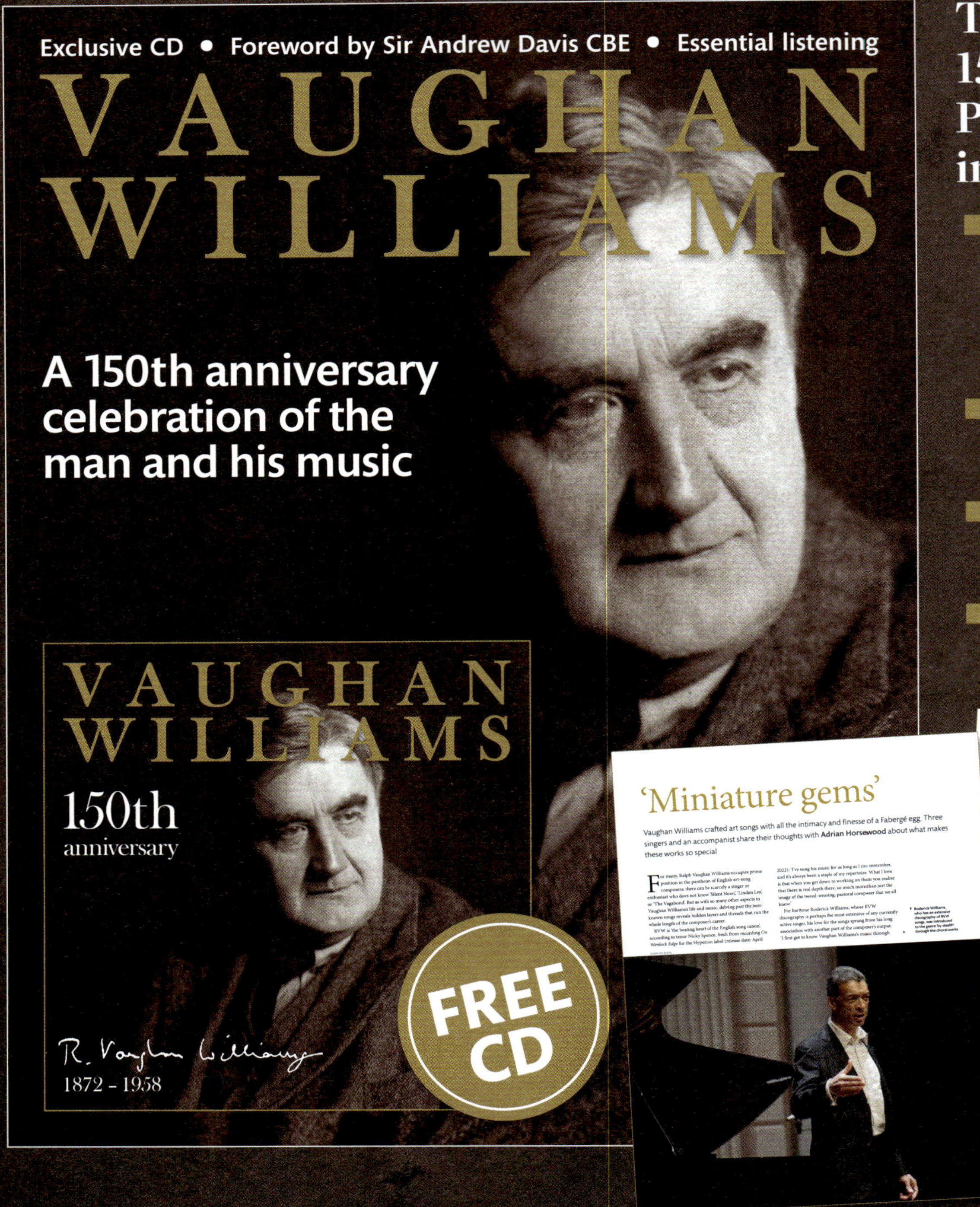

sculpted finesse from the Berlin Philharmonic, though the large body of strings threatens to overwhelm the singer in 'Liebst du um Schönheit'. Ludwig's artistry and vocal mastery are irrefutable. Yet in the lighter songs she is too much the grande dame to charm and touch: 'Blicke mir nicht in die Lieder' comes across as a stern reprimand, 'Ich atmet' einen linden Duft!' as a solemnly impersonal statement.

Brigitte Fassbaender, eloquently partnered by the Deutsches Symphonie-Orchester Berlin under Riccardo Chailly, is less impeccable vocally (her deep-bronze tone can discolour on high notes) but far more involving. Where Ludwig relates, Fassbaender lives each song, intensely. She is never merely comfortable 'Liebst du um Schönheit', taken swiftly, is ardent and outgoing, utterly devoid of sentimentality. She spins a caressing line in 'Ich atmet' einen linden Duft!', while both the larger songs are magnificent: in the fearful unease at the opening of 'Um Mitternacht', the shocking stab of despair at the melisma on 'entscheiden', or the otherworldliness of the line 'I am dead to the world's bustle' in 'Ich bin der Welt abhanden gekommen'.

With her lighter, more pellucid timbre, **Anne Sofie von Otter** matches Fassbaender in urgency of communication. She and the fine wind soloists of the NDR Symphony Orchestra under John Eliot Gardiner are exquisitely delicate in 'Ich atmet' einen linden Duft!', and distil an ethereal serenity, very different from Fassbaender's bittersweet world-weariness, in 'Ich bin der Welt abhanden gekommen' – though I don't sense any quickening of the pulse, as specified by Mahler, at the section beginning 'Es ist mir auch gar nichts darangelegen'. In contrast to Fassbaender, 'Liebst du um Schönheit' is tender and intimate. If von Otter lacks the ideal reserves of tone for 'Um Mitternacht', she compensates with her acute response to each phase of Mahler's dark night of the soul.

On an enterprisingly planned disc that juxtaposes the *Rückert-Lieder* with Ravel's *Shéhérazade* and Dvořák's *Biblical Songs*, **Magdalena Kožená** combines still-youthful beauty and evenness of tone with intensity of expression. 'Liebst du

Poet Friedrich Ruckert: for Mahler, a pure lyrical source

um Schönheit' is surpassingly tender, with an exquisite floated *pianissimo* on the climactic 'Liebe'. Cushioned by the infinitely delicate playing of the Berlin Philharmonic under Simon Rattle, she exudes a rarefied, secretive bliss at the line 'and rest in a tranquil realm' near the close of 'Ich bin der Welt abhanden gekommen'. In 'Um Mitternacht', founded on a seamless *legato*, she vividly dramatises the desolate self-questioning. She and Rattle are careful never to let the song become statuesque, and build to a glowing climax, excited rather than grandiose.

Kožená is equally intense and involving on a DVD recording from the Lucerne Festival. A batonless Claudio Abbado conjures miracles of refinement from the Lucerne Festival Orchestra. Mahler's contrapuntal lines are fastidiously sifted. And has any orchestra ever sounded so magical in the transfigured *ppp* (Mahler's marking) coda of 'Ich bin der Welt abhanden gekommen'? I loved the shot of the Hoffnung-esque bass tuba in 'Um Mitternacht'. But what David Gutman, in his original review, dubbed Kožená's 'wild-eyed gurning' does not take kindly to close-ups.

Forced to nominate a single version of the *Rückert-Lieder* with mezzo and orchestra, I should be hard-pushed to

choose between Kožená, von Otter and Fassbaender. For vocal radiance and touching vulnerability I should plump, just, for Kožená, with either Rattle or Abbado (perhaps with the picture turned off). But the version of these glorious songs that has moved me more than any other is the 1969 recording from **Janet Baker**, with the New Philharmonia Orchestra under Sir John Barbirolli. With Baker at her vocal peak, this has justly become a classic. True, one or two tempos are slower than Mahler probably envisaged. Flute and clarinet replace oboe and horn in 'Ich atmet' einen linden Duft!', the brief violin solo in 'Ich bin der Welt abhanden gekommen' is played by violins *en masse*, and there's the odd audible edit. But it hardly matters when the playing and singing are so lovingly attuned to these most private of Mahler's songs.

In its burning directness and subtle feeling for atmosphere, epitomised by the fearful *pianissimo* before the final apotheosis, Baker's 'Um Mitternacht' has never been eclipsed. 'Liebst du um Schönheit' captivates with its candour and freshness, 'Ich atmet' einen linden Duft!' with its floating grace. And not even Fischer-Dieskau quite equalled Baker's self-communing *Innigkeit* in 'Ich bin der Welt abhanden gekommen', from the opening phrase, perfectly *ruhevoll* (peaceful) – as the composer asks – to the hushed, transfigured close. Mahler, who needed to escape from 'the world's bustle' in order to create, called this sublime song 'my very self'. In Baker's hypnotic performance you sense that the singer is revealing as much of herself as the composer. **G**

TOP CHOICE

Baker; New Philh Orch / Barbirolli

Warner Classics

Tenderness, grace, impassioned directness, sublime Mahlerian inwardness: Janet Baker,

in glorious voice, has them all, abetted by Barbirolli's loving, yet never indulgent, accompaniments. Baker's recording is immensely moving.

PHOTOGRAPHY: LEBRECHT AUTHORS / BRIDGEMAN IMAGES

THE GRAMOPHONE COLLECTION

Mahler's Des Knaben Wunderhorn

These Lieder have enjoyed numerous recordings in both their orchestral and piano versions. In October 2016 **Richard Wigmore** surveyed those featuring all 12 songs and recommends the ones to own

What would one have given to be in the Brahmssaal (as it's now known) of the Vienna Musikverein on January 29, 1905. In one of the most celebrated of all Lieder concerts, an audience of cognoscenti heard an all-Mahler 'Lieder-Abend mit Orchester' that included the *Kindertotenlieder*, four of the *Rückert-Lieder* and seven songs from *Des Knaben Wunderhorn*. Two baritones shared the programme, while a slimmed-down orchestra ensured that Mahler's fastidiously imagined orchestral textures (each *Wunderhorn* song has its unique sound palette) emerged with maximum clarity. Conservative-minded critics – and the epithet usually went with the job – were unimpressed. But the composer's supporters in the capacity audience enthusiastically hailed what was in effect a new concept – the orchestrally accompanied song recital.

In the previous decade Mahler had found relief from the frustrations of his job as director of the Hamburg Opera in his long vacations in the Salzkammergut. It was during these summer respites that he composed most of his songs with orchestra from *Des Knaben Wunderhorn* ('The Boy's Magic Horn'), drawing on the volumes of folksongs and folk poetry published in 1806-08 by Achim von Arnim and Clemens Brentano. These examples of popular, 'natural' art – some newly invented, others adapted to contemporary taste – were nostalgically cherished by the German Romantics in a world of encroaching urbanisation. As Heinrich Heine put it, 'In these songs you can feel the heartbeat of the German people.'

Mahler had surely known many of the *Wunderhorn* poems since his childhood in the Moravian garrison town of Iglau, where bugle calls, fanfares and marches were part of his everyday experience. It is no accident that he remained haunted by the tales of hussars, drummer boys and sentries, some rooted in the Thirty Years War that had devastated the German lands in the 17th century. In his *Wunderhorn* songs Mahler treats folksong, military band music, Ländler and Viennese waltzes with mingled affection, irony and tragic realism. As in so much of his music, he delights in juxtaposing seemingly incongruous elements and using popular music (though there are no folk-tune quotations) to distorted, sometimes disturbing ends.

Several of the *Wunderhorn* Lieder are comic and/or parodistic. The singer dons her dirndl for 'Rheinlegendchen', a fairy tale in which the orchestra/pianist mimics a folk fiddler, as well as for the yodelling nonsense song, 'Wer hat dies Liedlein erdacht?'. Another bucolic Ländler, 'Des Antonius von Padua Fischpredigt' (later expanded into the *scherzo* of the Second Symphony), is Mahler's caustic commentary on smug bourgeois piety. In 'Lob des hohen Verstands', a donkey judges a singing competition between a cuckoo and a nightingale, with predictable results. All his adult life Mahler had suffered at the hands of hostile and cloth-eared critics. How he must have relished getting his own back at his tormentors.

Two of the humorous songs – 'Verlor'ne Müh' and 'Trost im Unglück', an edgy sparring match between a hussar and his (ex-?) lover – are conceived as a duet for one voice. Several recordings use two singers, here and elsewhere, though Mahler never did. Around half of the *Wunderhorn*

settings are tragedies, replete with Mahler's compassion for suffering, downtrodden humanity: the dialogue between mother and starving child in 'Das irdische Leben', or the doomed, phantasmal soldiers of 'Der Schildwache Nachtlied', 'Wo die schönen Trompeten blasen' (a Housmanesque colloquy between a girl and the ghost of her soldier-lover), 'Der Tamboursg'sell' and 'Revelge'. In the last, the most bitter of anti-war songs, a defeated regiment parades through the village as a mass of spectral skeletons, to the strains of a heartless quick march.

With dozens of releases featuring only selections from the *Wunderhorn* Lieder, I have limited my (emphatically *not* complete!) survey to recordings that include all 12 of the songs composed between 1892 and 1901 and subsequently published as a collection (10 of the songs had appeared in 1899 under the title *Humoresken*). Some recordings add 'Urlicht', incorporated into the Second Symphony, and/or the child's view of heaven, 'Das himmlische Leben', which became the finale of Symphony No 4.

SALON INTIMACY

Mahler conceived the songs in terms of the orchestra and its kaleidoscopic colours, then swiftly produced publishable voice-and-piano versions. While I always tend to hear the orchestral originals in my mind's ear, it would be unfair to dismiss the piano versions as mere sketches. By 1978, when he recorded the *Wunderhorn* Lieder with Barenboim, **Dietrich Fischer-Dieskau**'s tone could fray at climaxes. He was never a natural charmer; and heartiness can creep into 'Rheinlegendchen' and 'Wer hat dies Liedlein erdacht?'. A hectoring 'Lob des hohen Verstands' reminds me of the old saw that a German joke is no laughing matter. Abetted by the hard, brassy timbres that Barenboim conjures from the piano, Fischer-Dieskau delivers swagger galore in the equestrian opening of 'Trost im Unglück', though he tries too hard to characterise the girl, arms akimbo, upper lip curled in mockery. But in the tragic songs he is, predictably, in his element. If he can sound too imposing in 'Der Tamboursg'sell', he is compelling here and in a magnificently mordant 'Revelge', with Barenboim brilliantly 'orchestrating' the keyboard part.

A more recent version with piano uses two singers, **Diana Damrau** and **Iván Paley**; and, as on several of the recordings with orchestra, they perform some of the songs as duets. I'm ambivalent about the use of two singers in the hallucinatory nocturne 'Wo die schönen Trompeten blasen'; also in 'Der Schildwache Nachtlied' and the political prisoner's song of defiant bravado 'Lied des Verfolgten im Turm', where the girls' words have a dreamlike unreality. But 'Verlor'ne Müh' (where simpering girl vainly woos lumpen swain) and 'Trost im Unglück' are that much more vivid when they are sung as mini quasi-operatic scenas. Damrau always gives pleasure with her fresh, gleaming tone and immediacy of response. She catches just the right note of amused scorn in 'Trost im Unglück'. 'Wer hat dies Liedlein erdacht?' is pitch-perfect in its smiling caprice, 'Das irdische Leben' graphically characterised. Paley characterises lustily, too, though his baritone lacks colour and firm focus. Why he was allotted 'Rheinlegendchen' (here quavery and graceless) and, even more improbably, 'Urlicht' is anyone's guess.

If you want the complete *Wunderhorn* songs with piano, the version to go for is that by **Stephan Genz**, in tandem with the ever-sympathetic Roger Vignoles. In 'Revelge', Genz is a match for Fischer-Dieskau, giving a hard, sardonic edge to his naturally warm, rounded tone. 'Rheinlegendchen' is unselfconsciously charming, and the other humorous songs are nicely understated. Beginning in a tense, barely whispered half-voice, 'Wo die schönen Trompeten blasen' is moving by way of its tender restraint. The relentlessly whirring accompaniment of 'Das irdische Leben' depicts both the threshing of the corn and, by extension, the pitiless grind of human existence. In its piano version, this song loses less than many of the *Wunderhorn* songs, especially when Vignoles is involved. He and Genz choose

'Im Walde, des Knaben Wunderhorn' - oil on canvas, by Moritz von Schwind, *c*1848

a restrained tempo; and while Mahler's direction *Unheimlich bewegt* ('with sinister motion') gets its due, Genz emphasises lyrical poignancy, with a mournful colour in the starving child's pleas for bread.

LIEDER-ABEND MIT ORCHESTER

For obvious financial reasons, piano performances of the *Wunderhorn* Lieder predominate in the concert hall. On disc, the reverse is true. With two exceptions, all the orchestral recordings use two singers, a baritone (usually Mahler's preferred voice) and either a soprano or a mezzo. The exact allocation of the songs varies from version to version, as does the ordering, though this can of course be tweaked at the press of a button. It's worth remembering, too, that Mahler did not think of the songs as a cycle, and never performed more than seven of them in any one concert.

If sexual intercourse, according to Philip Larkin, began in 1963, the modern cult of Mahler was not far behind. By the end of that transformative decade, integral symphony cycles from Bernstein and Kubelík were well underway and three *Wunderhorn* recordings had appeared in quick succession. First out of the blocks was an all-British affair, with **Janet Baker**, **Geraint Evans** and the LPO under Wyn Morris. The conductor, once-labelled 'our Celtic Furtwängler', is bafflingly prosaic here, with minimal feeling for Mahlerian *rubato*. Tempos, usually on the fast side, are rigidly held. A pity, as both Baker, singing with her trademark emotional candour, and Evans strike a near ideal balance between vivid character and good, wholesome singing. Baker's radiance and unsentimental compassion in 'Wo die schönen Trompeten blasen' are as memorable as Evans's vigour and directness in the military songs. He sings 'Lob des hohen Verstands' with the resourceful glee that marked his Leporello, Papageno and Fra Melitone.

The conductors on the other two versions from the 1960s are far more natural Mahlerians, with a deep understanding of the music's central European background. Pride of place goes to the recording from Leonard Bernstein, who did more than anyone to make Mahler palatable to the Viennese, with the husband-and-wife duo of **Christa Ludwig** and **Walter Berry**. A drawback here is the dry, boxy recorded sound and the dominance of the New York Philharmonic in the balance. But the performances, with Bernstein at his most incandescent (one or two oddly slow tempos apart), are often compelling. Both artists are singers who place a premium on firm, evenly produced tone and a true, bound line.

Two recordings by Leonard Bernstein merit mention here, with one a close second to the top choice

With Bernstein relishing Mahler's garish orchestral palette, Berry sings 'Revelge' with controlled viciousness, finding a new, ghostly colour for the final section. Ludwig contrasts naturally the two voices of 'Das irdische Leben', sung in a single, desperate sweep; and her intense *legato* pays rich dividends in a poignant, broadly phrased 'Wo die schönen Trompeten blasen' and a rapt 'Urlicht'. The duets all work well, too, not least 'Der Schildwache Nachtlied', where Berry swaggers without forcing (many singers are tempted to shout here) and Ludwig brings an aching pathos to the (illusory?) girl's responses.

More commercially successful in the UK, then and (I suspect) now, was the near-contemporary version from **Elisabeth Schwarzkopf** and **Dietrich Fischer-Dieskau**, with the LSO under George Szell. The combination of the world's most famous (in 1968) Lieder singers, Britain's then finest orchestra and the gimlet-eyed Szell, renowned for his fastidious attention to balance, promised great things. With superb recorded sound, the promise was largely fulfilled, though you could never accuse either singer of artlessness. I confess I have never been a

paid-up Schwarzkopf fan, and the disparity between bright, open vowels and darkly hooded tones, characteristic of her later singing, does disconcert me. For me, she sounds too nudgingly knowing in 'Rheinlegendchen' and 'Lob des hohen Verstands' (the demotic was never her forte). But her mastery of mood and colour are irrefutable, above all in 'Wo die schönen Trompeten blasen', sung here as a duet. No one else matches her haunted sense of foreboding at the opening, or indeed Fischer-Dieskau's plangent *legato* in the soldier's answering Ländler. Abetted by the LSO's glitter and virtuosity, Fischer-Dieskau brings a harrowing intensity and command of colour to the military songs. 'Der Tamboursg'sell' is almost unbearably moving.

A decade later, Philips entered the *Wunderhorn* stakes with the young **Jessye Norman**, its new star soprano, in partnership with baritone **John Shirley-Quirk** and the Concertgebouw Orchestra under Bernard Haitink. The Amsterdam players and the recorded sound are at least a match for the EMI/LSO recording. Norman's sumptuous tone is heard at its most persuasive in 'Wo die schönen

PERIOD SONORITIES

Connolly *mez* **Henschel** *bar* **Champs-Elysées Orch / Herreweghe** HM HMC90 1920
Recreating a late-19th-century sound palette, Herreweghe proves a natural Mahlerian, not

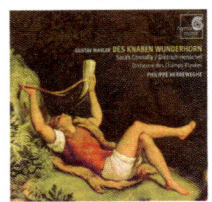

least in the easy lilt he brings to the Ländler. Henschel precisely gauges the military and comic songs, while Connolly's 'Urlicht' is one of the loveliest on disc.

CHAMBER SCALE

Bonney *sop* **Fulgoni** *mez* **Winbergh** *ten* **Goerne** *bar* **RCO / Chailly** Decca 467 348-2DH
There is an ideal transparency of texture here. Goerne is perfect in Mahler's *innig* mode;

Bonney is delightful in duet-for-one 'Verlor'ne Müh'; and Winbergh's distinctively open, Scandinavian tone and dramatic flair make for a magnificent 'Revelge'.

A CLOSE SECOND

Popp *sop* **Schmidt** *bar* **Concertgebouw Orch / Bernstein** DG 477 5744G 36
Bernstein, at his most magnetic here, notices everything and exaggerates (almost) nothing.

With that distinctive sharp edge to her tone, Popp sings a nicely acerbic 'Fischpredigt' and a nonpareil 'Wo die schönen Trompeten blasen'.

Riccardo Chailly's recording features four singers

Trompeten blasen', floated on seemingly infinite reserves of breath. Elsewhere, she can be straight-laced and word-shy. The duets never quite come alive. Shirley-Quirk, always intensely musical, is too refined for St Anthony's fishy sermon and the avian singing contest (where Haitink also downplays the vulgarity) but evinces a grave tenderness in 'Der Tamboursg'sell'.

Bernstein's second *Wunderhorn* recording, made at concerts in 1987 with **Lucia Popp**, **Andreas Schmidt** and the Concertgebouw Orchestra, suffers from an erratic balance and the occasional ensemble imprecision that goes with live recording. But the performances are often magnificent, not least the duets: in 'Lied des Verfolgten im Turm' (more urgent than in Bernstein's recording with Berry), Schmidt is ruggedly incisive, heroically refusing to compromise his political principles even when enticed by the enchanting Popp. In 'Wo die schönen Trompeten blasen', Bernstein's eccentrically slow tempo only just avoids sentimentality, and Popp occasionally squeezes her tone both here and in a rapt 'Urlicht' (more personal, less hieratic than Ludwig two decades earlier). But criticism seems impertinent in the face of singing of such plangent intensity, simplicity and sophistication held in perfect balance. Schmidt, with his fine dark resonance, is superb in the tragic military nocturnes. Mahler requires the opening lines of 'Der Tamboursg'sell' to be sung 'naively, without sentimentality', which is exactly what we get here: Schmidt vividly suggests the boy's feigned stoicism at the start, and then (as the composer indicates) a sense of horror seeps into his tone at 'O Galgen, du hohes Haus'.

WUNDERHORN AS CHAMBER MUSIC

Writing to Richard Strauss in 1905, Mahler stressed that the *Wunderhorn* songs should be performed 'in the manner of chamber music'. Allowing for the four horns demanded by many of the songs, and the mighty battery of percussion in 'Revelge', this is how he performed them in that pioneering concert in the Brahmssaal. Strings were scaled down to three or four per part, radically altering the string-wind balance. Two recordings follow Mahler's lead; and in both, the composer's characteristically unblended orchestral palette has an added transparency and bite, with each line standing out vividly, not least the snarling muted trumpets. There is much thoughtful, intelligent singing from **Thomas Hampson**, with the aptly named Wiener Virtuosen. Hampson

is effective in sardonic or military mode. But his once-velvet tone has now lost its lustre. He makes heavy weather of the girls' responses in the duets, while the yodelling 'Wer hat dies Liedlein erdacht?' sounds grittily determined rather than blithe.

More wholly recommendable is the version from Riccardo Chailly and a slimmed-down Royal Concertgebouw Orchestra, with the lion's share of the songs taken by **Barbara Bonney** and **Matthias Goerne**. Chailly is another idiomatic Mahlerian, and the reduced forces ensure an ideal lucidity in Mahler's fantastically intricate textures. Goerne sounds miscast in 'Rheinlegendchen' and, left to himself (none of the songs are performed as duets), misses the sardonic raillery of 'Trost im Unglück'. But there are superb things elsewhere. Bonney sings an irresistible 'Wer hat dies Liedlein erdacht', woodwind in chuckling collusion, and a pristine, delighted (but not *faux naif*) 'Das himmlische Leben'. As ever, Goerne's singing is founded on a scrupulously produced *legato* line, heard to eloquent effect in his desolate 'Tamboursg'sell' and the coda of 'Der Schildwache Nachtlied', where he distils an unearthly remoteness unmatched in any other recording. It is good, too, to hear 'Revelge', Mahler's sole song for a tenor, performed with an ideal mix of desperate bravado and lyrical pathos by **Gösta Winbergh**. A fourth singer, contralto **Sara Fulgoni**, sings 'Urlicht' with lovely deep-amber tone but rather fuzzy diction.

After its forays into Bruckner, Philippe Herreweghe's period Champs-Elysées

SELECTED DISCOGRAPHY

DATE / ARTISTS	RECORD COMPANY (REVIEW DATE)
with piano	
1978 **Fischer-Dieskau** bar **Barenboim** pf	EMI/Warner Classics ② ⊞ 476780-2
2003 **Damrau** sop **Paley** bar **Lademann** pf	Telos ② TLS1001; Profil Medien ② ⊞ PH14018
2007 **Genz** bar **Vignoles** pf	Hyperion CDA67645
with orchestra	
1965 **Baker** mez **Evans** bass-bar LPO / Morris	IMP Classics 1035
1967/69 **Ludwig** mez **Berry** bar New York PO / Bernstein	Sony SMK47590 (2/70ᴿ)
1968 **Schwarzkopf** sop **Fischer-Dieskau** bar LSO / Szell	EMI/Warner Classics ⊞ 567236-2
1976 **Norman** sop **Shirley-Quirk** bar Concertgebouw Orch / Haitink	Philips ② ⊞ 454 014-2PM2
1987 **Popp** sop **Schmidt** bar Concertgebouw Orch / Bernstein	DG ⑥ 477 5174GB6; ⑯ 459 080-2GX16 (6/89ᴿ)
1998 **von Otter** mez **Quasthoff** bar BPO / Abbado	DG 459 646-2GH (9/99)
2000 **Bonney** sop **Fulgoni** mez **Winbergh** ten **Goerne** bar RCO / Chailly	Decca 467 348-2DH (5/03)
2005 **Connolly** mez **Henschel** bar Champs-Elysées Orch / Herreweghe	Harmonia Mundi HMC90 1920 (11/06)
2009 **Oelze** sop **Volle** bar Gürzenich Orch, Cologne / Stenz	Oehms OC657 (11/10)
2009/11 **Iven** sop **Müller-Brachmann** bar SWR SO, Baden-Baden & Freiburg / Gielen	Hänssler CD93 274 (4/12)
2010 **Hampson** bar Wiener Virtuosen	DG 477 9289GH (2/11)
2010 **Kožená** mez **Gerhaher** bar Cleveland Orch / Boulez	
	DG 477 9060GH (11/10); Accentus DVD ACC20231; Blu-ray ACC10231 (10/11)

Claudio Abbado: an ear for Mahler

Orchestra reached to the brink of the 20th century in a recording with singers **Sarah Connolly** and **Dietrich Henschel**. Immediately striking here are the orchestral sonorities with the slightly veiled gut strings set against the relatively soft-toned woodwind. On the whole, this is a gentler sound picture than we're used to in Mahler. Connolly, with her glowing, supple mezzo, is well-nigh ideal, singing 'Rheinlegendchen' and 'Wer hat dies Liedlein erdacht?' with unaffected charm and grace. In 'Trost im Unglück', she catches the hussar's alpha-male bravado without straining for effect, and then suggests a depth of feeling behind the girl's mocking indifference. Henschel's high baritone is a splendid instrument; and if he occasionally rants, he brings an aching tenderness to 'Wo die schönen Trompeten blasen', done as a solo, like all the songs here. He is magnetic, too, in 'Der Tamboursg'sell', and earthily exuberant in 'Lob des hohen Verstands', with an apt touch of roughness in his tone.

PICKING A WINNER

Two German recordings made during the past decade are finely played and astutely conducted, but variably sung. With Markus Stenz's Gürzenich Orchestra, the sturdy baritone of **Michael Volle** is more appealing than the pleasant but cool soprano of **Christiane Oelze**. In 'Wo die schönen Trompeten blasen', Oelze sounds detached, outshone in tragic pathos by the Cologne woodwind. Casting a leading Sachs and Beckmesser in 'Rheinlegendchen' was always going to be a leap of faith. But Volle comes into his own in the sermon to the fishes and harnesses the power of his baritone to chilling effect

in 'Revelge', with the orchestra second to none in lurid violence.

As David Gutman noted, the veteran 'modernist' Michael Gielen proves a highly perceptive, and idiomatic, Mahlerian, with an acute ear for textural clarity – though, in the lively acoustic, a true *pianissimo* is at a premium. His singers are only so-so. Robust of tone and manner, **Hanno Müller-Brachmann** is better at characterisation than sustaining a line. His graceless 'Rheinlegendchen' is another piece of miscasting. Soprano **Christiane Iven** sounds uncomfortable in 'Das himmlische Leben', though she excels in the desperate race against the clock of 'Das irdische Leben' and uses the mezzo colouring within her soprano in a hushed, concentrated 'Urlicht'.

Given the cast list, expectations ran high in the live recording by **Magdalena Kožená** and **Christian Gerhaher** conducted by Pierre Boulez and caught on both CD and DVD. Although I hear more than the 'disinterested efficiency' noted by Richard Osborne, Boulez's scrupulously calibrated conducting can lack Mahlerian *Schwung*, as well as the feeling for the Viennese-Slavonic dance rhythms (say, in 'Verlor'ne Müh') caught so unerringly by Bernstein and Szell. Gerhaher sings 'Trost im Unglück' (as a solo) with incisive diction and a free ring to the tone. But his characterisation is fatally hampered by Boulez's dogged tempo. You'd never guess here that Mahler's direction is *verwegen* ('boldly', or 'jauntily'). Set against that is the sardonic brilliance of 'Revelge', its implacable rhythms tightly laced, and a compelling, ultimately heartbreaking 'Taboursg'sell', where Boulez notes Mahler's request for two in a bar (most conductors veer towards a slower four). Kožená and Boulez eschew charm in the Ländler – this is even more apparent on the DVD. But she 'sells' 'Lob des hohen Verstands', with the clarinet-as-ass outshrieking the competition; and, sounding like a mezzo Popp, she brings a touching purity and warmth – and a rarefied *pianissimo* – to 'Wo die schönen Trompeten blasen'.

Where Boulez's brisk conducting of 'Das irdische Leben' is neat and precise, Claudio Abbado's, with **Anne Sofie von Otter**, is eerily unnerving, with more extreme dynamic contrasts and more astringent sonorities. Von Otter graphically suggests the mother's mounting panic beneath her reassuring answers to the child's pleas for bread. In 'Verlorn'e Müh' she expertly catches both the girl's wheedling and the boy's sullen

responses, singing as it were through clenched teeth. And, given a delightful dance lilt by Abbado, she embodies Mahler's description of 'Rheinlegendchen' as 'direct, but whimsically childlike and tender… nothing but butterfly colours'.

Abbado's baritone is **Thomas Quasthoff** who, more than any other singer, notices how much of 'Revelge' is marked *piano* and *pianissimo*. With a care for a true singing line, even *in extremis*, Quasthoff evokes the pathos and pity of war as well as its fury and horror. Like von Otter, he brilliantly distinguishes the 'characters' in the duet songs, never straining for effect: in the contrasts of swagger and dreamlike tenderness in 'Der Schildwache Nachtlied'; or in a notably good-humoured 'Trost im Unglück'. And he and Abbado note Mahler's direction *behäbig* ('complacently, with an implication of portliness') in 'Des Antonius von Padua Fischpredigt'. If fish can lollop, they do here.

Time, then, to come clean. For all the insights on the justly famous Szell recording, Schwarzkopf tends to provoke more irritation than illumination. I could live happily with the versions from Chailly and his quartet of singers; Herreweghe with Connolly and Henschel; and Bernstein with Popp and Schmidt, who do several songs as duets – though, happily, not 'Wo die schönen Trompeten blasen', in which Popp is supreme. Yet confined to a single recording, I should plump, narrowly, for Abbado, with von Otter and Quasthoff. DG's engineers and Abbado's ear ensure that Mahler's orchestral palette has never sounded more vivid. And his singers not only have expressively flexible voices but also strike a fine balance between folk-like directness and sophistication: crucial in songs that mine what Mahler called the 'hidden treasure' within the ostensibly naive texts, transmuting the banalities and tragedies of the forgotten into unflinching commentaries on the universal human condition. **G**

TOP CHOICE

Von Otter *mez* **Quasthoff** *bar* **BPO / Abbado**
DG 459 646-2GH

As part of this dream Mahler team, Quasthoff sings 'Fischpredigt' with just the right

unexaggerated drollery, as the superlative Berlin wind cavort around him. Von Otter brings an unforced eloquence to her songs, culminating in a rapt, glowing 'Urlicht'.

Tennstedt's Mahler

In a fascinating and revealing interview from March 1987, **Edward Seckerson** visited the acclaimed Mahler conductor to talk through his views on the composer's symphonies

'It is not an oratorio. It is not Verdi's Requiem, Brahms's Requiem, or Haydn's *Creation*. Maybe a cantata – *maybe* – but never an oratorio. You see, you may argue that it is not a symphony. But the *colour* is symphonic: the chorus, the soloists are all a part of the instrumental texture – a "different-voiced" polyphony . . . Integration. That's very important.'

Klaus Tennstedt could only be speaking of Mahler's Eighth Symphony. And nobody does so more passionately. He shares none of those commonly-voiced doubts as to whether or not the Eighth truly commands a place among Mahler's finest works; whether or not the protracted *Faust* episodes of Part 2 actually hold up under close scrutiny; whether or not we are to some extent blinded by the sheer scale of the enterprise – its overwhelming sense of 'occasion'. The Eighth, he insists, is a masterpiece too often misunderstood by those who would search for secrets where none exist. Ask him which of Mahler's symphonies lie closest to his heart, and he'll instantly reply Nos 6, 9 and 8. In that order ('If I add No 2 then I must add them all!'). It's the affirmative, open face of

'This is not a symphony for the intellect. It is open, innocent, late-romantic music'

the so-called *Symphony of a Thousand* that stirs him so deeply, and he is plainly delighted that it should this month crown his long-evolving cycle for EMI: a project almost a decade in the making; the first Mahler cycle ever to carry the HMV/Angel logo.

I visited Tennstedt late last year at his high-rise apartment in Heikendorf near Kiel, the West-German port (Coventry's twin-town) where he was once General Music Director at the Opera. Our brief was 'his Mahler': a very personal, very intense response to the music born of many years' obsessive devotion. He conducted his first professional Mahler performance 25 or so years ago (and unlike others, began at the beginning, with the First Symphony). His recordings, with one notable exception (more on that later) are, he believes, a faithful embodiment of his thoughts so far. Who knows how tomorrow might re-shape those thoughts.

Later, Tennstedt 'conducts' me through the opening pages of the Eighth Symphony master-tape. His verdict: 'not bad'. The Westminster Cathedral organ has dubbed

well, he observes, as that arresting E flat pedal booms out. He is delighted with the lucidity of the choral writing, the 'integration' he spoke of earlier with regard to voices and orchestra. For recording purposes a more manageably-sized chorus had, he believed, paid dividends in the densely intricate counterpoints at the apex of the movement – the latter stages of the development. He was happy, too, with the 'matching' of his two sopranos, Elizabeth Connell and Edith Wiens (therein lies one advantage of Mahler's Eighth on record: the ladies – so sorely stretched in the concert hall – can conserve a little beauty of tone and line, secure in the knowledge that nearby microphones will be looking after their interests). And to watch him visibly coaxing LPO leader David Nolan though a sweetly piquant violin solo (Tennstedt himself once led an orchestra – it shows) or nudging into place every last accent, every startling pizzicato, at the start of the orchestral march 'interlude' (the first stage of the development) is to understand something of his Mahlerian instinct. 'People misunderstand this symphony: there are not so many secrets. This is *not* a symphony for the intellect. It is open, innocent, late-romantic music. Mahler wants you to *make music* that's all.'

Tennstedt goes on to talk about the explicit wide-eyed 'fantasy' of Part 2: the mysterious 'forest' music, the darker, wilder 'nature' music of the exposition; the sweet *naïveté* of the music which later speaks of angels and Heaven. He is right, of course. Suddenly one is back among the folkloric influences of Mahler's youth; closer than ever to the 'child of sorrow' from his twentieth year: his symphonic cantata *Das klagende Lied*. The Eighth, he says, draws together and develops all Mahler's achievements hitherto: the 'brand new orchestral polyphony and 'classical' roots of the Sixth and Seventh Symphonies, the very 'visual' programmatic character of the *Wunderhorn* symphonies. It is his ambition to perform the Eighth at full-strength in the Royal Albert Hall, using the arena for the orchestra and placing his hugely augmented vocal forces on the platform and beyond in the choir stalls. Rumour has it that next year might well see the fulfilment of that dream.

And so we begin looking back over the cycle in some detail. I am especially keen that we reflect a little first on Tennstedt's full-blooded approach to the Mahler sound: its inimitable character, colour and cast. Mahler, he says, 'pre-supposed' (Tennstedt's German-speaking American niece is on hand for tricky words like this; Mrs Tennstedt – Inge – has a dictionary

at the ready) an enormous range of colour possibility from his players, from the wind players especially. More, in fact, than the instruments of the day were capable of providing. Hence his legendary impatience and frustration in rehearsal. No such problems today. I wonder what Mahler would have made of the big-boned LPO horn sound, for instance. I watched Tennstedt closely during rehearsals for the Eighth (which he and the LPO had never before played, incidentally), and he was forever asking for more: not volume but tone – a filling-out of the note, the big uninhibited sonority every time. Modern instruments and orchestras as flexible as the LPO can at last realize what Mahler could only have dreamed: 'Oh, he would have been very happy! … You mention the horns. Yes, he wrote for the horns in a very special, very virtuosic, late-romantic way. They must be able to produce the nobility of a classical chorale and the lyric softness of Mahler's most romantic music, but also the unbelievably ugly "stopped" sounds at moments of great emotional anguish. The same with the woodwinds.'

And again, one can see Tennstedt physically tearing those raucous *Schalltrichter in die Höhe* ('bells in the air') wind passages from the texture. He is nothing if not

uncompromising in his approach to Mahlerian contrast. Incidentally, he positively eulogizes over the current LPO woodwind team. The acquisition of Gordon Hunt (oboe) and Jonathan Snowden (flute) make this, he says, 'one of the finest sections in the world. I can say this because I know most of the world's top orchestras.' And the LPO strings? He repeatedly reaches for the word 'flexibility'. By virtue of their flexibility, the LPO strings have – and this he has always maintained – a natural potential for the 'romantic' sound. I cite the Vienna Philharmonic and their instinctive, in-bred way with the Mahlerian/Viennese turn of phrase. 'Yes, beautiful. Always very sweet. But the LPO strings can be sweet too – and, where necessary, *they* can say *goddam*!' Point taken. It helps, of course, that Tennstedt himself is an ex-string player. 'That experience is pure gold when working with my orchestra. They trust you, they trust what you say when you offer advice. If you come from the piano and start to suggest fingerings and bowing … ! No, we have enormous respect for each other now. We understand each other's needs. You know, I would say that this Mahler cycle is a monument to my association with the LPO.'

Looking back though, are there not symphonies that he has rethought, that he would re-record given half the chance? I might have predicted his response. 'Yes; No 1, definitely. It was not bad. Not bad at all. But this was 1978 and not my style today. I think, perhaps, I thought of the First then as a work quite separate from the other symphonies: a much more classical, *early* romantic symphony. And that is not so.' Certainly Tennstedt's inaugural Symphony No 1 was much softer-grained in complexion than the higher-profile, craggier-based Mahler we have come to expect of him since. His response to the bitter-sweet ironies of the third movement, for instance, has definitely sharpened over the years. Besides, it bothers him that the First was not digital and that the hefty open-hall sound picture that was to become a hallmark of the series didn't really establish itself until John Willan (now, of course, LPO Managing Director) took over

'The Sixth is a terrible thing. Terrible. In this symphony Mahler was a prophet'

as producer four years later for Symphony No 2 (*Resurrection*). That's a remarkable performance; for me, one of the most successful of the cycle, bettered only by his live Royal Festival Hall account of that same year, 1982. It's the courageous breadth of line that impresses. The sheer daring of Mahler's vision is matched at every step of a long journey. Why are conductors invariably in such a hurry at the final revelation, I ask? (He and Bernstein are exceptions.) Here we are at one of the great perorations in all symphonic music and even Klemperer sounds too anxious to reach for the stars.

'Yes, yes, I know what you mean. This is where you must really b-r-e-a-t-h-e. You must allow yourself the same time and space that you would find for the coda of Bruckner's Fourth Symphony, last movement.' There is, of course, the other extreme. I still treasure an old World Record Club pressing of a performance from the great but eccentric Hermann Scherchen, whose cripplingly slow account of that coda would seem to suggest that he had ceased breathing altogether!

But back to Tennstedt's cycle. And if I am to be totally honest, the two symphonies which really do not work for me, the two symphonies which to my mind suffer from a surfeit of nervous impulse at the expense of repose and geniality, are Nos 4 and 5. The Fourth needs to relax more – Tennstedt still strikes me as a touch overwrought. The dark side of his Fifth – that most schizophrenic of creations – is everything that one would expect of him (and what a sonorous image EMI achieved there for the opening funeral march). But does the sun really break through for the final *Rondo*? Isn't the tension there screwed just a little too tightly, too earnestly? The maestro clearly doesn't think so. He is more than happy with the series, bar No 1 – and fair enough. Whatever my misgivings about this or that aspect of Tennstedt's Mahler, never for a moment have I ever doubted its integrity, its innate sense of stylistic 'rightness'.

We talk a little now about the Seventh – the 'black sheep' of the canon – and I'm sure that I speak for many when I ask first how it is possible to make music of the finale? 'We must be very honest. This is not good Mahler. The themes are good. The organization is not. It is too long and there is too little *substance*. Variations on the *Meistersinger* Prelude,

I call it! No, I understand what Mahler is attempting – the Viennese parodies, the dance music – you are right – but it just never works for me. It is a problem, like the Sixth of Bruckner. The other movements, though, are so wonderful – the *Scherzo* and two *Nachtmusiks* – unbelievable orchestration.'

Interestingly enough, Tennstedt has never regarded the Seventh as a radical departure, an experimental 'pure music' diversion between the more emotive Sixth and Eighth Symphonies (interesting how differently people view the cycle). In terms of form, tonality, 'neo-classicism', he still regards it as a brother or sister of the Sixth. We have arrived at the symphony closest of all to his heart. His brave, no-holds-barred reading – to my mind (and his) the finest performance in his recorded cycle prompted some controversy within these pages when it first appeared. Richard Osborne was not at all convinced. He spoke of 'cheap melodrama, a circus act of irredeemable vulgarity'. One or two readers begged to differ. For my own part, Tennstedt's Sixth seems to me to represent all that is most compelling – and most dangerous – about his Mahler. Like Leonard Bernstein (whom, it transpires, Tennstedt much admires – 'a great Mahler conductor'), he is not afraid to go wherever this music takes him – to the edge, and even beyond. Temperamentally speaking, both men are self-evidently at one with its psyche. Like all 'kindred spirits' they look these pieces squarely in the face, unafraid and unashamed to expose their best, and worst, excesses. Extreme music – music forever teetering between pathos and bathos – demands an extreme response. Tennstedt grows visibly heated when he talks about the Sixth. 'The Sixth is a terrible thing. Terrible. In this symphony Mahler was a prophet. He knew nothing of the wars that were to come. How could he? But, during his time in Vienna he saw the beginnings of the Jewish persecution – he saw the stones being thrown through the windows of Jewish shopkeepers – and somehow in his music we feel he is foretelling the future. Just listen to the march in the first movement. Now Mahler loved marches – the Bohemian, Hungarian, Austrian marches. He loved the music of the military band. He grew up with these sounds and we hear them throughout his symphonies. The joyous March of Summer in the Third.' (Tennstedt's gaudy Dionysian procession is another of his cycle's highspots – that entire first movement seemingly plucked from the elements that inspired it.) 'Then there is the first movement of the Seventh, and the funeral marches of the Second, Fifth and Ninth Symphonies – very slow, very serious. But never anything like the Sixth. *Never*. This is a *German march*, a *Nazi* march – a terrible march of war. A premonition.'

'Not one of his works came as directly from his innermost heart as this,' wrote Alma Mahler at the time. 'We both wept that day. The music and what it foretold touched us deeply.' Tennstedt is quick to remind me of those words and goes on to talk of 'so many other things' that were crowding in on Mahler as he began setting down the Sixth: feelings of guilt at the death of his student friend Hugo Wolf, his problems in Vienna, his failing health, the birth of his second child, his love for Alma – the one healing light in a work of almost unremitting gloom, but that too wracked with insecurity. I don't think anybody conveys more of an 'ache' in the ecstasy of the first movement second subject (Alma's tune) than Tennstedt. Again it's a question of the Mahlerian sonority: in no other performance do the clarinets (doubling violins) sing out so plangently from the texture.

'You must identify with him completely. Only then, can you conduct the symphonies'

But what of the disputed order of *Scherzo* and *Andante*? Does he have any doubts at all about the original published order: i.e. *Scherzo* second, *Andante* third? Having changed his mind once, did Mahler do so again just before his death? Yes, Tennstedt believes he did. In any event, he is absolutely adamant that the Mahler Society were correct in reinstating the original order. Alma's theme takes the first movement from A minor to a triumphant A major at the close; the threat, it seems, has for the moment been lifted. How much more effective then to shatter this false sense of security by wrenching the music back into A minor and hitting us again with the same relentless march rhythm, albeit hideously distorted now with a limp in its second beat. To opt for the 'safer' contrast at this point – to soothe the senses with the *Andante*'s remote E flat major, takes the sting, the obsessiveness, out of the piece. Tennstedt suggests that Mahler may have thought twice about the order believing that his first movement and *Scherzo* in quick succession would be more than the work's first audiences could endure. In short, a compromise, later reconsidered. He is anyway in no doubt that the consoling balm of Mahler's *Andante* is greatly heightened coming after that 'terrible caricature of a *Ländler*. The main third movement is a wonder. To me, this is Mahler's only slow movement without uncertainty – without a contrasting undercurrent. This movement is love; nothing else. No caricature, no cynicism. Love. I don't know, but maybe, just maybe, Mahler would like to have said to Alma: "Excuse me for the other three movements" ….'

Clearly then, Tennstedt and Mahler's Sixth have grown inextricably a part of one another. Anyone who heard his last two London performances will have noticed changes, quite dramatic changes. The later reading, coloured no doubt by Tennstedt's intervening illness, was definitely tougher, uglier, its precious moments of repose at that much more of a premium. 'With Mahler, perhaps more than any other composer, you have to change your conception with your life. No composer's life was more closely bound up with his music than Mahler's – Mahler's music is his life – and any change in your own life, in your own physical or mental state at the time will reflect in your performance of his music. But you must identify with him completely. Then, and only then, can you try to conduct the Mahler symphonies.'

But how completely does Tennstedt identify with Mahler, the man? One observes the volatile temperament, the perpetual animation, the passionate nervous energy, the childlike enthusiasm, be it for the passing steamers he'll point out to you from his wind-swept balcony or his early Edison cylinder player – a proud possession. One suspects that he and Mahler might have had a lot in common. This is one question that I direct to Inge Tennstedt. 'Yes. Read Alma's two books and you'll see that in life, in his temperament, his philosophies, there is a lot of Mahler.' The maestro nods. 'Of course, he is not so very clever as Mahler[!], but you know, I sometimes see him in his little hut and the maid nervously going to take him breakfast – that's me!' I trust she is not called upon to ward off intrusive bird-life from their balcony, just as Alma was forever discouraging inquisitive cows from Mahler's back yard! 'No, but when he wants to work, then we must all be quiet!'

I have one more question. Deryck Cooke's performing version of the Tenth? 'I think that was an interesting experiment, and we must be grateful to him. But when you know how much revision Mahler made to his scores once they had been tried out in the orchestra, how much he changed after performances he conducted with different orchestras, you begin to realize how much he would have discarded of these sketches, how he would have re-thought his scoring. I am sure that the conception of the Tenth would have developed greatly had he lived. These were sketches, for the most part, nothing else. Even the *Adagio* of the Tenth – a *wonderwork* – even this I am not entirely happy playing.'

And with that, Tennstedt insists that we brave the elements once more and venture out on to his balcony. The view is spectacular. To our right, the open sea – the Baltic. On a good day, he tells me, you can see over 50 kilometres to the coast of Scandinavia. And I am just about to ask why it is that we have never heard any Sibelius from him (such profoundly elemental music would seem to be eminently suited) when he reveals that he has been preparing the Fifth Symphony and will conduct the Violin Concerto this month (in a mainly Sibelius concert), in London. He has always loved this music and we can expect to hear more. Meanwhile, on record, another great love, Richard Strauss, beckons. A number of the tone-poems are planned (initially, *Zarathustra*, *Don Juan* and *Till*) and he still hopes that before too long he will find the right cast for his projected *Elektra*. At the piano, a full score of Bartók's *Duke Bluebeard's Castle* sits open. I mustn't say any more about that for the time being. **G**

Tackling THE taboos

As he left the Berlin Philharmonic in 2002, Claudio Abbado met with Rob Cowan – among the topics discussed was whether he would find the time to take on that unfinished Tenth

While late spring showers slooshed the walls of Paris's Cité de la musique, Claudio Abbado was inside rehearsing a delightful Schubert female chorus. 'I want more articulation,' he insists, 'and that top B flat, don't force it, you're making it a little sharp.' Suddenly there's a burst of communal laughter. Dissension among the ranks, perhaps?

Not quite, but then this is no ordinary chorus. A group of players from the 21-year-old Chamber Orchestra of Europe 'anyone with a voice' as producer Christopher Alder puts it – is collaborating with the radiant mezzo of Anne Sofie von Otter for a potential extra track on a CD devoted to Schubert song orchestrations. Von Otter will be sharing the solo honours with Thomas Quasthoff. 'Now you have to get Thomas to do it with all the *men*!' she jibes, prompting a further burst of laughter.

Abbado had been delighted when on an earlier occasion he had heard the girls singing a chorus from Rossini's *Il viaggio a Reims* at a party. 'Now tell me,' he says later, smiling impishly, 'what other orchestra could sing like that?'

Whether or not the delightful *Ständchen* (D920) makes the final cut remains to be seen but the rest of the sequence is more or less settled. The idea was not new. 'We started in Salzburg some years ago,' Abbado tells me. 'We had two programmes, one with Anne Sofie and another planned with Thomas, who fell sick, so we used other singers.

'I already knew some of the orchestrations: the Brahms, for example, the Reger and the Webern. Then I found others by Berlioz, for example, and Liszt.' Quasthoff is happily reinstated for the concerts and recordings, which will juxtapose fascinating reinterpretations of favourite songs.

Thin but vital, Abbado has emerged from obvious overwork and the far side of serious illness with a heightened sense of mortality. His Schubert is distinguished by conversational intensity whereas Mahler remains a salutary and beloved presence. The release of three live recordings is eloquent testimony to Abbado's commitment to the Mahler canon and to his respect for Mahler as an all-embracing creative force.

'Mahler is always about life, death, love – about everything!' exclaims Abbado with palpable passion. 'Every symphony has its own story; but there's more to him than that. He was a revolutionary, the most modern of composers. He wrote after his Sixth Symphony that it would take 40 years to understand his music. Even now it's too early.'

Isn't it true that the lure of Mahler's muse seems especially powerful to the young? 'Yes,' replies the maestro, 'but then the young are full of questions. They don't *know* about life, death or love. But they *need* to know, need to have some answers, to understand how to choose life. That's one of the most difficult things for young people. They need to make decisions.'

I've always sensed that Mahler's music contains coded messages about death in the midst of life. 'Most people don't like to think about death,' affirms Abbado, 'but with Mahler death is always a presence. He was probably born like that. When his brother – who was also a musician – committed suicide, that was a most terrible moment for him. But nobody speaks about this. It's almost as if they don't want to.'

Taboos about death have their musical parallels in 'completed' last works that some interpreters would rather leave to the annals of history. The performing version of Mahler's Tenth Symphony, for example, which Abbado has never tackled in concert. 'To be honest, I would like to know more about it,' he says. 'I have spoken with Simon [Rattle] who knows it very well, which is what makes him such a good judge. It's a question of time and when I have more of it then probably one day I will conduct the full version. Also, I would want to compare different performing versions.'

These and other Mahlerian reflections were prompted by the first commercial release on DG of three live Mahler recordings with the Berlin Philharmonic: Symphonies Nos 3, 7 and 9. Was there a specific reason why these symphonies where chosen?

'We have played the Mahler symphonies many times in concert performance, for the BBC, or in Paris or in Berlin,' Abbado explains. 'I listened to various tapes and some concerts were so beautiful and I thought they were better than my commercial recordings. By now, those first versions are old, so I thought we should make new recordings. And in any case, now I prefer to do live recordings.'

The Seventh is especially memorable. It sweeps forward in a way that it never quite managed in his Chicago reading and while Abbado recalls a third version – again live but on a 'pirate' disc with the Gustav Mahler Youth Orchestra, he concedes that the Berlin players are ultimately superior.

Of past Mahlerians, Dimitri Mitropoulos was a significant influence. 'I heard him live and he was for me one of the greatest conductors of Mahler. He had such an acute sense

'At the moment I would like to know as much as possible about other cultures'

After 12 years in Berlin, Claudio Abbado was looking farther afield – to the (re)foundation of the famed Lucerne Festival Orchestra

of fantasy. When I first heard Mahler's music I already knew Schoenberg and the music of the Second Viennese School, so for me it was the most natural thing in the world.

'I even knew Bartók before I knew Mahler. I remember that after the war critics and audiences would complain that Bartók was "barbaric" music – no, worse, that it was noise and not music at all' But this is great music, no? And the same applied to Schoenberg, Berg, Webern, Stravinsky and so on. That was the difficulty. For me it was very clear, but not for everybody. Nowadays the same principle applies. The difficult challenge is to understand which of today's composers will in 30, 40 years' time remain great.'

And what of his own efforts on behalf of 20th-century music? 'No, no, that's not the point,' he interjects. 'For me music is … just music. Think what they said about Debussy when he was writing *Pelléas* – "this isn't music any more". Schoenberg's contemporaries said the same sort of thing, and so did Beethoven's.

'It's been the same for almost for every great composer. There's always some resistance to new music. What is important is that everybody understands the best in music

as it happens, which for us would be, for example, Kurtág, Ligeti, Nono, Rihm.'

By contrast, isn't it also true that when considering older music we can, through the medium of recording, learn from an earlier generation of performers? Or is that more the province of collectors?

'But I love old recordings myself,' insists Abbado, 'though it depends on which music is being played. We can discuss the interpretations of Beethoven and Schubert by Furtwängler, who is still for me one of the greatest conductors of all. Of course I do it differently but that doesn't mean that his interpretations aren't wonderful to listen to.

'Then take the old recording of Toscanini, of the *Falstaff* – which is still the best recording that I know of. And there's Mengelberg and the older [Erich] Kleiber – there is always something to learn from them. It's one of the great aspects of music, that you have all these different ways, different possibilities for interpretation.

'Of course, today I think I'm doing it the right way, but who knows? Everybody thinks that he's getting closer and closer to what the composer wanted!' The truth is that Abbado would rather listen to old Furtwängler records than to his own older recordings, 'which mostly I don't like!'

Future plans include various British appearances and, in 2003, the formation of a new Lucerne Festival Orchestra – 'something similar to the one they formed for Toscanini before the war, he says, with a justifiable touch of pride. It will call on some of the best musicians in Berlin and Vienna, plus 'many soloists, like Natalia Gutman, Sabine Meyer, the Hagen Quartet'.

And repertoire for the new orchestra? 'Good music!' says Abbado, with a chuckle. 'We'll play a lot of Wagner because the Wagner villa is there. The Second Act of *Tristan* is perfect for performance in concert.'

Abbado's other lines of intellectual enquiry reach far and wide. 'At the moment I would like to know as much as possible about other cultures,' he says. 'We just don't know enough about other religions and that's one of the reasons why the world is plagued by so much misunderstanding, war or negative speculation. If people would learn more about the positive aspects of other cultures, the world would be a far better place.'

He serves as an occasional educational adviser at a top-grade school in the Bologna and Parma region. 'Sometimes they come to me and ask for ideas and suggestions,' he says. 'They know that I don't have time to give concerts so I give some ideas! And one of these ideas is to get children to know more about different cultures.

'We live so much with a sort of tired, touristic image of people you know the sort of thing: German people are like this, the Swiss like that, the Italian people like some other cliché. It's stupid, superficial – whereas you can find in any different culture something positive, something constructive. That, I think, is the most important area to develop. But it needs time.'

As to 'cross-over', it depends who does the crossing, he says – 'especially when you think how great composers such as Beethoven, Schubert and Bartók used folkloristic music and themes in their works. So it can be done if there's a great composer or writer involved. In art, you can use anything, but if it's going to work, you have to use it with genius!' Ⓖ

THE *music* OF *life*

For Sir Simon Rattle, Mahler's Ninth Symphony encompasses
the big questions, as he told Peter Quantrill in March 2008

To misquote the legendary football manager Bill Shankly, Mahler's Ninth Symphony isn't a matter of life and death. It's much more important than that. Another doughty figure from Liverpool is sitting opposite me in a corporate hotel room, sheltered from a chill January morning. It's a fair bet that Sir Simon Rattle knows as much about football as Shankly did about Romantic music, so, resisting the urge to quiz him on the puzzling rotation policies of Shankly's current successor in the Liverpool FC hot seat, I get down to business. What does Mahler's Ninth mean to him? 'When Berg saw the first movement he said that this is a movement full of the joy of living. That's really important for us to remember, that it is not just Dirk Bogarde with his make-up running or whatever other sentimental picture we might have. It's completely haunted by death but is actually all about life.'

Later on he applies this description to the symphony as a whole, which he recorded with 'his' Berlin Philharmonic last October. Such a view doesn't sit easily with the orthodoxy promoted by Leonard Bernstein, that whereas the *Pathétique* Symphony peers over the abyss, Mahler's Ninth plunges into it. But then Bernstein had no truck with the Tenth, as completed by Deryck Cooke, which showed that Mahler could move on even after taking the most apparently final of adieus, just as he had done with the Ninth after composing *Das Lied von der Erde*. Together, they form a symphonic triptych: three different ways of saying goodbye?

Rattle and his Berliners brought this insight home with unusual force last autumn by touring a three-concert programme to New York, 'Berlin in Lights'. Bearing in mind the designation of *Das Lied* as a 'Song Symphony', it placed Mahler's last three symphonies in order, each accompanied by a modem work (from Christian Jost, Thomas Adès and Kaija Saariaho). Rattle has always taken pride and perhaps a subversive delight in showing that 'anyone who sits down with the sketches of the Tenth and plays them from start to finish on the piano will realise that, like it or not, there is really a complete work there. And that is what people don't seem to get. They think it's something like the Elgar Third Symphony – or let's be heretical and say the Mozart Requiem, a lot of which is so clearly not by Mozart'.

So the Ninth is not the end. In fact this is clear on the most basic level of continuity. The descending whole-tone of those repeated 'Ewigs' at the end of *Das Lied* survives to the Ninth, where it metamorphoses into the melodic fragment (or seed? We come back to that) of the Ninth's opening theme. The

Ninth in turn closes with the softest imaginable cadential caress from the violas ... and it is they who introduce the very uncadential, irresolute, questing melody of the Tenth.

Rattle finds the strongest links between *Das Lied* and the Tenth, where the pain emitted by the famous dissonance (over which Mahler scrawled "Almschi!!!", in agony over his wife's affair) is so strong as to transcend instrumental abstraction. On a less exalted level, however, all three are connected by the fact that Mahler never heard them – and crucially never conducted them. Rattle is talking of Michelangelo when he refers to 'those wonderful sculptures which are not finished but look as though they're actually trying to struggle out of the granite ... it's ... I find them incredibly moving'. Such as the *Moses*? 'Absolutely. It looks as though it was designed like that. It's how we respond to it and of course, for Mahler no piece was ever quite finished anyway. He spent his whole life revising and revising and revising, even details of scoring and balance. With *Das Lied* he would have made changes to the orchestration. You have to change dynamics in the first and the fourth songs. There are areas in the fourth song where I sling the orchestration around a lot, particularly if we're using a mezzo. And I have no doubt that the Ninth would have been revised.'

> *'For Mahler no piece was ever quite finished... he spent his whole life revising and revising and revising'*

Later on, to prove his point, we huddle over my pocket score. There is singing. His is unusually good for a conductor. He points out where a return to the first tempo is marked, but no prior indication of how to get there. '[The conductor] Karl Anton Rickenbacher came up to me in Lucerne and asked, Simon, who do you think started off the tradition of speeding up here [the second theme of the first movement]? Where did that come from? And I'd never thought of it before. It was Bruno Walter who did this. Klemperer didn't." There must even be the memory of a funeral march about this countervailing, passionate theme, Rattle thinks, that looks forward to the explicit instruction of 'Wie ein Kondukt' in the wake of the movement's death knell (the indication itself casting us back to the first movement of the Fifth). 'Mahler had no impression of a solid tempo, a rigid tempo in a Toscanini-like sense, but I believe he was right.'

Even so there are more than enough pernickety admonitions in the Ninth, as in every Mahler symphony, to test the patience of most orchestral players. Very much in the line of Weber whom he championed so ardently, Mahler is a conductors' composer, because he was a conducting composer. Elgar is the same. 'The wonderful thing with

'It is not just Dirk Bogarde with his make-up running or whatever other sentimental picture we might have. It's completely haunted by death but is actually all about life' – Rattle on Mahler's Ninth

Elgar is that whatever the level of the orchestra, it sounds marvellous from the beginning. Maybe all his work with the lunatic asylum orchestra and learning every instrument gave him something. Mahler is something else, he's a hyper-realist. Not only do you see the mountain but every little lichen and every little butterfly and it's important for him to see all those things simultaneously. This is particularly true of the Ninth.'

This nature-imagery perhaps unconsciously chimes with Mahler's own feeling for *Naturlaut* – the cows in the meadow, the birds in the forest and the drunkard in spring – that many thought Mahler had left behind. Again, Rattle talks about the 'organic' nature of the symphony's opening D minor theme: 'it's like watching a flower open'. Rattle had made earlier reference to the letter Alban Berg wrote to his wife Helene, with its famous identification of the first movement as 'an expression of an exceptional fondness for this earth, the longing to live in peace on it, to enjoy nature to its depths'. But against that stands the no-less-holy writ from Arnold Schoenberg: '[The Ninth] contains what may be termed objective, almost dispassionate statements of a beauty which will be perceived only by those who can dispense with visceral warmth and who feel comfortable in a climate of intellectual coldness.'

'I could not find my score, marked up with everything everyone has ever said to me...gone'

Rattle is having none of it: 'Schoenberg was always deeply ambivalent about Mahler anyway. The only piece he really loved was the Seventh because it was the piece that was most like him. In a way the First Chamber Symphony is the one fan letter that Schoenberg wrote to Mahler – he used a lot of the same intervals, even the same kind of scoring.'

Certainly there has been no 'intellectual coldness' about Rattle's journeys through the Ninth. They started in Birmingham, naturally. I remember the broadcast from the old Town Hall on January 17, 1991, when there was already the sense of fully fleshed, all too human interpretation, on which survived the main road traffic noise but not the depredations of the restless Proms audience the following summer. The Ninth has not been a talisman for him like the Second, the Seventh or the Tenth, but in making his debut with the Vienna Philharmonic in 1993, he chose this symphony, that '"belongs" to this orchestra as much as any symphony does: the Austrian Radio broadcast became, at Rattle's request, the EMI recording to document 'an immensely happy time, where I think I was more nervous that I have ever been at any moment in my life, even waiting before the headmaster's study aged 11'. The Viennese have

'For Mahler as for Haydn, the symphony is where you could tell the most important truths'

not always done the piece justice, but they put something on the line for Rattle that made the first three movements sound as though every bar could be the last, a spontaneous desperation that eluded two plusher and somewhat distant concert performances with the London Symphony Orchestra in 1999.

Now the Ninth has landed back in Berlin, where the performing tradition is at least as strong as Vienna. Never mind Barbirolli's speculative recording and Karajan's elusive relationship with the work, the orchestra asked Rattle to go easy on the piece when he took charge in 2002, because they had played it with Claudio Abbado no fewer than 51 times. When they and he returned to it, did he go back to the attic of the mind to look for clues, or decide to have a clear-out?

'It's very Freudian but I moved house a couple of times and I could not find my score. The set of parts I used for all these other performances I have, but my score, marked up with everything everyone has ever said to me, everyone I've ever worked with … gone. Maybe it's good when you're forced to start again. A lot of the physical habits and tics have disappeared – this physical memory you have as a conductor. And that's quite good.'

He may have lost his workings, but Rattle has not forgotten the teachings of his mentor Berthold Goldschmidt. It was Goldschmidt who alerted Rattle to the odd *hinaufziehen* [drawing up] marking for the cor anglais in the fourth movement of the Third Symphony, producing an alien, swooping accompaniment for Nietzsche's poem of desolation that many conductors have since copied. It was also Goldschmidt who memorably described some of the emptier pages of the first movement of the Ninth as 'cosmic dust'. I mention that extraordinary passage where the solo winds

'The middle movements are the blackest and most vicious music he ever wrote'

grope for a theme in flat counterpoint, before the strings find it – 'and is it becoming the next line or is it the debris, being thrown out by a comet, of everything that's happened before? Then it's suddenly like the complete works of Webern, it's just frightening'.

What's more extraordinary still about the symphony is how it holds such music of the future within a fairly classical structure. The old forms increasingly took hold of Mahler. The concerto grosso of the Seventh, with its virtuoso solo parts and ritornello-based finale, the closed fugues and arias of the Eighth, what Rattle calls 'the exploded Suite' for *Das Lied*, and then the eternal verities of Classical form for the Ninth. 'For Mahler, as for Haydn,' notes Rattle, 'the symphony is where you could tell the most important truths. The Ninth is the one Alfred Brendel likes,' he adds. 'He has real problems with a lot of the others.' Indeed, and just as the influence of Mahler's contemporaneous study of the *Pathétique* comes to mind when considering the form of the Ninth, so does Brendel's scabrous remark about Tchaikovsky's 'crocodile tears'. 'But not the *Pathétique*,' counters Rattle. 'Then he's really writing about himself. This is a different situation. I don't know what the very latest research is, but the idea that you would write a symphony about your own enforced suicide does give another perspective on the piece.'

Be that as it may, are Mahler's life and work so inextricably linked? Rattle offers a comparison informed by his continuing work on *The Ring* with the Berlin Philharmonic (they are halfway through). 'Those of us who are not privileged – who are not cursed – to be geniuses need to know everything we can. For this generation of composers, everything was in there and so it is a gold mine. What is dangerous for an interpreter is when you get lost within that. It's fascinating and what's important then is to remove it to the back of the brain. With Wagner I choose not to know because I find the more I know about him as a human being, the harder it is to conduct his astonishing music. With Mahler I really choose to know because I find that it enlightens. And Wagner's music is transcendentally beautiful and very often deeply benevolent and good and I don't think any of those phrases could be used about him as a person. That's really a mystery, whereas Mahler as a personality is so completely tied up with his music that I find it helpful.'

What about the inner movements of the Ninth? If we decided not to apply the terms ironic or satiric to the second and third movements, would they not still be a Ländler and a rondo? Rattle's answer comes characteristically sideways on.

'At the end of *Così fan tutte* it is perfectly clear that Mozart knows how to write a joyous release in C major but it is equally perfectly clear that this is not a joyous release. This is not Mozart trying to write in C major and it hasn't quite worked because he's perfectly capable of doing that. He's saying something else and [the melody of the coda] is no kind of resolution. With Mahler it's more complicated. For me the two middle movements are in a strange way – particularly the second, the blackest and most vicious music he ever wrote – everything you most hate about the country followed by

Responses to the Ninth

Alban Berg
The first movement: 'An expression of an exceptional fondness for this Earth, the longing to live in peace on it, to enjoy nature to its depths.'

Arnold Schoenberg
'[The Ninth] contains what may be termed objective, almost dispassionate statements of a beauty which will be perceived only by those who can dispense with visceral warmth and who feel comfortable in a climate of intellectual coldness.'

Leonard Bernstein
'We are cleansed, when all is said and done; no person of sensibility can come away from the Ninth Symphony without being exhausted and purified. And that is the triumphant result of all this purgatory ... we do ultimately encounter an apocalyptic radiance, a glimmer of what peace must be like' The last page of the score, he said, 'is the closest we have ever come, in any work of art, to experiencing the very act of dying.'

Herbert von Karajan
'The Sixth is for me one of the greatest symphonies - and so seldom played in the past! There we have complete catastrophe. It is there in the Ninth but in the Ninth there is great beauty and a sense of harmony with death. Coming to the end of the symphony is one of the hardest tasks in all conducting ... I know was madly, madly involved with the symphony to the extent that when it was done - and it is one of the few works I say this of - I would not dare touch it again.'

everything you most hate about the city. But the movements outside, despite these immense convulsions, really end in a kind of peace.'

Yet by writing the *Adagio* in D flat, rather than the expected D, is Mahler really offering closure? So often performances of the Ninth enter a different realm at this point, as though the first three movements hadn't happened. Perhaps this is Rattle's point. 'What is extraordinary is that it's some kind of release. It's the opposite process to the Fifth which is moving from C sharp to D, and the Fifth spends almost its entire length attempting to make a climax which doesn't work, which is one of the reasons why it is so hard to conduct. Whereas in the Ninth it's particularly after these paroxysms of rage and sarcasm in the second and third movements (and having shown us what a D major can be in the middle of the third movement) that when you finally come to the *Adagio*, there's a feeling of – [sigh] – "I accept this" – which is why, for instance, a performance by Klemperer, who was maybe the conducting world's great stoic, can be so very moving.'

Where in the *Adagio* 'there are no solutions' for Bernstein, for Klemperer 'there is only the majesty of death … come as a friend, and not to punish'. Rattle, after Berg, is happier to court sentimentality. 'I think some of it comes from the other side. This is music from an unknown region – in some ways it's already taken this leap of what the future was going to be.' Eh? 'What Kurtág says is that Haydn was very influenced by Stravinsky. There is the idea of Mahler saying farewell to music that had not yet been heard or that he was not yet going to have time to explore. Mahler loved things that encompassed everything. It's no coincidence that his favourite novel was *Don Quixote*.'

Our time is almost up, and Rattle is about to go and do *Desert Island Discs* for BBC Radio 4. He too has selected Cervantes' *omnium gatherum*, 'because it has the seeds of every single opera plot ever written. It's all there, and it's not all perfect, but it says "this can happen and this can happen". There are wonderful stories about Mahler loving to read this aloud at parties and laughing with tears streaming down his face, and I can imagine it's something to do with the potentiality which is so vital for him'.

Rattle, it turns out, is a Ted Hughes man. 'That great Northern bluntness' – and here he puts a Scouse fist to the side of his head. We exchange recommendations – *Tales from Ovid* for me, the newly published diaries for him. It's a long time since any Ovid passed my eyes – 14 blessed years, actually – but on the way home I take his advice and buy a copy. I stand chastened, and enlightened. Hughes's account of Ovid's Augustan age, when 'the obsolete paraphernalia of the old official religion were lying in heaps, like old masks in the lumber room of a theatre, and new ones had not yet arrived': this is also Mahler's age, 'at one extreme wallowing in the bottomless appetites and sufferings of the gladiatorial arena, and at the other searching higher and higher for a spiritual transcendence'. The first movement of the Ninth is in Ovid and Hughes's cosmogony: 'Air was simply darkness. Everything fluid or vapour, form formless.' The Rondo here too, with 'These madhouse brothers, fighting each other, all but shake the earth to pieces'. It takes art to understand art. **G**

Simon Rattle's recording of Mahler's Symphony No 9 with the Berlin Philharmonic is available on Warner Classics

MAHLER
from a new perspective

François-Xavier Roth and Les Siècles' period-instrument recording of Mahler's Fourth Symphony looks set to bring about a renewed understanding of this music, as **Hugo Shirley** found in this recent interview

The ever-growing recorded catalogue of Les Siècles would be the envy of any ensemble, let alone a period-instrument orchestra. But Les Siècles, which celebrates its 20th anniversary next year, is no ordinary period-instrument orchestra, built as it is upon the idealistic desire to be equally adept and informed in tackling music from across different centuries – as its name implies. Indeed, in just the four years since Mark Pullinger last interviewed the ensemble's founder and conductor, the charismatic François-Xavier Roth, for *Gramophone*, it has added not only to the number but also to the range of recordings: there's been more Ravel (including last month's Recording of the Month) to join its *Gramophone* Award-winning *Daphnis et Chloé*, Debussy's *Pelléas et Mélisande* and symphonies by Beethoven, Berlioz, Mahler and Saint-Saëns.

All those recordings have appeared on Harmonia Mundi, the orchestra and conductor's home label for half a decade now, while they have also garnered one of their several Editor's Choices with a rare opera, Saint-Saëns's *Le timbre d'argent*, on the Bru Zane label. 'The recording itself is tremendous,' wrote Tim Ashley in his review of that set, 'conducted with infectious energy by François-Xavier Roth, and with Les Siècles really relishing every shift of colour in Saint-Saëns's gorgeous orchestral palette' (10/20). Similar words, or variations on them, pop up with unerring regularity in reviews of their releases.

For their newest album, it's a return to the heart of the Austro-German repertoire with Mahler. Having already recorded *Titan*, an early hybrid version of the First Symphony, they now turn to the Fourth, with Sabine Devieilhe as soprano soloist. When I sit down with Roth to discuss the release via Zoom, I begin by asking why he's turning to the Fourth Symphony now.

'It's a symphony I've been looking at on the side for years,' he tells me, 'being a little bit scared of it – because of its simplicity, because of its structure and shape. Then suddenly I found my way to it and I wanted to do it with Les Siècles. Sabine Devieilhe is such a close friend and a partner in many projects. I said to her she would be ideal for doing it now, and she said, "Yes, let's do it." Sometimes the reasons for doing something can be very banal,' he says in conclusion, with a shrug. It's a refreshingly honest response.

In conversation, even via a computer screen, Roth's easy-going charm shines through, his excellent English playful and delivered with irrepressible Gallic flair. And while he talks with what seems like a permanent twinkle in his eye, his seriousness, intelligence and honesty are unmistakable. This becomes clear when I ask what, if anything, makes the Fourth – the most intimate of Mahler's symphonies – suited to the approach of Les Siècles?' He answers, straightforwardly: 'This is difficult to describe.'

The lessons they learnt with *Titan*, he goes on to explain, are many. 'When we performed *Titan* we could already feel the benefits of going back to instruments that Mahler used,' he says. 'He used them in a certain way that pushes them to their limits, for example when he asks the instruments to be played with their bells up, which produces such an amazing effect with the instruments he knew – much more so than with modern instruments.'

Roth also identifies a requirement for what he terms a 'virtuosity of dynamics', with Mahler making special demands on the players. 'In one bar they have to play loudly and with lots of passion, and in the next

'With gut strings or Mahler's winds and brass, the effect of dynamics is so strong that you better understand their purpose'

bar they have to be something like invisible,' he says, 'and if you do that with either gut strings or the winds and brass he used to have as instruments, the effect is so strong that in the end you better understand the purpose of it.'

When it comes to sourcing those instruments, though, things are rarely straightforward. 'It would have been much more practical', the conductor admits, 'if, let's say, he had premiered all his symphonies with his Vienna orchestra. But that was not the case, starting with the First Symphony, which premiered in Budapest and then went to Hamburg. The Fourth was in Munich, the Fifth in Cologne. The Seventh, which I conducted last week, was premiered in Prague.' There are more general questions to be answered, too, as Roth points out: 'When a piece was performed for the first time in 1913, like *Le sacre du printemps*, do you use an instrument that was made in 1912 or one made in 1890?'

The ultimate decisions about which instruments to use in Les Siècles are made collaboratively, with the musicians presenting different options to the conductor, having located and often renovated the instruments themselves before trying them out in rehearsals. 'I mean, the rehearsals!' Roth says enthusiastically. 'One day we have to do a movie about that! My musicians, they train and they are so professional and passionate, but it's sometimes like starting from zero with the different instruments. We have surprises, and sometimes the instruments are not so steady. All these adventures are totally exciting, and totally exhausting – but at the end it's great, even if doesn't succeed on day one.'

As well as the instruments, though, there's also the need for his musicians to step into the shoes of their forebears from over a century ago. How do they go about that, I ask? 'Portamento, vibrato, the way you articulate, the way you make your instrument sound – what's normal these days is completely new. To play Mahler, we have to research not just the instruments but the people behind the instruments, what their habits were and their level of culture. For sure, we don't have direct answers. It's research, and we try to achieve a truth, but we won't have the definitive truth – and that's the magic of the music!'

What's clear, I venture, having listened to an early edit of the new album, is that it's not just the instruments and the textures, but also the whole approach to rubato – the ebb and flow of the pulse – that seem to have been pondered afresh from the conductor's perspective as well. Roth responds with an

Roth chose Sabine Devieilhe as the ideal soprano for Mahler's Fourth Symphony

Les Siècles recording Mahler's Fourth, a process that involves capturing live performances and then following up with patch sessions such as this one – above and right

admission: 'The most difficult aspect of performing Mahler is trying to understand what he meant.'

It's something he spent a great deal of time discussing, he tells me, with Pierre Boulez. 'I was so lucky to be close to Boulez in his last years, and it's something we discussed quite often. I asked him why, at a certain point, he had focused on Mahler's music, and he told me he was fascinated by the way that Mahler describes the tempo journey, if we may call it that: the trajectory of the pulse or the tempo within a movement. Mahler very rarely lets us – the orchestra or conductor – have a long phrase without telling us something: don't rush here; here, maybe a little less passion; there, don't do a *ritenuto*. All these indications make the flow of the music something unique, and that was something Boulez was fascinated by.

'At the same time, Mahler leaves us lost when it comes to many things. So he decides to make a new phrase *meno mosso* but doesn't indicate when the original tempo comes back. The fact that he doesn't give metronome markings is also a very strong statement. The metronome is something so practical for a composer, but Mahler just doesn't do it. He doesn't want to give us a number; he tries to inspire our creative imagination. Those are the mysteries and enigmas in the scores. And there are many enigmas in the Fourth Symphony, which make it exciting and challenging. But I think generally speaking his music remains a labyrinth: you have to find your way.'

In finding a fresh approach to Mahler, Roth would seem to be at several further advantages, not the least of which is that he is so active in performing contemporary music. Does he also see it that way? 'This is something that's completely complicated to describe,' he begins. 'When I conduct Helmut Lachenmann or Boulez, or a new work by George Benjamin, and then I go back to Haydn or Bach, or if I visit Mahler having conducted, for example, *Tristan*, the journey at the end is an accumulation of experiences.' He goes on, more specifically: 'For sure, I have special eyes

> *'The moments where we collectively take a decision and go for it, not knowing if it's going to succeed, make a group very special'*

looking at a score because of my experience of so many different repertoires. For a premiere, my eyes have to read music that nobody has heard before, and this makes me look differently at scores by Mahler or Wagner or Debussy or Mozart.'

I mention Boulez again, who must have been an inspiration when approaching Mahler from a new-music perspective, and all Roth offers is, 'Definitely,' accompanied by a chuckle, playfully withholding – or so it feels – the longer answer that I'm after. He's more forthcoming when I probe deeper into his own personal journey with Mahler. 'When I was a kid in Paris in the '70s Mahler was not very often performed,' he tells me. 'In the '80s there were maybe some Mahler cycles in Paris, but not so much.' His father, the renowned organist Daniel Roth, also played a role in steering his early tastes. 'He always said to me: "Mahler's too long. Richard Strauss is much more to the point."'

So the young François-Xavier didn't really discover Mahler until adulthood, and his first professional engagement with the composer was a modest one: 'I think I was 19 or 20 – I played second piccolo in the First Symphony with the Orchestre Philharmonique de Radio France at the Salle Pleyel.' But it's also significant, Roth says, that the first complete set he heard was conducted by Michael Gielen, a predecessor at the SWR Symphony Orchestra Baden-Baden and Freiburg (Roth spent five years as Music Director of the orchestra before it was controversially disbanded as part of a merger with the Stuttgart RSO). 'So my first approach to Mahler was, let's say, with the opposite of Leonard Bernstein – with a conductor who was more intellectual and associated with the modern stuff.'

Roth has also recorded Symphonies Nos 3 and 5 with the Gürzenich Orchestra in Cologne, of which he has been Kapellmeister since 2015 (as well as Music Director of the city, with responsibility for the opera company too). The

orchestra has a very distinguished Mahler history, having premiered the Fifth under the composer's own baton, and Roth is very much aware of the special authenticity it brings to the works. 'It's very interesting and moving', he says, 'when you conduct an orchestra that claims to have been the first one. For sure, none of the musicians are the same, but the first time I conducted Mahler's Fifth there was incredibly moving for me, because there's still something, no doubt, that's transported through the generations. So I have the Gürzenich-Orchester, which is almost 200 years old playing modern instruments; and then my 20-year-old French orchestra performing on instruments from Mahler's time. For me that's very interesting: a bit schizophrenic, but very complementary as well!'

Roth's Gürzenich Orchestra position is one of several posts he's held alongside his work with Les Siècles. Before the stint with the SWR orchestra he was Associate Guest Conductor of the BBC National Orchestra of Wales. Since 2017 he's been Principal Guest Conductor of the LSO, with which he's had a strong association ever since winning its Donatella Flick conducting competition in 2000. That breakthrough came only shortly after Roth had begun his conducting studies, taken up alongside his career as a flautist, and that led to two years as assistant to John Eliot Gardiner after which, in 2003, he founded Les Siècles.

The orchestra started, he has said elsewhere, almost as a 'garage band', meeting at first at his home. Did he imagine for one moment that nearly 20 years later it would be such a force on the international stage? 'Not at all,' he answers immediately. 'I didn't dare to think of our journey in terms of how we would be seen and appreciated. We all started out without being paid, without any support. We were there for the music and to try to do something differently.

> *'The most difficult aspect of performing Mahler is trying to understand what he meant – and there are many enigmas in the Fourth Symphony'*

'We have gained recognition because of the instruments we use in repertoire which has never been visited by period-instrument orchestras. But the orchestra is so much more than that. It's human beings who have travelled together through the years, so there is this deep connection between us. In rehearsals it can be so experimental that it's scary, but these experiences, these moments where we collectively take a decision and go for it without knowing if we're going to succeed, they make a group very special. I think that's also what audiences like about Les Siècles on stage. Very often people come to me and say they had the impression that it was our last concert, except everybody is smiling because we're having such fun!'

And right from the start, they have had a process of recording that is predestined to preserve that special atmosphere, capturing performances live in concert and following up with patch sessions. 'Nowadays, we do a few more patches, now that we are with Harmonia Mundi,' Roth explains, 'but the structure and the process of the recording has always been the same. Every recording we've done has had the same sound engineer, Jiri Heger, and I do the edit sessions with him every time.'

He doesn't deny that it's a model that was born of economic necessity, but there's little quibbling with the artistic results. 'In an ideal world I would certainly spend more time in a studio after an ideal tour, but I wouldn't like to do egocentric studio sessions. And it's true that the atmosphere of the concerts is something very interesting: we compare the takes between studio patches and the concert and very often you lose something, or you can't recreate something you created in the concerts. Music-making is concerts and concerts are, for me, really the ideal balance between preparation and giving to the audience.' **G**

Les Siècles and Roth's recording of Mahler Symphony No 4 is released on Harmonia Mundi

PHOTOGRAPHY: JEAN-BAPTISTE MILLOT

Mahler's Rückert-Lieder

In July 2017, mezzo **Alice Coote** released a recording of Mahler's most intense sets of songs, and ahead of it talked to **James Jolly**

For Hugo Wolf it was Eduard Mörike, for Robert Schumann it was Heinrich Heine, and for Gustav Mahler it was Friedrich Rückert (1788-1866) – three extraordinary partnerships between composer and poet, as Richard Wigmore reminded us in his *Gramophone* Collection on the *Rückert-Lieder* (1/13). In the case of Mahler, the poetry of Rückert – translator, philologist and professor of Oriental languages – struck a chord that would result not only in the five *Rückert-Lieder* (1901-02) but also in the *Kindertotenlieder* (1901-04). And one can't but help imagine that Rückert's Eastern-influenced aesthetic also opened Mahler's eyes and ears to the possibilities of Hans Bethge's translations of Chinese poetry that would result in the song-symphony *Das Lied von der Erde* (1908-09).

'Mahler seems to know, like no one else, how to utilise the "air space" so that it resonates as another instrument'

Alice Coote has recorded the orchestral versions of both the *Rückert-Lieder* and the *Kindertotenlieder* (plus the *Lieder eines fahrenden Gesellen*) with the Netherlands Philharmonic Orchestra under Marc Albrecht for Pentatone, but it's the first work that we choose to focus on. The mezzo-soprano comes prepared, armed with a handful of scores, from the full orchestral to a miniature score – all elaborately annotated.

The first thing to say about the *Rückert-Lieder* is that they do not comprise a song-cycle. They are five separate songs, usually performed as a group but – and it's quite a big but – in an order chosen by the performer, and very few recordings adhere to the same sequence. Alice Coote opts for (1) 'Ich atmet' einen linden Duft'; (2) 'Blicke mir nicht in die Lieder'; (3) 'Liebst du um Schönheit'; (4) 'Um Mitternacht'; and (5) 'Ich bin der Welt abhanden gekommen'. By comparison, Janet Baker and Barbirolli chose 2,1,4,3,5 (as did Fassbaender and Chailly), Ludwig and Karajan 5,3,2,1,4, and Kožená and Rattle 3,2,4,1,5. The order is an obvious opening sortie. 'I think one powerful influence is what you've grown up with – you just expect a particular song to come next,' Coote explains. 'But for a recording, someone like the producer sometimes reorders it later. The only thing that really upsets me is if anything follows "Ich bin der Welt". I can't go anywhere after that piece. That's the only really strong feeling I have when it comes to the order. When you're recording them you tend to do them in an order that works best for the different orchestral groupings anyway.' ('Um Mitternacht', for example, dispenses with all strings, 'Ich atmet' omits cellos and basses but adds a celesta, and so on.)

In 'Ich atmet' einen linden Duft', the singer joins in quickly after a gentle ripple of harp, celesta and clarinet over a held note on the horn. It's a song that, unusually, describes a smell – the perfume of lime trees. 'It's a fiendishly difficult song because, when you're singing with the orchestra and they're doing their job properly, there's only the merest thread of strings, running up and down in quavers. It's just genius! Mahler is not setting a poem, rather he's *living* a poem, creating a reality in music, in sound. The harp is part of the scent, which touches underneath your nose and joins the oxygen in the room. Then suddenly the thread of that fragrance, or whatever it is, becomes an amazing quaver line

The historical view

Gustav Mahler
As recorded by composer Anton von Webern (1883-1945) in his diary, February 3, 1905

'After *Des Knaben Wunderhorn* I could not compose anything but Rückert - this is lyric poetry from the source; all else is lyric poetry of a derivative sort.'

Pierre Boulez
New York Review of Books, October 28, 1976

'The reckless extension of time, the surplus of instruments, the supercharged feelings and gestures...form had to break down under these excesses! What could be the value of music in which the relation of idea to form is lost in the swamps of expressivity?'

Roger Vignoles
Hyperion booklet-note, 2004

'In these songs [Mahler] has finally abandoned the stock characters of the *Wunderhorn*, with their generalised emotional expression, for a poetic world that could express his own feelings with uncanny accuracy and sensitivity.'

and the vocal line duets above it. The strings are the memory, they are the feeling, the reminiscence.' And, I point out, there's a constant change of time signature. 'He's always shifting things, and each time you think you've landed it rushes off again, but of course a fragrance *doesn't* land. The imagery that went into Mahler's guts when he read the poem just *becomes* the song, a completely new reality. It's magical.'

'Blicke mir nicht in die Lieder' finds the poet/composer in the act of creation. 'I like doing this second because he's still got those quavers running on in the cellos and clarinet. This is another activity that never stops – his mind in the act of creation, but he's also talking about the bees working to create the honey. It's so witty – it really is! Technically it's more like a speaking song, like being an actor. You should have your voice lined up so those intervals feel easy, like speaking. The interest is in the orchestra – the brewing of those creative ideas.'

The central song in Coote's cycle is 'Liebst du um Schönheit', in many ways the most traditional of the five – a strophic setting and a love song. 'It's strophic in that it's got sections that repeat, but there's no other song like it. Also, it's a very fragile idea – Mahler throws out a thought and you develop it. The vocal line is on its own – it's disjointed and doesn't really have a melody. I find it the most difficult because it's so simple.' What does the *Innig* marking at the start contribute? Is it a mental attitude, or a way of projecting? 'It's *everything* – it's about the way you breathe in, what you're thinking, the colour, the way you place the first consonant, the relationship of the breath to the voice, how you sustain the sound, how you link that sound to the next note, how you choose to be quiet. It shouldn't really be planned. All you need to do is read the poem, listen to the introduction and you know what it means.'

Coote places 'Um Mitternacht' fourth and it's the darkest song, scored for winds, brass, harp and piano, with no strings at all. 'It's the most sparse, orchestrally – until the last page when all the brass return from their tea break! And the score *looks* empty. You *feel* that emptiness and that sense of being on your own: the vocal line is utterly alone. That opening phrase is right in the crack of your voice – it's in a dark place between the certainty of the lower voice and the head voice. You mustn't sing it in a chest voice. You are in the crack between day and night, the crack between knowing and not

Alice Coote is enraptured by the genius displayed in Mahler's Rückert-Lieder

knowing, between life and death, and from then on Mahler keeps on with those long, sustained lines that just ask, "What's going on? Help!". And when you sing the words "Um Mitternacht", it nearly always returns to those low opening notes. Mahler often goes down there for very direct, very truthful emotions.' And what happens when she reaches the word 'entscheiden', spread over 14 notes? 'It's like a real scream to me. When I'm singing it, it feels like there's something "animal" there. Mahler doesn't just do one fall, he is desperate enough to add another one.'

Coote's desire for 'Ich bin der Welt abhanden gekommen' to be placed last stems from the fact she couldn't get to the end, emotionally, singing 'I'm dead to the world', then re-enter the world with another song. The opening, too, is pure genius with first two notes, then three, then four, before the whole phrase unfurls. 'Yeesss! It's like with the symphonies: the sound world Mahler creates is a painterly thing. I really can't think of anyone else who sets up that same kind of emotional and psychological mood. And you just glide into it. It's very fluid, you almost don't notice the bar lines. He seems to know, like no one else, how to utilise the "air space", the space around the instruments, so that it almost seems to resonate as another instrument. I think that's why there are actually fewer instruments playing than you think you are hearing. It's pure magic.' **G**

▶ Alice Coote's recording of the Rückert-Lieder is on Pentatone

MASTERCLASS

Symphony No 5 – Adagietto

A musical masterpiece went under the microscope in December 1999, with the help of its performers

CONDUCTOR'S VIEW

Riccardo Chailly
Music Director of the
Royal Concertgebouw Orchestra
When I conducted the Fifth for the very first time in 1988 in Milan, and then, a year later on my farewell concert tour with the Radio Symphony Orchestra in Berlin, I remember I was tempted to slow down – because the music is so phenomenal and intense – instead of moving forward. This tendency to do the opposite of what Mahler wanted is too easy and self-indulgent.

I am reminded of something else that occurred in Berlin, again in 1988. Before the final rehearsal of the Fifth, I asked the technician at the Philharmonie to play Mahler's historic Welte-Mignon piano-roll 'recording' of the *Trauermarsch* to the members of the orchestra. I announced that something very special would be 'on air' and asked the players to pay special attention to the floating freedom of the pianist's tempo. They

were greatly surprised, and embarrassed almost, when I then told them that the pianist was Gustav Mahler! The degree of elasticity he brings to the first movement is truly extraordinary.

From that historic Welte-Mignon recording, and also from Mengelberg's conducting score, I came to understand more about the freedom, tempo-wise, which Mahler brings to his text. It is quite different from modern practice. Today we are more cautious, too cautious almost; we approach the text with a certain austerity. I feel it is important to respect the text but not exclude one's own personality when interpreting it. Imagination is different from violation.

VIOLINIST'S VIEW

Alex Kerr
Leader of the
Royal Concertgebouw Orchestra
The question of tempos in the fourth movement is fascinating. Mahler actually writes *Adagietto*. It's not an *adagio*, so

shouldn't be played that slowly. When it's treated too lugubriously it becomes over-sentimentalized. There's emotion enough in the music already. Listen out for the constant dramatic, dynamic changes and for the climax in the middle of the movement – as if Mahler is suddenly afraid he has gone too far emotionally and slams on the brakes. His way with the music is so beautiful you first feel you're longing for something, then you've reached it, you're suspended there, then gently brought down.

There are a lot of tempo changes guiding you through the *Adagietto*; there are 32 commas just in the opening. They give you a clear idea of the phrase structure, a picture of exactly when to time the required motion forward. Imagine a singer singing this *Adagietto* – they'd need natural places to take a breath and that's what those commas are for. In fact, I can clearly envisage a singer performing it, even without words. There are different kinds of timbre – voices – that Mahler uses in the movement which moves from a dark, baritone-tenor-like tone to a high soprano at the climax. In relation to the rest of the symphony it's like finding a solo voice in Bach after a large choral passage.

There is a sense of stillness about the *Adagietto* which is too often translated into slow, ponderous playing. It is very easy to get caught up in the harmony, but I don't think that is what Mahler intended. To make it into a tragic, depressing, love-lorn thing is wrong. Mahler constantly says 'move forward', quite often writing *sforzandos* which, if done with just the bow arm, create a swoop of sound that pushes you forward and stops it being overly sentimental or kitsch. The use of F major, a very uplifting key played on open strings, is interesting, especially when its surface is broken by a hint of ominous D – the reality that interrupts the reverie.

WHAT WE SAID AT THE TIME

'*I understand that Mahler is not "well seen" by critics of good taste, but here is a good fruity tune with plenty of sugar, exquisitely recorded with concert-hall echo complete. It gives me a great deal of pleasure and I venture to believe that it will give 75 per cent of our readers a great deal of pleasure too. It is rather on the lines of the Intermezzo from Cavalleria. I hope that Columbia will give us some more of Mahler. We gramophone lovers are simple creatures, and we enjoy records like this.*'

Compton Mackenzie - January 1927
Columbia L1798: Adagietto. Concertgebouw Orchestra,
Amsterdam / Willem Mengelberg

The Adagietto from Mahler's Symphony No 5, best thought of as a song without words

The *Adagietto*'s ending is problematic because there is no definite end. The best way to play it is to follow Mahler's urging – move forward. The simplest way is the best way.

TRUMPETER'S VIEW

Peter Masseurs
First Trumpet of the
Royal Concertgebouw Orchestra

In the first movement the trumpet sets the tone for the rest of the symphony. You have to accept that and try to be as expressive as possible without overstating anything. Mahler wrote for the B flat trumpet but I play with a C trumpet, a more brilliant sounding instrument with cleaner intonation. The end of the first movement ought to vanish away; that's the emotional heart of the symphony, the sense of things dying away in their own natural time. There's a real difficulty in trying to achieve that quality within a work as large and loud as the Fifth.

The *Adagietto*, of course, is a resting point for the brass section. Sometimes it can be a bore, sometimes exciting. There's so much space in the *Adagietto* it can lift you up to heaven or drop you down to reality. But it's difficult to play because you have to do so with such delicacy. The strings play so hard in the first three movements, building pressure and drama all the time, then suddenly they're required to relax and play with

no vibrato on the bow, only with the left hand and that's very hard.

I sometimes feel the symphony could stop after the *Adagietto*. The step back into the *Rondo-Finale* is a clear change of pace, and requires huge control and concentration. Technically it isn't that difficult but to create a change of mood can be very difficult for the horn player who must reach a high E very quickly after a long rest. It is Mahler at his most demanding. **Interviews by Michael Quinn**

HOW IT WORKS

The *Adagietto* is heard out of context so often these days, that its original role as a relatively lightweight slow introduction to the *Rondo-Finale* – balancing the role of the symphony's opening funeral march and *allegro* second movement – is easily overlooked. It was Mahler himself who sanctioned its separate performance, launching the process of change that transformed the piece from a song-like intermezzo of just over seven minutes to a funereal dirge of nearly 15. That, at least, is the current orthodoxy, although the main direction is *sehr langsam* (very slow) and we know that the first great Mahler conductor Willem Mengelberg himself noted a performing time of nine-and-a-half minutes in his score. Bernstein may have had something to do with the go-slow – he conducted the piece at the funerals of Serge Koussevitzky and

Senator Bobby Kennedy – but it was Luchino Visconti's film, *Death in Venice* that confirmed the tendency.

If this music is 'meant to be' a love song for Alma Schindler, as Mengelberg maintained, it also encodes a bittersweet longing for the tenderness and intensity of love that works best at a middle-range tempo. The score is littered with detailed markings – Mahler was a conductor first and wished to leave nothing to chance – but the key indicators are all to do with feeling not pacing. A natural ebb and flow, and the markings *seelenvoll*, *mit Empfindung* and *mit Wärme* (soulful, with emotion and with warmth) are surely what count.

At a mere 103 bars, the *Adagietto* is Mahler's shortest symphonic movement, best thought of as a song without words, a haven of F major peace between the strenuous D major activity of the complex structures on either side. The expectant hush of strings and harp alone, a sound unprecedented in symphonic literature, is suddenly, subtly felt. Then, against the soft plucking of the harp, the main idea steals in with an opening phrase derived from the second of the *Kindertotenlieder*, 'Nun she' ich wohl'. It is tentative at first, the long upbeats and expressive *appoggiaturas* of the melodic line create the yearning, heartbreaking effect that, for many listeners, is quintessentially Mahlerian. The cellos take over the melody at 1'09" and, from 2'25", a further strain on the violins pushes forward, acquiring greater intensity.

Comparable to the contrasting verse of a Lied, the middle section from 3'59", marked *Fliessender* (more flowing), is darker, more passionate and developmental. Mahler may or may not have intended specific melodic allusions to the archetypal lovers of Wagner's *Tristan and Isolde*. There is an equivocal though undemonstrative implication of a D yet to be conclusively affirmed before the music comes to rest with a slow, barely grazed *glissando* on the first violins and violas. This serves as a bridge to reintroduce the main theme, now more frankly emotive than before. The extended Cs that usher in the section seem to float on air. The final climax comes closest to the *Rückert* setting, 'Ich bin der Welt abhanden gekommen' in its reluctant, highly emotional leave-taking, although there is no authority in the score for dragging out the final bars. **David Gutman**

PHOTOGRAPHY: LEBRECHT MUSIC ARTS / BRIDGEMAN IMAGES

Petrenko's magnificent MAHLER 7

In August 2021, **Edward Seckerson** praised this startling survey of the symphony from Kirill Petrenko and the Bayerisches Staatsorchester on the orchestra's own label

Mahler

Symphony No 7
Bavarian State Orchestra / Kirill Petrenko
BSO Recordings Ⓕ BSOREC0001 (73' • DDD)
Recorded live at the National Theatre, Munich,
May 28 & 29, 2018

I really thought I knew this work – every facet of it. But Kirill Petrenko has a way of hearing deep into textures and harmonies that is at times really quite startling. He gives us X-ray ears. Truly you don't need a score in front of you to believe your ears and eyes.

This piece was perhaps the greatest leap Mahler ever made towards the kind of 'pure music' that leaned less heavily on high emotion and instead explored an almost hallucinatory range of colours in terms of both texture and harmonic language. More colours, more layers – and that is where Petrenko leaves nothing 'unturned'. There is a passage from about 7'08" in the first movement where arresting pizzicatos in the violins (and by arresting I mean that for a moment I wondered if two different passages had been accidentally superimposed) skew the harmony in ways that suggest the Second Viennese School has already arrived.

'Petrenko takes Mahler at his word, pushing the stridency of his woodwinds so that the harmonic anomalies really pop'

Dynamics play a big part in this, of course, and Petrenko does more than take Mahler at his word, pushing the stridency of his finely honed Bayerisches Staatsorchester woodwinds so that the harmonic anomalies really pop. He's also mastered the sometimes wilful tempo relationships in the outer movements. It's hard to get these right in the first movement and some – in search of its atavistic character – grind to a halt at times (Klemperer is almost in reverse gear throughout). So there's an imperative about Petrenko's reading that is carried through to his ardent phrasing of the second subject in the fabulous departure to higher regions at the heart of the movement. What a rarefied and exotic passage that is.

You might suppose that the warmth and sophistication of Petrenko's Bavarians slightly detracts from the primitivism – I always feel a paganism in this piece – but that is countered by Petrenko's willingness to encourage coarse and even ugly sounds. The Scherzo, the dark heart of the piece, is (along with the Sixth Symphony's equivalent) Mahler's ultimate homage to 'things that go bump in the night', full of convulsive grunting and slithering and a moment where the natural

Petrenko's Mahler takes its place among the finest versions on record

Giving us X-ray ears: Kirill Petrenko and the Bavarian State Orchestra bring a clarity to Mahler's textures that allows the music to speak with unusual directness

order of things gives way in a snap-pizzicato that is officially the loudest note in the piece. Petrenko sees to it that it is.

There's another momentary 'collapse' in the first of the two Nachtmusiks – a collision of major and minor tonalities that Petrenko almost literally turns into a landslide. Like all such moments this conductor relishes the surprise of it, the newness of it. And if he can make seasoned Mahlerians even for a moment imagine that this is a first-time experience then he's got my attention. The opening of this movement may sound familiar (a motor oil TV ad hasn't helped) but the way Petrenko navigates this curious 'night patrol' through a constantly shifting landscape is testament to his understanding of Mahler the pantheist.

The second Nachtmusik, with its guitar

and mandolin tinklings – a wistful nocturnal serenade – sounds properly intimate. And this is where the humanity of Petrenko's reading and the refinement of the playing reminds us that Mahler always left us in no doubt of exactly how he felt at any given juncture. The scale may be modest but the blossoming of the big lyric idea in this movement can hardly contain itself and Petrenko lends it lots of heart.

You can't see for C major in the finale, of course, but where this movement can go horribly wrong is when conductors try to iron out the seemingly chaotic nature of this jubilant dance marathon – Mahler's 'apotheosis of the dance'. Again you have to take him at his word: awkward changes of tempo and daring volte-faces are what it is all about. This is a gathering of the clans and the way Petrenko characterises its

multifarious variants – sideshows, if you like, within the whole – is key to his success. It doesn't sound awkward or incoherent; it sounds joyful, a crazy collage wherein we pull focus on the small details as well as the grand gestures. The final scene of *Die Meistersinger* is often referenced – and with good reason: all humanity is here. And when that celebratory trumpet theme at the outset undergoes glorious transformation at the close, Petrenko could hardly make it more universal.

This is an auspicious first release for the Bayerisches Staatsorchester's own label and whichever favourite version of the symphony you might have in your collection – be it Bernstein or one of the Fischers, perhaps – Petrenko demands to be heard and attention paid. **ⓖ**

THE EVENT

Mahler's Symphony No 8 premiere – September 12, 1910

The day the world gathered in Munich

An earth-shaking musical explosion was imminent in Munich in the late summer of 1910. Everyone seemed to be waiting for it and Europe's cultural and political elite had flocked to witness it for the sake of posterity. Gustav Mahler had come to the city to conduct what Munich's municipal chronicle described as a 'monster-concert' for an audience of 3400. The venue was to be the enormous glass and steel Festival Hall of Music in the Exhibition Park, which had opened a few seasons before. The reason for all this excitement: the première of Mahler's Symphony No 8, which the concert's promoter, Emil Gutmann, dubbed the 'Symphony of a Thousand' in a no-holds-barred publicity campaign which saw hundreds of signed photographs of the composer in shop windows and a barrage of huge posters. Mahler had been annoyed by the Barnum-&-Bailey

success of Mahler's composing career and described by some as nothing short of his apotheosis – confirmed what many concert-goers and record collectors today take for granted: that Mahler was the greatest symphonic composer of his time – indeed, of the 20th century.

'A lightning vision' is how Mahler himself described the work's genesis in 1906. In a letter to his wife Alma – the work's dedicatee he wrote: 'On the threshold of my old workshop the Spiritus Creator took hold of me and shook me and drove me on for the next eight weeks until my greatest work was done.' He wrote it, in his own words, 'rapidly and half-unconsciously in two months … as if it had been dictated to me'. It was conceived in two massive parts, with human voices – deemed by Mahler to be 'the most beautiful instruments in the world' – used throughout: the first, a setting of ninth-

It was the first utterly resounding success of Mahler's composing career

style of Gutmann's campaign and nearly cancelled the performance from his base in New York where he was conducting a busy season at the Metropolitan Opera. But he yielded when Gutmann told him that rehearsals were already underway.

Munich wasn't the most obvious choice for a major Mahler première. It was the home town of his chief rival, Richard Strauss, who had tenuously – some would argue half-heartedly and only strategically – championed the slightly older composer's music, and was the city where Mahler's Fourth Symphony had been born with a thud 10 years earlier. But the monumental triumph of the Eighth – the first utterly resounding

century cleric Hrabanus Maurus's grandiose Latin hymn *Veni, creator spiritus*; the second a setting of the final scene of Goethe's *Faust*. Never afraid to think big, Mahler, in his choice of texts, aimed to unite the rivers of religion and humanism to form an ocean of ecstatically joyous affirmation. He did not know the words to the hymn by heart, and while waiting for the complete text to arrive from Vienna the inspiration-ravaged composer continued to write the music for the first movement, finishing half of it. To his astonishment – and as evidence in his mind of the mystical ties that bind life and music to the realm of the spirit – texts and music fitted together

perfectly. Alma described her husband as 'boundlessly happy and exalted' during this 'last summer of peace and beauty and contentment'.

Four years later, as final rehearsals for the concert were underway, the scale of the undertaking became clear to everyone. A caricature that appeared in the local paper showed Mahler on the podium receiving the news that no one was in the audience because everyone was needed on stage to perform the symphony! This wasn't too far off the mark considering the fact that 500 adult and 350 child choristers joined the 146-player orchestra (including organ, mandolin and harmonium) along with eight vocal soloists and 12 extra brass players positioned around the hall. (In one aside, Mahler assured the soprano Lilli Lehmann that, in the future, audiences of 20-30,000 would assemble to hear the work at popular festivals!) 'People are collecting in herds,' wrote Mahler to his wife. '[Arnold] Rosé with his quartet, R Strauss with the Philharmonic, critics from every nation, etc., etc! Lord, what visitations threaten me! But I will put a good face on the awful business.'

Though fighting a throat infection and severe back pain, Mahler couldn't resist reporting that at the first rehearsals

Mahler rehearsing the vast forces required for his Eighth Symphony, the so-called 'Symphony of a Thousand'

the effect of the massed sound was 'staggering … it does really sound overwhelming'. For Mahler it was indeed 'the grandest thing I have done, so peculiar in content and form that it is really impossible to write anything about it … there are no longer human voices, but planets and suns revolving'.

On the night of September 12, 1910 crowds gathered to watch the luminaries entering the hall, greeting them with lusty cheers to rival the biggest Hollywood premiere. Richard Strauss, Max Reger, Camille Saint-Saëns, Alfredo Casella and Anton Webern (who had assisted at the rehearsals) represented the composers; Mahler's protégé, Bruno Walter, was one of several prominent conductors; writers Thomas Mann, Stefan Zweig and Arthur Schnitzler were but three on hand. When Mahler stepped onto the podium he was greeted with an instantaneous, roaring standing ovation. More than two hours later, when the work ended in its final blaze of glory, the composer was greeted with a near-hysterical 20-minute frenzy of applause, screaming and foot-stamping. Mahler, who had suffered so many personal tragedies, professional setbacks and incomprehension, was overwhelmed with emotion and moved to tears.

Diary entries from many dumbstruck audience members recounted their awe at the work's miraculous blending of pure, innocent emotion and soaring philosophical aspiration. Luminaries wrote about the 'great days of the Mahler 8 in Munich'. Lilli Lehmann noted with reverence: 'His work, which was given by 1000 performers, sounded as from one instrument, from one throat … for the whole of the second part I gave way to emotion which I could not control.'

Months later, Nobel Prize-winning author Thomas Mann captured the spirit of this historic occasion with a note he sent to Mahler, along with his latest novel: 'I was incapable of saying, that evening in the hotel, how deeply indebted to you I was for the impressions of 12th September … [the book] is certainly a very poor return for what I received – a mere feather's weight in the hand of the man who, as I believe, expresses the art of our time in its profoundest and most sacred form.'

Mahler's Eighth was premiered not long after the composer's 50th birthday, but tragically, just eight months later, he died of a heart ailment. Europe lost its greatest composer, and only a few more summers would pass before the world would lose its hope that great art might lead man to heights beyond the ravages of war. **G**

ALSO IN 1910

This is the year in which Mahler, at 49, became the conductor of the New York Philharmonic Orchestra.

JANUARY 13
First live musical radio programme – radio pioneer Lee De Forest broadcasts the voice of Enrico Caruso from the Metropolitan Opera in New York

FEBRUARY 22
Beecham conducts the premiere of Delius's *A Village Romeo and Juliet*

MARCH 9
Samuel Barber born

MARCH 19
Béla Bartók's String Quartet No. 1 receives its first performance in Budapest

MARCH 28
Henri Fabre makes the first flight in a seaplane (Martigues, France)

APRIL 14
Debussy's piano Préludes published

MAY 3
Alban Berg marries Helene Nahowski

MAY 6
George V ascends to the throne of the United Kingdom on the death of Edward VII

MAY 18
Halley's Comet passes close enough for the Earth to pass through its tail

JUNE 22
Zeppelin's airship makes its first flight carrying passengers

JUNE 25
Paris première of Stravinsky's *The Firebird*

JULY 4
Jack Johnson the black world boxing champion knocks out white Jim Jeffries, sparking race riots in the US

SEPTEMBER 26
Richard Strauss completes his opera *Der Rosenkavalier* at Garmisch

OCTOBER
Arnold Schoenberg mounts a one-man exhibition

OCTOBER 5
Portugal becomes a republic with Teofilo Braga as the first President

OCTOBER 12
Première of Vaughan Williams's *A Sea Symphony* (Birmingham)

NOVEMBER 7
The musical comedy *Naughty Marietta* with music by Victor Herbert opens on Broadway

NOVEMBER 10
Edward Elgar conducts the première of his Violin Concerto, with Fritz Kreisler as soloist (London)

NOVEMBER 20
Leo Tolstoy the great Russian novelist dies of pneumonia aged 82

NOVEMBER 27
Penn Station in Manhattan opens as the world's largest railway terminal

DECEMBER 10
First performance of Puccini's *La fanciulla del West* in New York (at The Met)

Classics RECONSIDERED

Hugo Shirley and **Richard Fairman** sat down in January 2015 to listen to the 1952 recording of Mahler's Das Lied von der Erde by Kathleen Ferrier and Bruno Walter with the Vienna Philharmonic

Mahler

Das Lied von der Erde. Three Rückert-Lieder
Kathleen Ferrier *contr* **Julius Patzak** *ten*
Vienna Philharmonic Orchestra / Bruno Walter
Decca Ⓜ 466 576-2DM (76' • ADD)

Bruno Walter's deep understanding of Mahler is given every chance to show itself in this carefully balanced recording with its sense of space: and one can appreciate to the full Mahler's wonderful handling of his large orchestra, in its most delicate as well as in its most strenuous moments. The charming chinoiserie of youth is beautifully caught: the glittering oriental march in 'Beauty', and the brooding sorrow of the last song, 'Farewell', with its tragic funeral march and its exquisite lyrical passages (which Kathleen Ferrier makes almost intolerably moving) are very memorable. One's critical sense, however, has to note that Miss Ferrier is placed rather too close to the microphone, and thus one is more aware than would otherwise have been the case of a certain sense of strain in one awkward passage in the last great emotional outburst. She recovers at once and sings the last words 'blauen Licht die Fernen' with a superb *legato* and beautifully manages the toneless repetitions of 'ewig' at the end. It is a pity that the celesta is not clearly heard enough on these last pages – one gets some but not all the notes of the arpeggios; the triangle, also, is elusive at the start of 'Youth'.

I can only briefly allude to two other outstanding things in this recording: the melancholy beauty of 'The Solitary in Autumn', in which Kathleen Ferrier excels, and Patzak's singing at the moment when the bird calls to 'The Drunkard in Spring'. **Alec Robertson** (10/52)

Hugo Shirley Although we're talking about 'classics' reconsidered here, I can't help feeling there's a special significance in that this recording is one of Decca's 'Legends' series, and that that particular rubric seems to carry an awful lot of weight here. After all, without wishing to be too morbid or sentimental, this is Ferrier in 1952, a couple of years before her tragic death, singing the work in which Mahler himself started coming to terms with his own mortal illness, and which he began composing just after his elder daughter had died.

Richard Fairman Somehow I don't feel that morbid colouring as strongly as you do. However tragic Ferrier's life was, the events are far enough back in time that they fall outside most people's experience and memory now. The very positive message that comes across to me from a 'classic' recording like this is that great music-making lives on, and is alive and moving to us now, even though all the major protagonists are deceased. I hope you feel the performance itself feels like a living creation.

HS There's certainly nothing morbid or sentimental about the recording itself, no, which is what makes it so successful over 60 years later. And, although we shouldn't ignore Patzak in the tenor songs, it is very much about Ferrier. There's the remarkable rich voice, a proper contralto which also has a certain vulnerability at the top. There's not really anything like it these days, is there?

RF That question sounds like a challenge. How about Nathalie Stutzmann or Ewa Podleś? I've checked on Google and both of them have sung the work, though as far as I can see there aren't any recordings. In any case I haven't heard them in this music. Ferrier is certainly unique in my experience for the depth and richness of her contralto. So much seems to flow from the sound of the voice – grandeur, generosity of feeling, a sense that the songs are addressing monumental and timeless issues.

HS There are other impressive contraltos today, but none, as you seem to suggest, really comparable. And it's almost impossible to separate the character of the voice from the character of the interpretation.

RF Exactly – they seem to be one and the same.

HS There's a phrase in Michael Kennedy's booklet essay, which he applies to 'Um Mitternacht', one of the *Rückert-Lieder* couplings, but which actually seems just right for describing Ferrier's performance: 'stoical solemnity'. There's also that characteristic you often get with great interpretations of not noticing any actual 'interpreting'.

RF That's probably because the quality of Ferrier's voice is already so individual. The number one way that she seeks to represent the feeling of the music is the choice of tone colour she employs. You mentioned the 'vulnerability' at the top. At first, I thought that was because she was a bit unsure and cautious up there, which I still think might be the case, but the end result is so luminous and intimate, it is like the flickering of half-repressed emotions deep within. Sorry about that –

Kathleen Ferrier and Bruno Walter, two of the artists behind a Mahler recording that remains moving today

I can't think how to describe it without getting poetic!

HS It's also quite difficult to point to any specific moments in the interpretation that stand out – as one normally might in this feature – since it all feels so of a piece. Going back to that apparent weakness at the top of the voice, though, you also realise what a difference it makes to have a true contralto in these songs: the whole colour is changed (when compared to a mezzo – let's not get started on the 'baritone question') and the voice seems to fit within the orchestration differently. The effect in 'Der Abschied', of course, is especially hypnotic.

RF One more point before we move on. I would have liked more words from her. Her German isn't that clear, though I do appreciate the way she phrases in complete arcs, or sentences, helped no doubt by Walter keeping the music on the move.

HS Yes, and picking myself up again after a first listen through, I returned to her first two songs, where I have to say I find her a little less convincing. I occasionally wished for a lighter touch, and she doesn't seem ideally comfortable when required to pick up her skirts and get a move on when 'Von der Schönheit', for example, gathers speed. Without Walter's sense of momentum (even 'Der Abschied', which often runs to over half an hour these days, comes in at just over 28 minutes) and his flexibility, the result might have felt a tad matronly and staid.

RF OK, I'll give you that. And Patzak?

HS I think Patzak is wonderful in the very different challenges of the tenor songs.

He colours the words naturally but vividly – the way he weighs 'wüst' and 'Freude' in the first verse of 'Das Trinklied vom Jammer der Erde' provides an example almost straight away – and never feels heavy or unduly effortful. I particularly like his dainty way with 'Von der Jugend', too.

RF He has that old-style way of communicating through the words, as if he automatically expects that the audience speak the right language. That's how the musical world was before singers started jetting around all the time. Against that I don't always feel his voice has the same outstanding quality as Ferrier.

HS The voice itself sounds a bit grainy and short on edge, granted. I get the sense, though, that he's not helped by the engineering – I'm not sure if it's a case of the balance of the voice against the orchestra, the slight muffling of the upper frequencies (at least in Decca's remastering), or a mixture of both. Anyway, what about Walter? We've really dealt with him only in passing so far, although we've both hinted at the quality of his contribution – and that of the Vienna Philharmonic.

RF I find him quite revelatory. Every time I come across a Walter recording (which isn't as often as I would like) I am bowled over. Do you know his Brahms Third? The end of the first movement is titanic.

HS I'm afraid I don't – I've just ordered a copy though!

RF Apologies for going off-piste! But the wholehearted emotion that sweeps him

along in the Brahms is just what I hear again here.

HS Certainly what he does here is wonderful, and it's remarkable the transparency and flexibility he gets from the orchestra, and a great amount of detail comes through in the sound too: those flutter-tonguing flutes that pop up occasionally; the sense of bustling, quivering life he conjures in the central interlude of 'Trinklied vom Jammer der Erde' is wonderful; the sense of yearning intensity he produces as passion breaks through the numbness in 'Der Einsame in Herbst' is glorious, and the way the lower strings really dig out their notes at 'Sonne der Liebe' in that song is viscerally exciting.

RF For me, he is the fount of inspiration in this recording because his emotional response to the music feels so uninhibited. Next to him, the other great conductors on record seem either inexpressive – Klemperer, impassive – or contrived – Bernstein, pulling the music around wilfully, and Karajan, all arty, technologically manipulated mysticism. Walter just lets the emotion in the music pour out.

HS The playing feels so natural, too, with instinctive string *portamentos*, and horn solos that would have given Dennis Brain a run for his money. You mention those other conductors, and that makes one realise how important Walter is in this performance. There's something especially moving in the way that his passionate outbursts and his sense of forward momentum contrast with that 'stoical solemnity' of Ferrier's. With a different conductor, her interpretation, I feel, might have felt very different.

RF Before we sign off we have to mention the recording. In many ways it is quite good for its day, especially the amount of orchestral detail it captures. You keep thinking, 'Oh, I've never heard that before', which is unexpected in a recording dating from the early 1950s. But, for all that, the sound isn't ingratiating, is it?

HS It's not at all bad but it is definitely a bit short on bloom and beauty, and it's difficult not to think about the sort of engineering Decca would manage in Vienna just half a decade later. But by then, of course, there was no Ferrier.

RF For this very special line-up of artists we could probably put up with a lot in the recording. Here is, truly, a 'classic'. **G**

Classics RECONSIDERED

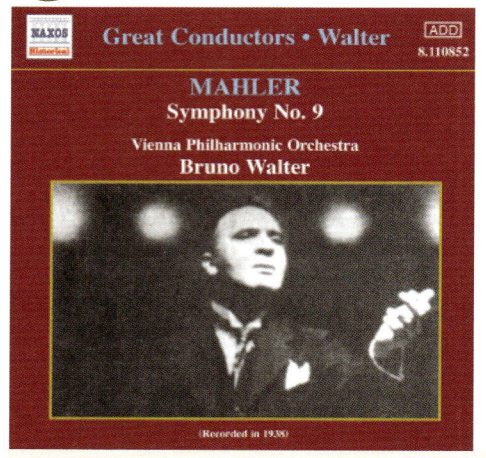

Great Conductors • Walter

MAHLER
Symphony No. 9
Vienna Philharmonic Orchestra
Bruno Walter

(Recorded in 1938)

Mike Ashman and **Peter Quantrill** discuss the merits and shortcomings of Bruno Walter's classic 1938 live recording of Mahler's Ninth Symphony

Mahler

Symphony No 9

Vienna Philharmonic Orchestra / Bruno Walter

Naxos 8 110852; Dutton CDBP9708
Recorded live in 1938

The conductor has written of Mahler with persuasive affection, and here is his testament of interpretation about a work that cannot be heard without deep sympathy for a composer who did not live to hear it.

The quieter moods of the first movement are so quickly broken by dramatic urgencies; here is obviously a powerful drive of interplaying forces; the most immediate reference is to the Strauss tone-poem style, but no 'programme' is given us.

The second movement turns to the simplicities of old German and Austrian life, by making use of the Ländler; but this is no happy motion of minds at rest and bodies glad to keep them so. Not only the very striking orchestration but the abrupt, perhaps harsh-feeling ejaculations bring a sense of doubt, which some might interpret as bearing a heart of sadness, expressed in a brusque heaviness.

The third movement adopts a more open wildness, and develops the contrapuntal art that Mahler so greatly esteemed. The word 'bitter' is much in one's mind; but it is not easy to define the nature of the music, as its so varying lights sweep the sky of the mind of composer and listener.

It is in moments such as the beginning of the finale that the faith of some who may have wavered about Mahler should be deepened. However we choose to regard late Mahler, I cannot think that so remarkable a revelation of the man's spirit at the end of his life can fail to impress any musical mind and move any open heart.
WR Anderson (1/39)

Mike Ashman As the first recording of the Ninth Symphony, conducted by one of Mahler's two closest disciples, this is surely a classic of its kind. It is not the greatest nor the best-played nor the best-recorded Ninth on disc. It is not (nor was ever intended to be) a trend- or style-setter for *echt* Mahler interpretation or performing. It is an exciting, at times thrilling record of a live concert of the symphony – including some overdubs from rehearsals – given by the performers who, some 25 years previously, had given the work's world premiere.

Peter Quantrill It's true that from the first bar you hear the kind of *rubato* and sanely Romantic, flexible phrasing that largely disappeared from Mahler performance and yet is entirely apt to it. The style has been revived in the last two decades but inevitably as a learned style, rather than just style.

MA All style is learned, isn't it?

PQ But where are the heightened contrasts, the bitonal indecision between D minor and major, which define the first movement's journey? A combination of the flattened recording sound and the regular metre has Karajan-ised the movement into a seamlessly integrated Romantic narrative. On the other hand, perhaps where now we wrestle with Mahler the ironist, it may be refreshing to hear a performance that bypasses the issue.

MA It may be – but this isn't it! This performance – and his *Don Giovanni* the previous summer at the Salzburg Festival – are the two that most contradict Klemperer's famous critique of Walter: 'He is a moralist; I am an immoralist'.

PQ In the light of a kind of Kantian naturalism in which Fine Art is an art 'so far as it has at the same time the appearance of being nature', then yes, the flexible play of tempi in the second movement might represent such naturalism. And it might make sense to perceive Walter as such a Kantian in view of the reasons for his rejection of 'the devious way' of Schoenbergian modernism that seem to me to harmonise with the *Don Giovanni* in which Walter's hero Mahler is as present (as conductor) as Mozart. But such a light casts an anachronistic shadow not only in our time but in Walter's own. May I reconcile you to an angled (no less crude) version of Klemperer's contention between naturalist (Walter) and alienated expressionist (Klemperer)? Aren't these the poles that lend the Ninth its magnetic tension?

MA The utter difference of their Mahler interpretations shows that both were keen followers of the composer's frequently repeated encouragements to keep his music alive for its time. His interpreters should make their own traditions. The point of this recording historically was to take down a performance by one of Mahler's disciples – before (as it seemed to the producer Fred Gaisberg) that whole culture collapsed and disappeared. The Nazis were at the gates of Vienna.

PQ And Kurt Schuschnigg was in the audience, yes, I know. But the playing! At the climax of the first-movement exposition it collapses into incoherence

Bruno Walter: conducted the symphony's 1912 premiere

MA These things can happen in concert – especially in a virtually sight-read performance. They didn't get the rehearsal time available now and probably no sectionals at all! All that happens is the recording overloads and the horns struggle a bit with the first of their high-lying phrases. There are moments of less good playing – not a 'collapse into incoherence'.

PQ When not all the orchestra has even reached base camp in the counterpoint of the Rondo, despite five rehearsals during the previous week, is there even the sense of a sense to this music? This performance is like a hastily wrapped parcel, held together with string by cadence points and double bars.

MA No! This is called adventurous conducting of a radical piece of music.

PQ So you're saying the mess belongs to the music.

MA Totally. You're confusing Walter's intellectual/musical aims with the

playing standard he was able to get. The inaccuracies don't matter at all when the interpretative aims are so clear and valid.

PQ OK, I did recently see Lachenmann remark that 'there is always in Mahler a situation of abyss'. But I would find it easier to hear the abyss in the Rondo as satirical if the contrasting idyll was more…idyllic than the insistent, aggressive brass chording here. Certainly there's little evidence of the 'warmth' and 'honesty' that have commonly been associated with Walter the interpreter.

MA Yes, very little – because they are lazy post-1950 critical terms that Walter would have been horrified by as a description of himself! And anyway, the Walter of 1938 was not the Rudolf Steiner-loving ersatz Californian of his last years –

PQ – when he made that final Columbia recording of the Ninth just a year before his death in February 1962. And this last Ninth is beset by its own problems, such as an enlarged chamber orchestra with four double basses, not wholly or successfully pimped by the engineers into a full-size band. I can't help wondering if the success of both Walter's Ninths has been as much down to marketing acumen and historical tragedy/serendipity as intrinsic qualities.

MA Neither Walter recording is a cynical marketing exercise – there was little room for that in 1938, and the Mahler revival was not under way enough for that to work in 1961 either.

PQ The executive shortcomings in 1938 still incline me to the view that this is a blueprint for a great performance (or 'interpretation'? I am not sure I can tell them apart as readily as you can) rather than the thing itself. Can't you hear a leap in nuance and atmosphere and all that makes a performance when you switch to the record we have of *Das Lied von der Erde* made two years earlier by the same performers? The recording is more distant, yet more truthful. The playing is more accurate in every way. Did the intervening political tensions really prevent professionals from doing a job to the best of their abilities? How can we know now?

MA It's not a blueprint, though it may be something of a memory of how things were in 1912. According to the memoirs of the VPO's chairman Hugo Burghauser the pressure to join (or resist) the Nazi Party had started, by 1938, to make an impact on orchestral morale. This Ninth was the last VPO concert for him and many

of the Jewish principals. In any case, the Ninth is a much harder piece to play and record than *Das Lied*. Despite all Mahler's personal psychological flimflam (the Ninth is really my Tenth, etc), *Das Lied* is a set of accompaniments to a song-cycle, not a symphony – and a work the orchestra had played during the 1920s, unlike the Ninth.

PQ In the original sleeve-note for the 1961 recording Walter writes that the *Adagio* 'voices a peaceful farewell: with the conclusion, the clouds dissolve in the blue of Heaven'. We'll never know, but I wonder if he thought so in 1938? Never mind the startlingly loud first violins or the bassoon intonation and rhythmic instability soon afterwards: the famously swift tempo feels hectic compared to Norrington, who at an almost identical speed finds just such a sense of hard-won but calm farewell. It's not as if Walter's recording preserves the kind of string tone and style that Mahler would have known, if Norrington is to be believed – the age of Kreislerian continuous vibrato is already upon us.

MA *If* Norrington is to be believed. I find Norrington's Mahler bland to the point of interpretative invisibility –

PQ – which, true to the original lights of a historically informed performance philosophy, may be his point; to stand within and not on top of the music.

MA Of course Norrington's *idée fixe* is interesting (if only because it's made a lot of people think) but there is a great deal of contrary evidence (not least in Robert Philip's book, *Early Recordings and Musical Style*). And by the time of this recording, it's already three decades after Mahler had any direct influence on Viennese playing. You've only got to read the accounts of the 'modernisations' Weingartner put into effect to see how much things had changed by the time Walter stood in front of this orchestra. It's all in the details. The mixed tempi of the *Scherzo*, the chaos of the Rondo, the *forte* marking for the violins at the start of the *Adagio*: these things that we both hear are all in the score –

PQ – though I'd argue that *forte* here means 'strong', in a conscious reference to the same place in Bruckner's Ninth, not overbearing –

MA – and Walter, like Klemperer, was always following Mahler's much-repeated instructions to his musical disciples: go your own way, do your own thing, make your own style. **G**

MAHLER
through the pages of
GRAMOPHONE'S ARCHIVE

A hand-picked selection of articles from the past century gives a flavour of how we've explored Mahler's music on record

Gramophone's own near-century of existence closely matches the growth in awareness of, followed by reverence for, the music of Mahler. As our archives reveal, recordings of the composer's music were initially thin on the ground – not helped, one suspects, by the sheer length of his symphonies – but persistence, technology and advocacy began to change things, and to do so in time for those who had known Mahler himself, or at least known his era, to share their understanding so extensively with listeners.

Foremost among these was the conductor Bruno Walter, and one of the most extraordinarily powerful and poignant historic documents captured in the early era of recording is his performance of Mahler's Ninth Symphony in Vienna, two months before the Nazis took over the city and Walter was forced to leave. Fred Gaisberg's recollections of that recording - and of meeting Bruno Walter in Paris two month's later to play him the results - are reproduced here.

A key figure both in the life of Mahler's music and in that of Gramophone's pages was Deryck Cooke, who appears in this section twice – firstly as reviewer, in this case sharing his thoughts on Sir John Barbirolli's recording of the Ninth, and secondly through his completion of Mahler's Tenth Symphony, recorded by Eugene Ormandy.

Finally, we hear from one of today's finest Gramophone critics, Richard Osborne, who in 1984 welcomed a classic of the catalogue, Herbert von Karajan's recording of the Ninth Symphony. There is much more where these came from, and we urge anyone interested to explore Gramophone's fully digitised archives for themselves. **G**

The Gramophone, June, 1925   40

(*To the Editor of* THE GRAMOPHONE.)

DEAR SIR,—In the March number of the gramophone you ask for comment from those who have heard the larger orchestral pieces from the Polydor catalogue. Voilá ! I have the good fortune to have the majority of those that I am pleased to consider interesting : the Mahler, the various Beethoven, the Anton Bruckner, and all the Strauss. For us in America it is a grand catalogue, and I was very lucky, I feel, in getting them in. We do not have the same outlay here that you do in England, nor the same chance to buy good music.

The Gustav Mahler is—what ? It is a stupendous thing and it took great courage to make it, but after all was it worth making ? That is, I'm afraid, not the question for these pages. It is well made, there can be no denying that. From all standpoints a fine set of records. Oskar Fried is a mighty conductor and he has done wonders with the records. The chorus and solos are exceptionally good, a thing rather rare in records. A thing which we can hardly say for the Beethoven *Ninth*. I have not heard either the H.M.V. nor the Parlophone versions, and so naturally can make no comparisons. The Beethoven No. 4 and 3 are well made and make a very valuable addition to any collection. The third because it is the only complete version I have ever heard, and the fourth because it is the only one that I have ever heard.

I anxiously am awaiting their supplements.

Yours very truly,

Chicago, Ill.   VORIES FISHER.

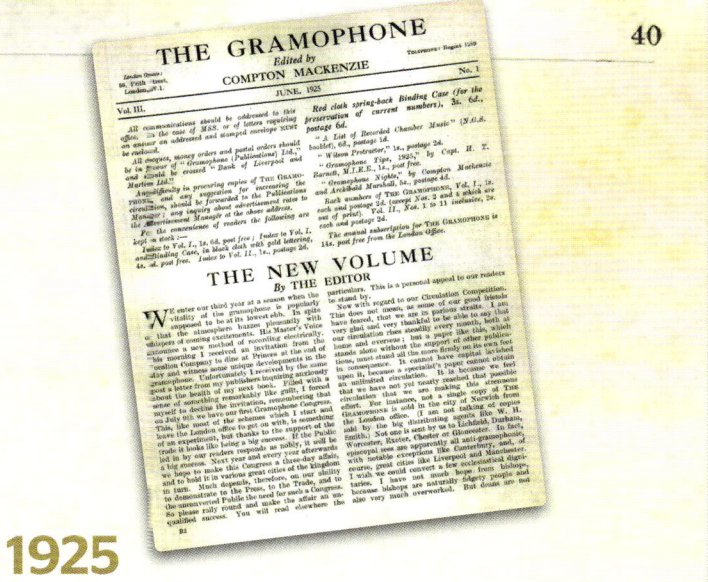

1925

Early Mahler mentions

Within a couple of years of *Gramophone*'s launch, Mahler was beginning to make our pages. A letter in June asked if a Polydor *Resurrection* recording was worth buying – something answered in the affirmative by Editor Compton Mackenzie in October (below)

The Gramophone, October, 1925   220

POLYDOR RECORDS

By THE EDITOR

The records that have given me the greatest pleasure are those of Gustav Mahler's *Resurrection Symphony* and Haydn's *Abschied Symphony*, which lie at the opposite poles of orchestral recording. I cannot understand why we don't ever get an opportunity of hearing the Mahler symphonies in England; the particular one recorded by Polydor is full of drama and melody ; it contains a superb contralto solo, and the choral part is most moving. Its length, of course, is tremendous, eleven double-sided records, but to my taste, at any rate for the moment, the length seems justified. It might be that a musician of more sophistication might find it *faux bon*, but I am perfectly sure that the man of average musical taste with enough leisure to play it right through occasionally will find it thoroughly enjoyable. It necessitates some tremendous orchestral effects being recorded and the success with which they are achieved deserves our warmest admiration.

'I cannot understand why we don't ever get an opportunity of hearing the Mahler symphonies in England; the particular one recorded by Polydor is full of drama and melody'

MAHLER'S RESURRECTION SYMPHONY
(No. 2 in C minor)
[*Communicated*]

GUSTAV MAHLER was born on July 7th, 1860, at Kalischt, in Bohemia, and was educated in Prague and Vienna. In 1886 he went to Leipzig to assist Nikisch and conducted for six months in that city. In 1888 he undertook the direction of the opera at Pesth, and in 1891 moved to Hamburg, remaining there till 1897. He came to London in 1892 to conduct at Covent Garden.

This symphony requires a very large orchestra, the dimensions of which have probably militated against frequent performance of the work. It is constructed as follows : 4 flutes, 2 piccolos, 3 oboes, cor anglais, 3 clarinets, bass clarinet, 3 bassoons, contra-bassoon, 6 horns, 6 trumpets, 4 trombones, tuba, organ, 2 harps, the usual strings, and a whole gallery of percussion instruments, including the "Ruthe" or whip, which Richard Strauss has used with good effect in the early part of his *Elektra*.

The *Second Symphony* of Mahler is of gigantic proportions and a detailed description of it would fill many pages. It runs into five movements, the general feeling being that of immense force and vigour mixed with tenderness (perhaps all too fleeting) ; the themes are big almost to clumsiness, the wealth of idea profuse. It is, in fact, a true successor to the symphonies of Beethoven and of Brahms, in stateliness and occasional stridence. Mahler is not afraid of insisting upon a theme, however stark and severe, though it may take a dozen pages of score to come to its own ; and as regards material and idea there is enough in one movement of this work to form a complete symphony by latter-day composers.

Perhaps the most astonishing feature is the exhibition of the diversity of Mahler's musical mind. Each movement is separate and distinct from the other. Each bears its own individual stamp, and so varied are the facets of the artist's outlook that the symphony gives one perhaps the impression of being the work of several composers. This, however, does not imply looseness of structure, weakness, or incoherence, for the whole is bound together by that distinct feeling of dominating force and power of will so characteristic of Mahler's music in general.

Frankly speaking, the work is far from being perfect in technique. In these days of economy of means as regards scoring Mahler's almost brutal energy of orchestration strikes one unfavourably. He employs the whole orchestra unceasingly and does not seem satisfied unless the complete machinery is in motion. This overloading not only becomes monotonous and wearisome, but tends to spoil some of the most lovely passages, and when Mahler occasionally gives his melody free and untrammelled play, it is, one feels, a trifle petulantly, as though he longed to set the wheels of the entire orchestra going again. But though this is perhaps the most serious blemish in Mahler's work, it is his personal outlook, his musical idiom, he himself.

The eleven Polydor records of the symphony (Nos. 69681 to 69691) which have been strongly recommended by the Editor (October, page 220), are played by the orchestra of the Berlin State Opera House and conducted by Oskar Fried. The performance is of great beauty and obviously realises the intentions of the composer to a marked degree. The flute and harp come out very clearly and if there is a little thickness and muzziness in the 'cellos and basses it is probably the fault of the composer and not of the executants. As an instance of perfect recording I would draw attention to ten bars before No. 23 in the score and for some bars onwards, where the strings, alone or accompanied by harps and horns, play gorgeous melody, left to their own devices.

The first movement opens with an upward rushing semiquaver figure in the 'cellos and double-basses, followed by a group of four triplets, reminiscent of the beginning of the *Third String Quartet* by Brahms. What may stand for the second subject is a soaring scale of melody given to the violins, used again in the last movement of the work. The general feeling of the music throughout the whole of the first movement is that depicting an unequal struggle between man and some more powerful hidden force, a striving against fate, which is the key-note of so many of the creations of Beethoven. The whole section is grim, almost dour in character, with a few moments of relief and resignation, such as the lovely passage at No. 23 (full score, Universal Edition) which would seem to show that the composer had, for a while, abandoned his hopeless combat.

The chief fault of the first movement, as indeed of the whole work lies in the over-elaborate scoring. As in Strauss' *Domestic Symphony*, handfuls of notes could be plucked and discarded from the score, not with detriment, but with advantage to the music. Even the extremely simple themes are weighed down and overloaded with extraneous thick accompaniment. By this process the ear soon wearies, and what is worse, when a powerful climax is intended, the composer has no remaining forces at his command, in spite of the huge orchestra he has at hand.

The second movement comes as a surprise and relief after the strenuous impotence of the first. It commences with a charming simple theme of *Ländler*-like quality and Schubertian grace, marred, later on, unfortunately, by the complicated orchestration already referred to, which would seem to be Mahler's besetting sin. The movement is short and ends with the same child-like simplicity, leaving one to marvel at the breadth of a musical mind which can encompass so diverse a range of expression.

With the third section we enter into another entirely different world, the realm of Liszt and Berlioz, in diabolical mood. Long running *legato* scale passages are heard alternately on the strings and wood-wind with *pizzicato* accompaniment in the bass, and occasionally interrupted by ejaculations from the brass instruments. The effect thus produced is devilish and Mephistophelian in character, but, through it all, there is more than one hint of the lighter side, of salon music and the waltz.

There is no break between the third and fourth movements of the symphony. The latter is the shortest in the whole work and consists of a beautiful contralto solo. The poem is taken from the old German collection, *Des Knaben Wunderhorn*, and is entitled "Urlicht," or "Source of Light."

A rough translation of the poem is as follows :—

Man is in great sorrow and deep distress !
I fain would be in Heaven !
I wandered forth upon a broad and beauteous path,
And met an angel who would have turned me back ;
But I cried : "I come from God and will to Him again,
For He will give me light,
And guide me to the realms of everlasting life !"

This lovely aria is somewhat akin in feeling to the *Alto Rhapsody* by Brahms, and though very short, deserves to be taken from the symphony and heard frequently in the concert-room.

From this moment of quiet and thoughtful ecstasy the listener is suddenly torn away and hurled, without pause, into the opening fury of the fifth and last movement, marked in the score *Wild herausfahrend*.

"Perfect Mahlerites" may probably deem it rank heresy to suggest that the first half of this last movement had better never been written. To others the section 1 to 31 in the full score, with its coarse orchestration and blatant march will appear too full of the worse Mahlerisms for their fancy. For undoubtedly the finest part of the whole work begins at the end. It is in the form of a chorale, the words of which speak of death, resurrection, and early preparation for a future life. A new facet of Mahler's genius is here made apparent—namely, the power to handle choral construction. The two solo voices (soprano and contralto) blend admirably with the choral mass, and by the composer's special instruction are never allowed to dominate it (*im Geringsten hervorzutreten*), thus giving the effect of unanimous prayer and undivided faith.

Some strange directions for conductor and performers are dotted about the full score. We read, for instance, at the end of the first movement : "An interval of at least five minutes must be made here." Later : "The bell of the trumpet to be raised high in the air" (though this, through Richard Strauss, has now become quite usual). In the fourth movement the bassoons, horns and trumpets are to be removed to the back of the orchestra, to return to their original places later on. Horns 7 to 10 then retire into the background *und so weiter !* Towards the end of the work trumpets in F, those in C, triangle, and other percussion instruments are banished to a position almost out of the building, to return, later, to their allotted places in the orchestra as quietly as possible, for fear of disturbing the beginning of the final chorus ! ! Odd as these directions may sound, there can be no doubt whatever that, nevertheless, the work, taken as a whole, with all its faults, remains a colossal product of a master mind.

G. R. H.

December 1925
Mahler's Resurrection
That Polydor set received a more extensive review in December that year – the first substantial coverage of the composer and his music in our pages.

'Perhaps the most astonishing feature is the exhibition of the diversity of Mahler's musical mind'

The GRAMOPHONE

TURN TABLE TALK

Mahler

How long is this Mahler starvation to go on? One hungry enthusiast has actually gone to the length of having the Ninth Symphony privately recorded from a radio performance. This, he says, is much better than nothing, but the Fourth, which was recorded from a foreign station, was a failure. Is it not rather discouraging that a search in Columbia catalogue should produce only a 1926 snippet from the *Fifth Symphony*, while the nearest thing to Mahler in H.M.V.'s catalogue is *Mah Lindey Loo*?

Who wants a Mahler Society? Postcards, please.

Mahler

Our question about a Mahler Society brought in a few post-cards, but not enough. If we can't manage a Society, surely we might be allowed a few of his songs. Sophie Wyss' broadcast of three of them on March 13th was an appetiser. They were lovely and delightfully sung. More postcards, please.

Mahler

This month's support for a Mahler Society is confined to three enthusiastic readers—one writing from Paris, one from Ohio, and one from Stockholm. This is slow progress.

A PLEA FOR THE RECORDING OF THE SONGS OF GUSTAV MAHLER
by ROBERT W. F. POTTER

GUSTAV MAHLER (1860–1911), besides being a brilliant orchestral conductor in the opera house and concert hall, was one of the greatest composers of modern times in the realms of symphonic music and *Lieder*. The permanent value of his symphonic works is a much debated point, but there can be no doubt that his songs will live. One gets an impression of their beauty and melody even in perusing the score, particularly of *Des Knaben Wunderhorn* (twenty-three songs) and *Lieder eines fahrenden Gesellen* (four songs). Their merits and beauty may also be judged from the spasmodic broadcasts of Mahler's songs, notably that by Maria Olszewska several years ago, and recently, those by Sophie Wyss, who on two occasions has sung several Mahler *Lieder*. A third means of assessing Mahler's contribution to the field of *Lieder* is the gramophone records of a few of his songs listed below, which give an indication of the qualities, worthwhileness, and variety of the songs as a whole.

Of Mahler's forty-two songs, nine (all sung in German) are available as electrical recordings:

Rheinlegendchen and *Der Tambourg'sell*—both from *Des Knaben Wunderhorn*—sung by Heinrich Schlusnus (baritone) with orchestra (Decca-Polydor 12 in. CA8082).

These songs are intensely fascinating. In the scoring one finds the brilliance of a Richard Strauss, the subtlety of a Hugo Wolf, and the brimming melody, *Ländler* grace and compelling rhythm of a Franz Schubert.

Kindertotenlieder—a cycle of five songs—sung by Heinrich Rehkemper (baritone) with orchestra (Decca-Polydor 12 in. CA8027-8-9).

Here again, the orchestral tone-painting is equal to the best work of Richard Strauss when he is writing *Lieder* for orchestra. The music seems to be born of the very words. The poems are in mournful vein, but melody is ever in the forefront.

Wer hat dies Liedlein erdacht?—from *Des Knaben Wunderhorn*—sung by Elisabeth Schumann (soprano) (H.M.V. 10 in. E555), and also by Lula Mysz-Gmeiner (contralto) (Decca-Polydor 10 in. PO5105), both with piano accompaniment.

A delicate trifle, which would gain by being recorded in the more attractive orchestral setting.

Um Mitternacht—one of the five lyrics by Rückert, set by Mahler—sung by Aaltje Noordewier-Reddingius (soprano), on two sides of a 10 in. Dutch Columbia record (DH81), with organ accompaniment.

This singer has been famous for many years as an interpreter of Mahler's songs, and was one of the principals in the Mahler Festival held at Amsterdam in 1920 to commemorate the twenty-fifth anniversary of Willem Mengelberg's conductorship of the Concertgebouw Orchestra.

The following electrical recordings are not now easily obtainable:

Urlicht—from *Des Knaben Wunderhorn*—is also the contralto solo from Mahler's Second Symphony. It is sung by Madame Charles Cahier (Ultraphon 12 in. E288), and by Emma Leisner (Polydor 12 in. 66295-6), both with orchestra.

Ich bin der Welt abhanden gekommen—one of the five lyrics by Rückert, set by Mahler—sung by Madame Charles Cahier. It is coupled with the above-mentioned Ultraphon record of *Urlicht*, and has orchestral accompaniment.

Mme. Cahier has probably given more Mahler *Liederabende* than any other singer in the world.

The following acoustical recording is not now available:

Ich ging mit Lust durch einen grünen Wald—from *Des Knaben Wunderhorn*—sung by Grete Stückgold (soprano) (Polydor 12 in. 19234), with orchestra.

A critical friend has pronounced this to be the most beautiful pictorial *Lieder* record in my large collection. I thought Miss Sophie Wyss's recent broadcast of this song with piano accompaniment was a delightful collaboration. The song in its orchestral setting, recorded under modern conditions, would probably prove even more appealing, but I would welcome a record of the song by this singer, with piano accompaniment.

One would like to see a Society formed to support a scheme for recording Mahler's songs, especially those which do not appear on the current gramophone record lists. I hope that Miss Sophie Wyss (soprano) will be entrusted with some of the songs.

1936
A Mahler society?

Letters and articles over several months allude to only slow progress being made of Mahler on record – the solution? Start a society!

'How long is this Mahler starvation to go on?'

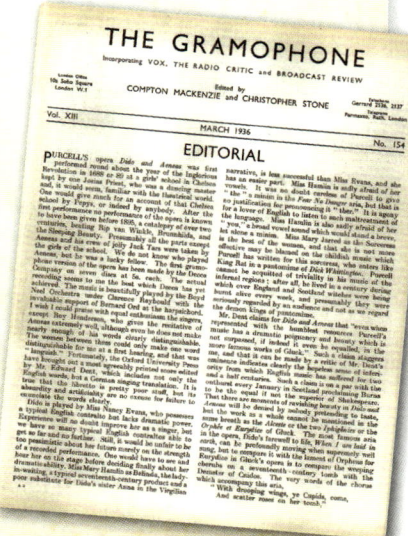

The GRAMOPHONE

SOCIETY ISSUES

MAHLER

Das Lied von der Erde (Gustav Mahler). **Kerstin Thorborg** (mezzo-soprano) and **Charles Kullmann** (tenor), with the **Vienna Philharmonic Orchestra**, conducted by Bruno Walter. Seven 12 in. Columbia records, ROX165-171, £2-2-0.

This recording was made at a public concert in Vienna last year, and conveys with striking fidelity the atmosphere of the occasion. Such incidental noises as the preliminary murmur of voices, coughing, and the sound of mutes being removed by the string players are clearly to be heard, and, in my opinion, are by no means to be considered as defects in the recording. The whole performance is most vividly reproduced, and I know of few sets which evoke so powerfully the illusion of actual presence in the concert hall.

Mahler's *Song of the Earth* is a song-symphony, and its six movements are based on German versions of ancient Chinese poems. These poems were further modified by Mahler himself in order to make them fit into his poetic design of a last farewell to the beauties of the earth. The work succeeded the gigantic eighth Symphony, and in it a new and chastened Mahler found expression. He had recently learned that his heart was dangerously weak, and the knowledge that his end might come at any time drew out the best that was in him and, perhaps for the first time, he expressed himself fully in *Das Lied von der Erde*.

The work is marvellously scored, and even those to whom Mahler's somewhat glutinous sentiments are antipathetic may be recommended to hear these records, just as a series of gorgeous orchestral noises. Almost all the details of the brilliant and delicate scoring are convincingly reproduced, except for the triangle which, as so often happens, is a mere ghost of its real assertive self.

The Drinking Song of Earth's Distress with which the work begins combines the praise of wine with despairing reflections on the brevity of human life. The often thankless voice-part is splendidly sung by Charles Kullmann, who is, I believe, an American. Let us be thankful to Hitler that he had made it impossible for any of the usual German tenors to take the part, in the recording of a work by one of Mahler's race. *The Solitary in Autumn* is scored, in strong contrast with the previous movement, almost in the style of chamber music. Kerstin Thorborg, Covent Garden's much admired Kundry and Fricka, sings this with lovely tone and slack rhythm. Three humorous poems follow. *Youth* is a delicate piece of *chinoiserie*. The vocal line of *Beauty* is a typically naïve Mahler tune, like a child singing itself to sleep. It is broken into by a glittering oriental march—one of the few places in the score where all the immense orchestral forces are employed. The end of this movement on side seven is a good example of the quality of the playing and recording in this set. Li Tai Po's well-known *Drunkard in Spring* follows, in which Kullmann manages beautifully the awkward high A's and *pianissimo* A flats. The central episode of the conversation with the bird is delicious. The long *Farewell* takes up the last six sides. It is the heart of the work, in which Mahler's rather esoteric art takes on universal qualities, and hesitating purchasers would be well advised to hear the whole of this movement through before deciding that these records do not appeal to them. The singer's faulty rhythm shows up again here. She makes several wrong entries and, at the beginning of side eleven, for nearly two bars she is a beat ahead of the accompanying flute. These are small defects in a performance of great distinction, for which the chief credit must go to Bruno Walter, whose Mahler performances are absolutely authoritive, being founded on a long intimacy with the composer himself. A great set of records.

F. W.

*Kerstin Thorborg (contralto) with Bruno Walter conducting the Vienna Philharmonic Orchestra : Ich bin der Welt abhanden gekommen (Rückert–Mahler) ; sung in German. Columbia LB45 (10 in.—4s.).

" To the world I am lost ; I often used to quarrel with it ; for a long time it has taken no notice of me ; it may very well believe I am dead. It does not matter in the least to me if it regards me as dead ; I cannot object if it does, for it is true, I am dead to the world. I am dead to the world's tumult, and rest in a quiet retreat ; I live by myself in my heaven, in my love, in my song." This is a rough translation of Rückert's poem, which Mahler set to music, and it may be useful to those who would appreciate the song, a feat of which I find myself incapable.

It is sung here by the Swedish contralto, Kerstin Thorborg, who has won golden opinions at Covent Garden. The recording was made at an actual concert performance in Vienna in May, 1936, and on this occasion I am sufficiently unmoved by the statement to consider that a studio recording would have been preferable. To me the authentic atmosphere of the concert room is represented only by the preliminary hum of conversation which rapidly subsides as the orchestra begins the performance. This is directed by Bruno Walter, a great friend of Mahler and an authority on his music ; the record should, therefore, be of great interest to lovers of Mahler's work.

'Bruno Walter's ... Mahler performances are absolutely authoritive, being founded on a long intimacy with the composer himself'

1937/8
Bruno Walter's Mahler

Two Columbia sets preserved performances by a conductor deeply associated with Mahler – as well as the interpretations of Swedish mezzo Kerstin Thorberg.

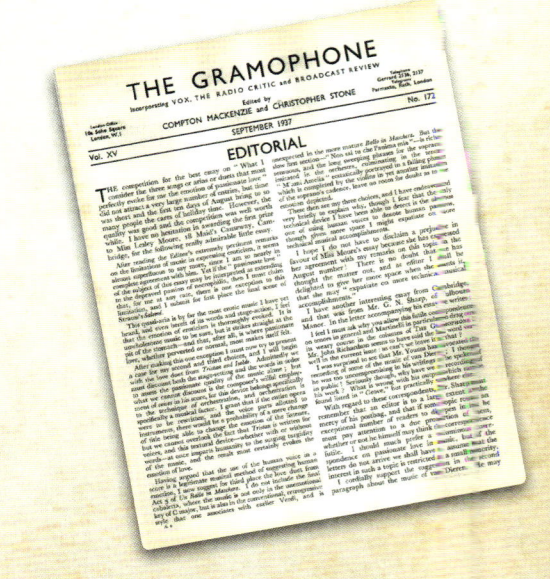

March 1938　　　*The GRAMOPHONE*　　　433

H.M.V. SPECIAL LIST No. 2

The following records are obtainable from all His Master's Voice dealers on special order only.

Minneapolis Symphony Orchestra (Ormandy) : **Symphony No. 2, in C minor** (Mahler), **Allegro maestoso, Andante moderato, In ruhig fliessender Bewegung** (Quiet, flowing motion), **Urlicht** (Primeval light), **Sehr feierlich, aber schlicht** (*with* Ann O'Malley Gallogly, Contralto), **In Scherzo tempo, Song of Resurrection** (*with* **Corinne Frank Bowen,** Soprano ; **Ann O'Malley Gallogly,** Contralto, **and Chorus**) H.M.V. DB2751–61 (12 in.—66s.).

Part of the Mahler problem (a problem that is part of a reasonable man's pleasure in him) lies in the diversity of his attack, in each symphony. A little while before writing this, I had heard the B.B.C.'s Eighth—part of it an inadequate performance, such as I certainly should not wish to hear recorded—but after hearing this specimen of the *Kolossal* a few times, and finding it decreasingly nourishing (for its swollen apparatus of ecstasy does not convince me that Mahler there brought his visions to any kind of universal life), one can still hear other works of his with a clear mind and a tolerably bright hope. It seems worth while, though, to realise the weight of his period, his peculiar mid-European culture, and his aspirations. One great delusion of these turn-of-the-century people seems to me this : they were afflicted with a vast pseudo-mystical-philosophical load, which eternally got in the way of their music ; and they were windy beyond belief. Nobody will ever convince me that the Eighth needed that huge choral and orchestral force (" the symphony of a thousand," it is called ; but the B.B.C. cannily employed only about half that number) with eight soloists, organ, piano, Old Uncle Tom mandoline and all, to rhapsodise about Faust's redemption. The psycho-analyst would have a lot to tell about some of these good megalomaniac souls, if that useful science had been working freely in their day. Or maybe it is simply that, as Thornton Wilder says in *The Woman of Andros,* " of all forms of genius goodness has the longest awkward age."

This performance, I take it, is the one which the Encyclopedia of Recorded Music speaks of as having been recorded three years ago at the University of Minnesota, from a public concert. The Twin City Choir took part (the cities are Minneapolis and St. Paul, separated by a river). The recording is mightily impressive, in its opening sonority. There should be no difficulty in anyone's rising to the exciting bait. So far, so good ; but Mahler always worked his notions too hard. He was, it appears, seeing the funeral grandeurs of a hero, and pondering on the old problems of mankind's end and purpose. This recording is a bit too massive for my liking, but perhaps if you are doing this sort of thing you may as well do it with plenty of *empressement* (for which, however, I strongly recommend a steel needle. My fibre found it ungenial). Five sides of this is a good deal too much. Beethoven achieved the heroic with less spread of canvas but finer sensibility. Yet you can enjoy the slow procession, if you are willing to allow something for the mid-European spread (not the middle-age spread, in this instance : it is clearly the declining years of a period—one has to think of, say, 1895–1910). If you look at it as a series of glimpses of the procession, and soak yourself in the *Zeitgeist,* you will enjoy this music as much as possible—according to your suitability or otherwise as a subject for its ministrations. There are too many ideas, and not many of them are first-class. Mahler so easily wound himself up to heights of excitement that I am afraid few listeners can attain. That is the defect of a curious temperament and a personality that, on the credit side, has facets of strong individuality. One can respect a spirit that is " different," even if its evocations do not deeply touch one's own. That, as I have often urged, is one of my pleasures in hearing music that is not very familiar. But the sort of rather simple-minded glory on, for instance, side 4, is not happy within a symphonic frame. Here even fibre provides sounds that I find immensely loud, rather edged, and not very pleasing, in my room. I think you ought to take a public hall, for this sort of thing.

Side 6 brings the second movement, a memory of good days once enjoyed with the hero. One may think of long walks (three sides are quite long enough), good cheer and (inevitably) good beer. I am occasionally irreverent enough to put down some of this late-nineteenth-century music to pure beer—pure beer ; is not there some effect of *bloating* in so much of the Mahler-Bruckner products ? But still, this movement has an ingratiating generosity of notion, and I think many people will enjoy its stir, even though that is rather heavy-going (and again too loud for my liking).

Drum-fans will gloat over the start of side 9. Here, I gather, we are to picture the ever-questing human being finding his fellows too much like phantoms, in (I suppose) their preoccupation with affairs which keep them from meditating about the Why, Whence, Whither of existence, that weigh so heavily on the composer-poet. This busy music, thus recorded very-much-in-the-ear, becomes oppressive in its loudness. I cannot think that this recording of an actual performance shows the music at its best. Studio conditions could have given a much better effect. The playing is good enough, though heavy. There are a few moments of raggedness (e.g., near the end of side 9).

But here we are at side 12, and so far there is only about half the time's value in symphonic quality, the rest comprising an expansiveness that has by now become tiresome. I like a good long chat, in which things can be argued out ; but there is too little argument, and too much talk.

The fourth movement brings in the voice, to tell of the soul's redemption (a good big contralto, that unfortunately wobbles badly. Whether the recording amplifies that or not, I cannot tell. The effect is uncomfortable). This is where Mahler comes nearest, I feel, to immediate, clearly-seen and directly imagined beauty. This is the best Mahler—you find him also in some of the other songs. And I venture to say that it is the best movement because (for one reason) it is the shortest.

Side 14 brings the Last Trump, no less, and the composer's vision of judgment, or rather, of the preparations for it ; since all, in the end, dissolves into beatitude. It was at von Bülow's funeral that Mahler had the idea for a chorus to end the work. The large canvas is now better filled, and I think one gets in this movement by far the best idea not only of Mahler's powers but also of his nature. It is far too long, but it has a more spacious basis, and treats some of the ideas better than the first three. Also, I suppose that, faced with the idea of the Last Judgment at all, one feels bound to give the composer every support in his attempting such a theme. Even here, there are striking weaknesses: as so often, one lies in the themes. When Mahler tries a long one, he falls into a cheap way. Mark, for example, that in the middle of side 16 : very thin, for such an argument as that of this movement. This kind of cheer-leading stuff simply isn't good enough for any symphonic purpose. It is only fit for the band parade before a football match. Before the chorus enters, near the end of side 18, one feels that Time is indeed finished, and Eternity growing grey. The choral writing is warm, heart-evoked, and readily acceptable if one is familiar with the German succession that had one climax in Beethoven, and others in Strauss, and its end in Mahler (though, of course, the Beethovenian cast was mightily different from the Straussian). This epilogue, though, is exceedingly long. It would have been four times as effective if a quarter the length. The choral singing is sound if not thrilling. I suppose one can't expect to hear many words.

The recording, with the proper armament of steel plate and record-piercing needles, may well be declared remarkable. Before I took to this equipment, I had ruined more fibres over the first few discs than in the whole of my life before. Those will enjoy the symphony best who have big instruments and town halls, ears that delight in the utmost sonority that a record can hold, ample time on their hands and—best of all—a relish for the long and discursive, the laboriously aspiring and mystagogical. Alas, I remain, as regards the Second, one of the unregenerate. After ploughing through it, I had to put on something for fun. A small prize will not be offered for the title of the chaser, but everybody is allowed one free guess.

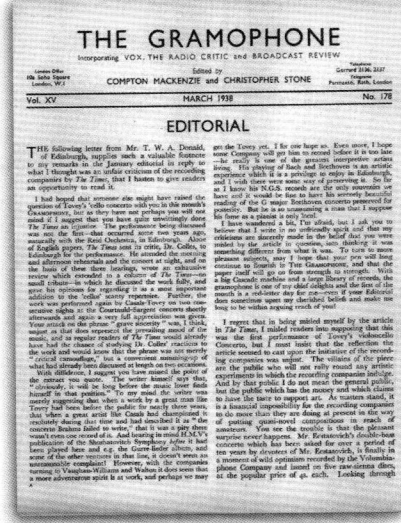

'The recording is mightily impressive, in its opening sonority. There should be no difficulty in anyone's rising to the exciting bait'

March 1938
Ormandy's Resurrection
Mahler's music was still taking time to earn the acclaim later generations gave it – WR Anderson was yet to be entirely won over by the *Resurrection* Symphony, here conducted by Eugene Ormandy.

Notes from my Diary

RECORDING OF ACTUAL PERFORMANCES

By F. W. GAISBERG

Recording during concerts has given a far higher percentage of successes, but I have to report two conspicuous failures. One was a fine set of records of the *Requiem Mass* (Mozart) with Elizabeth Schumann, under Bruno Walter, which the conductor would not accept because of faulty horn entries. The other was a splendid performance of *The Dream of Gerontius* during a Three Choirs Festival in Worcester Cathedral, which was spoilt by the coughing of the audience, and especially one chatterbox of a gossip who, during an unexpected pause, continued a dissertation about a bargain in camisoles she had picked up. Surprisingly successful on the other hand was Mahler's *Das Lied von der Erde* and the great Ninth Symphony, both recorded during concerts in Vienna with the Vienna Philharmonic Orchestra conducted by Bruno Walter.

The other afternoon (Monday, May 15th) I tuned in to the Home Forces programme and spent an hour of sheer delight listening to the great Mahler Ninth Symphony and recalling the scene and events leading up to the recording of the records just played. I started these notes as a letter to the B.B.C. expressing pleasure and gratitude. I wanted to pay tribute to their technical staff for the flawless linking together of the twenty sides in a continuous performance, and give praise to their Programme Planning department for courage in assigning space and time to so serious and unknown a work. They can sympathise with me when over five years ago I put forward the suggestion that the Gramophone Company should record the complete symphony at a performance in the old Musikverein to be held on Sunday morning, January 16th, 1938. That Bruno Walter, the direct link with Mahler, would be the conductor, and that there would be five rehearsals during which our engineers could make their tests and experiments in " mike " positions were arguments that clinched the decision. Another argument was that the work was difficult and could never be economically recorded in a studio, as it required many rehearsals and a big orchestra. For the same reason it rarely made its appearance in a concert programme ; so this opportunity of using Mahler's own orchestra and his pupil as conductor was historic and not to be missed. So on that cold, grey morning of January 16th, 1938, we set out to record what amounted to being the Swan Song of the Vienna Philharmonic Orchestra under their old conductor Bruno Walter ; because from then on until the Germans overran Austria two months later political upheavals absorbed all social life and made music-making impossible. In fact all the orchestra leaders like Dr. Arnold Rosé, Professors Bauxbaum, Berghauser, Starkmann, and Anton Weiss disappeared from the scene shortly after this concert, and the next time I saw them was in Paris or London. As I watched the crowd of Mahler music-lovers filing into the hall (over 2,000 of them) I thought how their shabby

respectability contrasted with the elegant and rich audiences of the old Franz Joseph days. Present also were the high officers of the State, including Chancellor Schuschnigg, who after the concert congratulated Walter and the orchestra on their performance. In the Green Room I made this photograph of Bruno Walter just before he stepped on to the platform. He is leaning against an old Bösendorfer piano and on the walls are signed photographs of many great artists including Brahms and Pablo Casals, the latter one of the patrons of the old Vienna Philharmonic Orchestra and responsible for raising big funds that carried them over trying periods of post-war depression.

Over one hundred players filled the tiers of the stage, and I took my place in the top corner amongst the timpani, facing the conductor. Through me passed the conductor's signal to the engineers for the start of each movement of the work. That was their cue to drop the cutter on to the revolving wax disc. Two recording machines, each in charge of an engineer, were used alternately ; while one was recording the other was being loaded with wax and was ready to take up the thread as number one record was finishing. A switchboard control box was in charge of the senior engineer, Charlie Gregory, who was advised by a musician who followed the performance with a full score and indicated the " traps " that had to be avoided, such as sudden *forte* timpani blows or extreme *pianissimos* or *fortissimos* ; also when at the end of a movement the current had to be closed off before the applause began. The well-filled hall toned down the resonance of this great orchestra to a rounded out sound of rich mass and depth, yet without dissipating the higher frequencies of the instruments.

A few weeks after this Walter turned up, a bewildered refugee, in Paris, where I met him to play over and obtain his approval of the twenty records recorded that Sunday. So delighted was he with the results that his usually sober face brightened up considerably. At lunch he told me the story of his long friendship with Mahler as assistant and sub-conductor of the Vienna Hof Opera from 1901 to 1907, one of the most glorious pages of its history. When the great man resigned, Walter was appointed Co-Director with Franz Schalk. Walter studied with the master all his compositions and discussed with him his aims and ambitions. Indeed the Ninth Symphony is dedicated to Walter, who with the Vienna Philharmonic Orchestra gave its first performance a year after Mahler's death.

I classify as of equal artistic and historic importance the very fine records of Mahler's greatest work, *Das Lied von der Erde*, made in May 1936 at a concert arranged in Vienna to commemorate the composer's death (May 18th, 1911). Again the orchestra was Mahler's own Vienna Philharmonic and his disciple and pupil Bruno Walter the conductor. Particularly fortunate was the selection of the tenor Charles Kullmann and the mezzo-soprano Kerstin Thorborg to take the important vocal parts in this work. Their fresh young voices are a joy to listen to, and easily surmount the difficulties of this exacting music.

September 1944

The Ninth Symphony from Vienna in 1938

The powerful performance – and recording – of Mahler's Ninth by Bruno Walter, made in Vienna just two months before the Anschluss, is vividly recalled by the producer Fred Gaisberg.

'On that morning of January 16th, 1938, we set out to record what amounted to being the Swan Song of the Vienna Philharmonic under their old conductor Bruno Walter'

sense of strain in one awkward passage in the last great emotional outburst. She recovers at once and sings the last words " *blauen Licht die Fernen* " with a superb legato and beautifully manages the toneless repetitions of " *ewig* " at the end. It is a pity that the celesta is not clearly heard enough on these last pages, one gets some but not all the notes of the arpeggios : the triangle also, is elusive at the start of *Youth*. I can only briefly allude to two other outstanding things in this recording, the melancholy beauty of *The Solitary in Autumn*, in which Kathleen Ferrier excels, and Patzak's singing at the moment when the bird calls to *The Drunkard in Spring*.

Ich bin der Welt abhanden gekommen is far and away the best of the three songs to poems by Rückert (a poet set by Schubert, Schumann and Brahms and by Mahler, again, in *Kindertotenlieder*) on the reverse. The music, reminiscent of the *Adagietto* in the composer's Fifth Symphony, is beautifully orchestrated and Kathleen Ferrier's singing is surpassingly lovely and tender. The middle song, *Ich atmet einen linden Duft*, has a charmingly devised accompaniment, but is not otherwise remarkable : and the last one, *Um Mitternacht*, is scored without strings : the wood-wind used include an oboe d'amore and a double bassoon, the brass, trombones and bass tuba.

This scoring was dictated perhaps by the grandiose hymn-like ending, which is undeniably effective and in which Kathleen Ferrier pours forth glorious tone. The recording of all three songs is extremely good.

The German words of all these songs, with English translations, can be had from Decca for sixpence and I urge all purchasers of this disc to take advantage of this praiseworthy publication.
A.R.

'Bruno Walter's deep understanding of Mahler is given every chance to show itself in this carefully balanced recording'

*MAHLER. Das Lied von der Erde. Three Rückert Songs. Kathleen Ferrier (contralto) Julius Patzak (tenor). Vienna Philharmonic Orchestra (Walter). Decca LXT 2721-2 (12 in., 79s.).

It will be remembered that the Columbia recording of *Das Lied von der Erde*, with Kerstin Thorborg and Charles Kullmann, and Bruno Walter conducting the Vienna Philharmonic Orchestra, was made at an actual performance in Vienna on May 24, 1936 and suffered somewhat from the prevailing conditions. It is, nevertheless, a recording one has cherished : but now the greatly improved methods of recording and the avoidance of the many breaks in the music make it difficult for one to listen to it patiently after hearing the present one : and there seems little point in making comparisons.

It must, however, be said that Kathleen Ferrier's singing is even more beautiful than that of Kerstin Thorborg and that her rhythmic sense is much superior. It was complained that Julius Patzak could hardly be heard in the Edinburgh Festival performance this summer : but however that may have been the placing of the microphone sees to it that we get his every note in this recording so that we are able to hear what a fine and sensitive performance he gives ; a remarkable one, in this taxing part, for a singer no longer young. Bruno Walter's deep understanding of Mahler is given every chance to show itself in this carefully balanced recording with its sense of space : and one can appreciate to the full Mahler's wonderful handling of his large orchestra, in its most delicate as well as in its most strenuous moments. The charming *chinoiserie* of *Youth* is beautifully caught : the glittering oriental march in *Beauty*, and the brooding sorrow of the last song, *Farewell*, with its tragic funeral march and its exquisite lyrical passages (which Kathleen Ferrier makes almost intolerably moving) are very memorable. One's critical sense, however, has to note that Miss Ferrier is placed rather too close to the microphone, and thus one is more aware than would otherwise have been the case of a certain

October 1952
Ferrier's farewell
Few recordings have taken on such a beloved place in the history of a work: listening to Kathleen Ferrier's recording of *Das Lied von der Erde* is a profoundly moving experience many decades on (see the discussion on page 76).

September 1964   *The GRAMOPHONE*   133

September 1964

Barbirolli's Ninth Symphony

Deryck Cooke's status as a Mahler authority was cemented by his completion of the Tenth symphony; his views on any interpretation – as here with Barbirolli's Ninth with the Berlin Philharmonic – are fascinating reading.

MAHLER. Symphony No. 9 in D major. **Berlin Philharmonic Orchestra** conducted by **Sir John Barbirolli.** HMV Ⓜ ALP2047, ALPS2048: Ⓢ ASD596, ASDS597 (three 12 in. sides, 53s. 6½d. plus 8s. 8½d. P.T.).

VSO, Horenstein   (7/61) Ⓜ VBX116/1-3
LSO, Ludwig   (10/61) Ⓜ CM16-7: Ⓢ SCM16-7
Columbia SO, Walter
     (9/62) Ⓜ BRG72068-9: Ⓢ SBRG72068-9

Barbirolli is the first English conductor to be invited to make a recording with the Berlin Philharmonic Orchestra since Beecham's famous *Magic Flute* twenty-six years ago; the invitation came as a result of his concert performance of Mahler's Ninth Symphony with the orchestra last year, which was hailed by the Berlin Press as "the finest Mahler heard in a decade"; Barbirolli himself was called the finest conductor of the orchestra since Furtwängler. These are quite phenomenal encomiums to live up to, but one can easily understand them: he is one of very few remaining conductors who puts not only his head and technique into his performances, but his whole heart and soul.

Barbirolli has been really absorbing Mahler for some years now; he has the tremendous Ninth firmly in his repertoire, having conducted it with the Hallé Orchestra many times. Of course, his own way with Mahler is not the traditional way; but then, as I discovered when I listened to recordings of the Fourth by Mengelberg, Walter, and Klemperer, it is extremely dubious if 'the Mahler tradition' has any real meaning. The great first movement of the Ninth is usually taken very broadly; even the passages marked to be taken quickly are normally given much weight at a fairly steady tempo. Barbirolli, on the other hand, varies widely between powerful breadth and some really swift accelerations towards the climaxes, full of his own volatile kind of urgency; the ascent to the first climax—after figure 6—is a typical example. Personally, I find this just as impressive in its way as the much more spacious approach of both Walter and Horenstein (Ludwig I find merely superficial). The tempo of the second movement is a continual subject for argument: the very slow tempo of both Walter and Horenstein has led to criticisms of the movement as "wearisome *ländlerizing*", and I do prefer the more lively tempo Barbirolli uses (not anywhere near the beyond-the-pale *allegro* of Ludwig). The grotesque brilliance of the movement, and the infinite nostalgia of its Trio, are beautifully brought out. In the clattering uproar of the Rondo-Burlesque, Barbirolli is entirely at home, again taking a tempo midway between the steady *allegro pesante* of Walter and the *presto* of Ludwig, but he seems to be open to criticism in that this tempo has slackened when it comes to the reprise (owing to a combination of two different takes?). In the final heart-rending *Adagio*, as may be imagined, Barbirolli digs as deep into the emotion of the music as anyone, and is unique in insisting on a real *pianissimo* in the many places where it is indicated. The only stylistic criticisms I have to offer are of the characteristic Barbirolli string portamento, which I find a little excessive, and of a curious interpretation of Mahler's odd marking of a "wind porta-

mento" (third movement, just after figure 40). What Mahler meant by this impossible marking is anyone's guess, but Barbirolli's idea of letting the flute and oboe trail down, taking in a few other notes on the way, is hardly a successful solution.

My main criticism of the record, curiously enough, is the playing of the Berlin Philharmonic, who in fact are nowhere near as used to Mahler as some of our own orchestras; although there are many beautiful and brilliant sounds, there is not that absolute precision and virtuosity which one ideally expects in this fantastically complex and difficult work. Nevertheless, the orchestra puts across the work as a whole with tremendous punch, and the string playing in the finale is a dream. The recording, in both mono and stereo issues, is excellent, though I personally like more vivid clarity of detail in Mahler myself. HMV offer a more general picture, which does not really help in the places where the texture is rather opaque (one feels that if Mahler had lived to conduct the symphony himself, he would have pruned the orchestration, as he did with several of his earlier symphonies). All in all, though, this is an extremely fine issue of the Mahler Ninth, which at least holds its own with those already available. Choice between it and the others can only be a matter of personal taste, based on careful comparison.   **D.C.**

'Barbirolli has been really absorbing Mahler for some years now; he has the tremendous Ninth firmly in his repertoire'

MAHLER. Symphony No. 10. **Philadelphia Orchestra** conducted by **Eugene Ormandy.** CBS Ⓜ BRG72408-9 Ⓢ SBRG72408-9 (two 12 in., 64s. 6d. plus 10s. 6d. PT).

As Mahler enthusiasts will know, Deryck Cooke, taking time off from his monthly stint in THE GRAMOPHONE, prepared a Third Programme broadcast with extracts from Mahler's unfinished Tenth Symphony back in 1960. Four years later his 'Performing Version' of the whole work was conducted at a Prom by Berthold Goldschmidt. Last November Eugene Ormandy gave the first American performance and later recorded it.

After writing the Ninth Symphony, in which he was obsessed with thoughts of death, Mahler roughed out this much less gloomy one in the summer of 1910. He wrote first a sketch on four staves with very few instrumental cues; you can seldom be sure who is to play either the tunes or the harmonies, and in some passages he achieved no more than a single line of melody. Yet every bar exists. The symphony is in five, as it were, palindromic movements, starting with an Adagio and a Scherzo, having a tiny movement called 'Purgatorio' in the middle, and then unwinding with a second Scherzo and second Adagio. Mahler also wrote a good deal of a full score, getting nearly to the middle of the 'Purgatorio' movement but leaving many blanks in the first Scherzo. On his death-bed he asked his wife to burn the sketches, but he later agreed to leave their fate to her discretion. In 1924 Mrs Mahler published the manuscript in photographic facsimile, and this same year Krenek and Alban Berg prepared the opening Adagio and 'Purgatorio' for performance. (This two-movement version was published with ill-considered changes in 1951.) It was felt that if anyone was to complete the symphony it should be Schoenberg, but Schoenberg decided the task was beyond him, and this view influenced Mrs Mahler, who, when she heard of Deryck Cooke's Third Programme broadcast, put a ban on any further performances of any kind. She was persuaded to relent in 1963 and wrote congratulating Cooke. Since then she has died, and Mr Cooke's score has been played in Germany and Italy as well as in England and America.

I am told that the copyright problems are formidable. Apart from one or two other musicians who have completed the symphony from the facsimile, the International Gustav Mahler Society of Vienna published a good score of the first Adagio in 1964 (Universal Edition), and Erwin Ratz has explained at length in the preface that to arrange, publish or perform any of the other movements would be a monstrous indiscretion. (Incredibly, he says that those in the past who made a piano score from the facsimile for their own private use did so "with a feeling of guilt".) The views of Mahler's daughter may well be all-important, and she must be under pressure from more than one direction. Thus it is not certain if Mr Cooke's version will be published, if some other version will be published, or if no version will be published. I put the possibilities in order of desirability.

To serious-minded Germans it may seem a terrible thing to tamper with incomplete sketches by a dead composer. The issues raised are both moral and aesthetic, and it may be hazarded that interests more than a little vested are involved as well. To you and me the issues will seem simple enough. Mr Cooke's version is not quite the symphony Mahler would have published had he lived, but it is a thousand times better than nothing. In essence this *is* a Mahler symphony, and a good one; much more interesting, to me at least, than No. 7; enthralling, uplifting music that I hope to hear at regular intervals for the rest of my life. The alternatives, then, are either to give deep pleasure to thousands of music lovers by playing the Cooke version, or to limit all knowledge of the last four movements to the tiny handful of people prepared to pore over the manuscript. The choice seems an easy one to make; after all those who choose the manuscript don't have to buy the record.

Much of what I have said can only have validity if Mr Cooke's version shows a profound knowledge of Mahler's methods. It does. Personally I cannot tell from the sound what has been added, and, uninformed, I would not have suspected that anything had. I have been able to borrow a photostat of Mr Cooke's manuscript, and it shows quite clearly throughout what Mahler wrote and what Mr Cooke wrote. Footnotes make a good case for the additions, and they have been made with quite remarkable insight. Nevertheless, Mr Cooke, for reasons that will be obvious, has been underplaying his contribution all along the line, explaining that he has not attempted to complete the symphony but merely to prepare Mahler's preliminary sketch for performance, and stressing in a fascinating article in *The Composer* (the Journal of the Composers' Guild, July 1965) that the substance of the music remains unchanged, that substance in music is always more important than orchestration and final titivating (important though these are), and that his additions are mostly by analogy with passages elsewhere that the composer did complete. All this may be true, but the fact remains that the last two movements and much of the first scherzo are almost entirely scored by Cooke, and short passages here and there, some of them climaxes, are harmonized by him too. His contribution to the success of the work has been enormous, and it would be impertinent for anyone else to pretend otherwise.

Ormandy's recording will be welcomed by the great mass of people who crowd into public performances of Mahler these days, and the short-comings I shall mention are of small account compared with the opportunities these discs give you of getting the music under your skin. The wonderful opening Adagio, with its warm luscious tunes and unexpected sense of optimism, could do with the touch of a Barbirolli, so to speak; the tempo is too inflexible, and it cannot be right to take the Andante sections at the same speed as the main Adagio. But there's lovely playing here, especially from the strings. As often in the past I found myself wishing the first and second violins could have been placed on opposite sides of the platform. Here, as elsewhere, Mahler obviously planned much of his violin writing with antiphonal effects in mind, and though nothing can be done about them on mono discs, it can on stereo. I thought the first time round, as I felt at the Prom performance, that the first scherzo does not quite come off, but it's remarkable how it improves on acquaintance; I find myself liking it better and better. In places the brass are not quite rhythmically precise.

The sleeve-note explains, as soon becomes obvious, that the very short central 'Purgatorio' movement is really the start of the second half of the work, for its tunes dominate the remaining movements. It would therefore have been better to put it at the start of Side 3, where there is plenty of room, than at the end of Side 2; the change of discs would then have coincided with the best moment for a short break. The title is a mystery, and Mr Cooke has suggested that Mahler might have dropped it on revision. Ormandy takes it rather faster than Goldschmidt, and this emphasises the charm at the expense of the wryness, but he plays it beautifully and his tempo accords well enough with Mahler's marking. (My difficulty is that I don't really know what Purgatory suggests to me, let alone to Mahler, but I would find the title more convincing if it applied to all the last three movements.) The subsequent scherzo is exciting in spite of some undistinguished material here and there and a slightly flagging rhythm in this particular performance, while the final Adagio in which Mahler passes from pessimistic nullity to confident affirmation is superlative music. It is compellingly played on this record.

The sound in both mono and stereo is vivid, though the balance has occasional touches of unreality; for instance both solo violin and harp sound much too close. In general the recording is satisfying, but you will not, surely, buy this record for its quality of sound. It's the quality of the music that I'm recommending, and I'm recommending it as forcibly as I can.

R.F.

June 1966
Cooke's completion
Two years later, and it's Deryck Cooke's completion of the Tenth, conducted by Eugene Ormandy, that earns exploration and acclaim from fellow *Gramophone* writer Roger Fiske.

'Much of what I have said can only have validity if Mr Cooke's version shows a profound knowledge of Mahler's methods. It does.'

MAHLER. Symphony No. 5 in C minor. Rückert Lieder*. **New Philharmonia Orchestra** conducted by **Sir John Barbirolli** with * **Janet Baker** (mezzo-soprano). HMV ASD2518-9 (nas, 87s. 6d.). Notes, texts and translations included.

Symphony No. 5—selected comparisons:
NYPO, Bernstein   (7/64)   72182-3
Boston SO, Leinsdorf   (1/65)   SER5518-9

This new Barbirolli version of Mahler's Fifth starts with two enormous advantages: the recording quality is far fuller and richer than either of the other two (good and bright as the RCA was) and on the fourth side comes one of the most enthrallingly beautiful Mahler performances I know on record—Janet Baker in the five Rückert Lieder. For myself I would add the quality of devotion to the performance of the symphony, but on that there will inevitably be disagreement among Mahlerians. As we know from Barbirolli's earlier Mahler recordings, his style could hardly be more affectionate, and to that he adds a fondness for tempi slower than usual. Sometimes, as in his Berlin recording of the Ninth Symphony, the result has all the inner intensity of a great performance heard live; sometimes as in his more recent version of No. 6, the expansiveness stretches the music too far and the tension wanes. Though in the Fifth some will clearly prefer a sharper, less indulgent reading like Leinsdorf's, I don't think there is any doubt that in commitment and intensity this interpretation matches and even surpasses the Berlin Ninth. If the aching tragedy of the opening "Trauermusik" is more deeply conveyed by Barbirolli than his rivals, so is the buoyant optimism of the final movement with its tongue-in-cheek foundation on the *Knaben Wunderhorn* song about the cuckoo and the nightingale.

As it happens those two outer movements bring the two most sharply controversial tempi. In both Sir John chooses speeds very much slower than we are used to, and dangerous though that course is (as we found in the Sixth) the performance completely justifies it. The very opening at Barbirolli's tempo inevitably loses something in sheer dramatic bite, and that despite superb brass playing sumptuously recorded. But the sense of power in reserve is very clear, and the change of tension when the dramatic music of the opening gives way to the main sustained melody of the funeral march provides the sort of *frisson* one experiences in the concert hall but all too rarely on record. The phrasing of that melody is characteristically affectionate but without the underlinings which in Bernstein's performance quickly sound self-conscious. Barbirolli is comparably on the slow side for the quicker section at fig. 7, and after Bernstein he may not seem to be observing Mahler's marking "Wild" so effectively, but in its context the contrast is just as sharp, and the surge of the melody with its Brahmsian triplets across the march rhythm is superb.

The advantages of a slowish tempo in the finale are, if anything, even more striking. I imagine that few will resist an initial sense of disappointment when after the preliminaries on horn, bassoon and oboe the main theme enters in so leisurely a manner. "Allegro giocoso. Frisch" Mahler puts on the score, and Barbirolli's initial statement seems to belie that. But Barbirolli then goes on to demonstrate, to my mind conclusively, just why the rest of the movement gains by not being rushed, becomes genuinely "giocoso" instead of just brilliant. In the first place the busy fugato in quavers at fig. 2 sounds much more comfortable (particularly for the horn), and when the main theme returns at fig. 5 the warm, Brahmsian quality in the resonant G-string violin writing is more naturally conveyed. But the rightness of Barbirolli's tempo is confirmed by all the many references to the cuckoo and nightingale song, "Lob des hohen Verstandes". Where normally the reference seems slightly outlandish (and is arguably intended to be so as a deliberate source) Barbirolli recaptures the intense humour of the song by being far closer to it in spirit as well as tempo. Later too when towards the end Mahler grows even richer and more expansive, Barbirolli's interpretation brings one closer to the innocent heavenly joy of Mahler's *Des Knaben Wunderhorn* world.

In the second movement I am less certain that Barbirolli's comparative relaxation is right. The marking is "Stürmisch bewegt. Mit grösster Vehemenz", and I am not sure that Barbirolli is quite stormy or vehement enough. Both Bernstein and Leinsdorf bring more biting dramatic contrasts, but in compensation one has more feeling in Barbirolli's reading of a symphonic, sonata-form development of "Trauermusik" material and not just an emotional outburst. In the third movement Barbirolli uses his slowish tempo to achieve lightness, where Bernstein with an even slower basic tempo is rather heavy, with the Viennese waltz references underlined. Admittedly Barbirolli's Viennese lilt for the second trio is extremely heavy too, but there his tongue-in-cheek intentions are very evident indeed, so that the humour of the passage is what comes out. Leinsdorf is generally fresher and brighter with a nice hint of grotesquerie in the pizzicato trio and a stunning coda, but lightness and humour are not so evident.

But if there is a justification for Barbirolli's reading, it lies in the achingly tender performance of the Adagietto. In advance I was rather afraid that he would sentimentalise it, laying too heavy a layer of expressiveness over the simple string melody. But not so. Barbirolli lets the melody speak for itself in the most hushed tones, and the lead-back after the middle section (meticulously marked with tempo indications) brings a moment of *Innigkeit* that it would be hard to match. Nor does Barbirolli let the marking "Noch langsamer" a few bars later bring the music to a halt as Bernstein virtually does in his deeply felt but more extrovert performance. I am sorry the NPO violins do not have quite the resonance of their American colleagues on the climactic phrase of the movement ("Viel Ton!" writes Mahler—with an exclamation mark) but I am happy enough when it is their ability to play softly that matters.

The recording is one of the very finest I have heard from EMI. I knew in advance that their engineers were particularly pleased with it, but even so I was surprised just how rich it is. The superlative brass-playing of the NPO is a particular joy throughout.

As to the fill-up, I find myself reluctant to dissect anything so deeply affecting in its apparently spontaneous expressiveness. Even by Janet Baker's standards the range of vocal tone-colour is glorious and in every bar one has ample evidence of the inspiration reciprocated between soloist and conductor. Janet Baker did an earlier version of "Ich bin der Welt abhanden gekommen" with Barbirolli, as a fill-up for the coupling of *Kindertotenlieder* and *Lieder eines fahrenden Gesellen*, and it is fascinating to compare the two performances in their equal spontaneity. The new one is some 25 seconds shorter (quite a substantial margin) and gains from the easier flow of the phrasing. The NPO players are more naturally flexible than their Hallé colleagues were (though the Hallé violins managed the hint of a glissando in the final coda more neatly) and the faster tempo brings a mood no less relaxed. One point of detail: Janet Baker this time follows the orchestral score just before fig. 5 with a simple D natural on "Häid", where previously she had an E flat-D appoggiatura from the piano version. Rightly I think this song is placed last in the group. And perhaps the most striking contrast between the two versions lies in the extra fidelity of the recording to Miss Baker's incomparable voice. If anyone hesitates about Barbirolli's approach to the symphony, I am sure the fourth side will provide the entrée to a uniquely warm experience.   E.G.

'Barbirolli lets the melody speak for itself in the most hushed tones'

December 1969
Barbirolli and Baker
Edward Greenfield praises a superb Fifth and Rückert-Lieder

September 1972   *The GRAMOPHONE*   471

MAHLER AND THE CONCERTGEBOUW ORCHESTRA

By MARIUS FLOTHIUS

LET me start with a personal recollection: on October 25th, 1931, I heard for the first time Gustav Mahler's Third Symphony, played by the Concertgebouw Orchestra under Willem Mengelberg. This event made an indelible impression upon me. Some days after the performance I attended a youth concert where only two movements of this symphony were performed—the second and the third. That occasion made no impression at all. Despite many assertions that Mahler's works fail as far as their form is concerned, the cohesion of the six movements was so strong that the complicated whole made a stronger impression on a young listener than the two movements extracted from their context. At that time, the history of Mahler and the Concertgebouw Orchestra, which began in 1903 and now spans nearly seventy years, had already reached its third phase. Willem Mengelberg, then principal conductor and music director of the Concertgebouw Orchestra, had become associated with the Orchestra in 1895, seven years after its foundation.

It is not to be assumed that the unprepared listener of 1903 experienced the Third Symphony the same way as I did in 1931. Although the spirit of this highly romantic music probably fitted in with the general outlook on life of that time, a number of factors may have stood in the way of real understanding: its length, an Adagio for finale as long as a Haydn symphony, the enormous size of the orchestra, the complicated structure. It therefore required courage indeed to schedule two works by Mahler within a short period of time. Nevertheless, on October 22nd, 1903 the composer conducted his Third Symphony in Amsterdam and three days later his First. The following year, on October 23rd, Mahler conducted the Fourth Symphony before the interval after which he joined the audience to listen to a second performance, given under Willem Mengelberg. These events marked the starting point of what might be called the first phase of the association between Mahler and the Concertgebouw Orchestra of Amsterdam, a phase which lasted from 1903 to 1911, the year of Mahler's death. Usually the works were thoroughly prepared by Mengelberg; Mahler then came to the final rehearsals and conducted the first performance. The subsequent performances, which took place not only in Amsterdam, but also in other Dutch cities like The Hague, Rotterdam, Haarlem, Utrecht and Arnhem, were directed by Mengelberg himself.

During these years six of the nine symphonies were performed (Nos. 1 to 5 and No. 7) as well as the *Kindertotenlieder* and *Das klagende Lied*. Taking into account the excessively large orchestral forces required for the Eighth as well as the fact that neither the Ninth Symphony nor *Das Lied von der Erde* was performed anywhere during Mahler's lifetime, the introduction of the eight works just mentioned seems no small achievement.

Between 1911 and 1920 those of Mahler's works that had not so far been performed were added to the repertoire—the Sixth, Eighth and Ninth Symphonies, *Das Lied von der Erde* and the *Lieder eines fahrenden Gesellen*. The *Rückert* and *Wunderhorn* Lieder also followed in due course, though not as complete cycles. The crowning event of this period was the famous Mahler Festival of 1920 (May 6th—21st). To celebrate

Willem Mengelberg's twenty-fifth anniversary as the conductor of the Concertgebouw Orchestra, three important series of concerts were organised, of which the Mahler Cycle is undoubtedly the most vividly remembered. It is probably unique in the history of any orchestra that for the celebration of a *conductor's* jubilee all attention was directed to the nearly complete output of a contemporary *composer*. In this case, however, it seemed only natural, in view of the close ties between Mahler and his works and Mengelberg and his Orchestra. Nine symphonies, *Das klagende Lied*, *Das Lied von der Erde* and fourteen songs—were all performed within sixteen days. Some of them belonged to the Orchestra's regular repertoire, some others had been given in the course of the winter season, which ended only ten days before the beginning of the Mahler Festival. In fact, the preparation of the greater part of the Festival programmes was done in little more than a week!

Another fact is worth mentioning. At the beginning of the 1919-1920 season the membership of the Orchestra had been extended to ninety players, but still it could not meet the demands made by works like the Third and Eighth Symphonies. So for these works supplementary musicians had to be engaged, both instrumental and vocal. Among these 'extras' were several eminent musicians who were highly respected in their own right, as soloists, teachers or both, but who did not consider it beneath their dignity to collaborate in this event as mere members of the orchestra or the choir. Among them were the violinists Oskar Back, Adolf Busch, Carl Flesch, Alexander Schmuller and Hendrik Rijnbergen; the pianist Leonid Kreutzer; the singers Mia Pettenburg, Di Moorlag, Meta Reidel and Willem Mengelberg's wife Mathilde also sang in the choir.

Between 1920 and 1940 Mahler's works, thoroughly established by Mengelberg in the Netherlands, remained a regular part of the Concertgebouw Orchestra's repertoire, but they were no longer given under Mengelberg exclusively. Foreign conductors and assistant conductors performed them from time to time. Bruno Walter, himself a pupil of Mahler, was appointed first conductor (next to Mengelberg) from 1934-1939 and gave wonderful readings of several Mahler works, like the Third and Ninth Symphonies, with the Orchestra. During the months following the capitulation of the Dutch Army on May 14th, 1940, many people, in their innocence, thought there would be a military occupation in accordance with standing international rights, and that public life, in particular cultural life, would continue much as before. On October 10th, 1940, Mengelberg gave his last performance of Mahler's First Symphony. Part of the letter written on October 7th, 1940, by the occupational authorities to the Board of the Concertgebouw Orchestra deserves to be mentioned. Translated literally it runs as follows: "The 'Reichskommissar' has decided: 1. The Mahler concert 1st Symphony [*sic*] can be given in Amsterdam and The Hague, each once, in a sense as a conclusion to the performances of this composer given so far. 2. Compositions by Mendelsohn [*sic*] should be cancelled under all circumstances. 3. Hindemith *can* be performed, but he is not really desirable in the future". This marked the beginning of the darkest period in the Orchestra's history and with it that of the bond between the Concertgebouw Orchestra and Gustav Mahler. As a result of his ambiguous attitude during the Occupation, Willem Mengelberg was not allowed to return to the Orchestra after the Liberation. Eduard van Beinum,

Marius Flothius is the Artistic Director of the Concertgebouw Orchestra, Amsterdam.
A review of the Festival/Concertgebouw Orchestra set of Mahler symphonies appears on p. 549.

Left to right: Cornelius Dopper (composer and assistant conductor of the Concertgebouw Orchestra); Gustav Mahler (seated); H. Freyer (manager); Willem Mengelberg and Alphons Diepenbrock (composer—one of the first musicians in Holland to recognise Mahler's significance).   [*photo: Phonogram*]

appointed in 1931 as assistant and in 1938 as principal conductor next to Mengelberg, took over completely. It goes without saying that one of the first works to be played after the war, was a symphony by Mahler—on August 2nd and 4th, the Second Symphony, the *Resurrection*, was performed—a symbolic gesture indeed.

Prior to 1940 Van Beinum had conducted very few works by Mahler, probably as a result of the strong tie between Mengelberg and Mahler. In the beginning this special bond may have lent an air of authenticity to Mengelberg's interpretations but on the other hand the arbitrariness with which Mengelberg approached almost every score he performed gave rise to some doubt. Before 1940 both the presentation of Mahler's work and the attitudes towards it often suffered under the heavy burden of extra-musical, philosophical and even religious considerations. It took Van Beinum some time to develop an affinity with a world which by nature was almost alien to his own character and which in addition was so completely identified with the Mengelberg era. Once he had overcome this he came to present Mahler's music with a surprising freshness and a considerable degree of faithfulness. That he did not take his task lightly is obvious from the fact that he not only presented the more accessible works, like the First and Fourth Symphonies and *Das Lied von der Erde*, but also the complicated Third and the rather neglected Sixth and Seventh Symphonies.

The years following Van Beinum's death in 1959 were marked by a strong desire for both the renewal and continuation of the traditions of the past, and even before his appointment as Principal Conductor in 1961, Bernard Haitink, who had conducted the Concertgebouw Orchestra for the first time in 1956, had shown a great affinity for Mahler's music. The idea to put on record Mahler's complete works had been thought of long before 1960 but the final impulse for the project came with the Jubilee Season 1962-1963, the seventy-fifth season of the Concertgebouw Orchestra. One of the principal works of that season's repertoire was Mahler's First Symphony. This work was a particularly appropriate choice since Mahler completed it in the year of the founding of the Concertgebouw (literally "Concert Building") and of the foundation of the famous orchestra that bears its name. With this work the foundation stone was laid for the integral Philips recording and the management of the Orchestra had an important task for within the next ten years the nine symphonies and the song cycles had to be reintroduced to the repertoire—not an easy task for either conductor or Orchestra. It is also interesting to note that during the same period Bruckner's complete symphonic works were also being performed and recorded by the same forces and the fact that all these recordings were being made with one orchestra and one conductor is unique in the history of gramophone recording.

The performances and recordings all took place in the same hall, the Great Hall of the Concertgebouw. It is rightly famous for its acoustics, probably because of its architectural proportions and the fact that the orchestra is seated some distance from the rear wall. It has often been said, and is also the conviction of Bernard Haitink, that the conditions in the Hall do add to the sound quality of the orchestra; and this special sound appears to be an appropriate one for Mahler's music.

The merits of both the Concertgebouw Orchestra and Bernard Haitink as Mahler interpreters have been internationally recognised: the Orchestra received the Gold Medal of the International Gustav Mahler Society in 1955; in 1962 Bernard Haitink was made an Honorary Member and in 1971 was awarded, after a remarkable Holland Festival performance of the Eighth Symphony, the Gold Medal of the same Institution. The recording of the Eighth, a few months after the performance, was certainly one of the most demanding tasks for the Phonogram engineering staff. Credit for the excellent result of this and other recordings must go to the producer, Jaap van Ginneken, who over the years has assisted Bernard Haitink and the Orchestra with remarkable knowledge, patience and insight.

It seems that Mahler's prophecy, "Meine, Zeit wird noch kommen" ("My time is yet to come") is finally being fulfilled. It is certainly a great honour and satisfaction for the Concertgebouw, its conductors and artistic management to have made such a large contribution on Mahler's behalf.

September 1972
Mahler in Amsterdam

Marius Flothius served as Artistic Director of the Concertgebouw from 1955 to 1974 – and his involvement stretched back further still – so was well placed to reflect on the orchestra's relationship with the music of Mahler, from Willem Mengelberg's early advocacy (culminating in a 1920 Mahler festival) to that of Bernard Haitink.

'It is probably unique in the history of any orchestra that for the celebration of a conductor's jubilee, all attention was directed to the nearly complete output of a contemporary composer ... Nine symphonies, Das klagende Lied, Das Lied von der Erde and fourteen songs – were all performed within sixteen days'

July 1984

Karajan's Ninth

A final archive review that takes us into the CD era: another Ninth, again from Berlin but this time with Herbert von Karajan on the podium reviewed by a leading critic of our own era, Richard Osborne.

MAHLER. Symphony No. 9 in D major. **Berlin Phil-**
★ **harmonic Orchestra / Herbert von Karajan.**
DG ① Ⓕ 410 726-2GH2 (two discs, nas).
Recorded at performances in September 1982 at
the Berlin Festival. Only available on Compact
Disc.
Comparative CD version:
Chicago SO, Solti (11/83) 410 007 2-2DH2

In 1980, Karajan and the BPO made a memorable LP recording of the Ninth Symphony in excellent analogue sound (DG). As a performance it went further than any extant recording in distilling the music's essentially impersonal, other-worldly character whilst at the same time suggesting what EG, writing in the *Guardian*, aptly called "the emotional thrust of a live performance". One or two critics here and in the United States thought Karajan held the work at arm's length; but the reading won plaudits from Mahlerians of many persuasions, for as Schoenberg observed, and as Karajan and his players so movingly reveal, "this symphony is no longer couched in the personal tone. It consists, so to speak, of objective, almost passionless statements of a beauty which becomes perceptible only to one who can dispense with animal warmth and feels at home in spiritual coolness" (*Style and Idea*, Faber, 1975).

And yet the reading continued to develop. It already had great precision, beauty and tonal clarity—all hall-marks, Schoenberg tells us, of the late Mahler style—but there was clearly more to say. Like Mahler, Karajan has been accused by some colleagues of achieving results through a super-abundance of rehearsals. But, says Schoenberg, the great conductor knows in the ninth rehearsal that there is more to say in the tenth, whereas most conductors have nothing to say after the third: "the productive man conceives within himself a complete image of what he wishes to produce".

All of which is germane to the present performance. In 1982, the BPO's centenary year, Mahler's Ninth was played in an unforgettable series of concerts in Salzburg, Berlin and New York. Two things were evident in the momentous first performance in Salzburg in April 1982. First, Karajan was bringing an added toughness and truculence to the opening measures of the second movement, strengthening still further an already masterly unfolding of Mahler's powerful essay in the metamorphosis of the dance. Secondly, the LP recording was no studio fabrication. Schwalbé and his men really did play the work from first note to last with a degree of technical address which, by normal standards of human perfectibility, was well-nigh incredible. As the 1980 LP recording was not in digital sound and as the reading had itself evolved, Karajan seems to have needed little persuasion to allow the taping of the final, Berlin performance in 1982. I say performance advisedly, for what we have here is a single performance, though the dress rehearsal was taped as a precaution and used (I would suspect in the concluding *Adagissimo*) where audience or platform noise was likely to be damagingly intrusive.

The result is again exceptional. Certainly this is the finest live performance of a Mahler symphony to have appeared on any kind of record since Mengelberg's 1939 account of the Fourth Symphony. Interpretatively and orchestrally, it is superior to the historic live 1938 VPO set of the Ninth under Bruno Walter (World Records SH193-4, 9/74—nla). Walter never realized the concluding *Adagio* (on record, at least) as steadily, as lucidly, as eloquently, as dispassionately as Karajan; and the old VPO is no match for our own latter-day BPO.

Only in one respect does the old Walter recording seem preferable and that is in some degree of distance that exists between the microphones and the orchestra. Make no mistake, the digital sound on this live Berlin recording is wonderfully clear and thrillingly actual; but I am not always at ease with the conductor's-ear-view of the proceedings, though of course long stretches of the score—the ruminations and chilly declensions of the first movement, the rapt Trio of the third (fabulous violin- and trumpet-playing here) and paragraph after paragraph of the fourth—derive immense benefit from the absolute clarity and absolute quiet of the CD.

Technically, there are similar swings and roundabouts with Solti's studio recording on Decca, as EG pointed out last November. But good as the Solti is, it isn't in the Karajan class as an interpretation. Which is no disgrace, for Karajan's reading and the Berliners' playing of it—the *Adagio* in especial but much else besides in this latest performance—is one of the seven wonders of the modern musical world. R.O.

'Karajan's reading and the Berliners' playing of it ... is one of the seven wonders of the modern musical world'.

RECOMMENDED

Mahler's music has inspired many of the finest conductors, singers and orchestras to achieve their most profound recordings. Choosing the best will always be a very personal thing, but we here offer a breadth of some of the most remarkable contributions to the catalogue.

The Symphonies

Symphony No 1

Bavarian RSO / Rafael Kubelík
DG

'Kubelík is essentially a poetic conductor, and he gets more poetry out of this symphony than any of the other conductors who have recorded it, except only Bruno Walter.' (5/68)

Symphony No 1

Royal Liverpool PO / Sir Charles Mackerras
Warner Classics

'Less self-consciously titanic than his big-name rivals, Mackerras delivers a lithe and naturally paced account that many will find especially rewarding, recorded as it is with great warmth and presence ... The music breathes with complete naturalness and nothing is vulgar or overstated.' (12/92)

Symphony No 1

Düsseldorf SO / Adám Fischer
AVI-Music

'This is a terrific account of Mahler's fledgling symphony – full of the rashness and impetuosity of youth and the wild imaginings that go hand in hand with it. Each time that eight-octave-deep "silence" of the opening page sounds, hazy violin harmonics tracing a haze of light on the dawn horizon, you have to wonder at this twenty-something's daring holding to the rules of symphonic form while seeking new dimensions with his nose for theatre.' (4/18)

Symphony No 1 with Blumine

London PO / Vladimir Jurowski
LPO

'Jurowski "hears" everything but better yet the reasons for everything. His precipitous way with tempo contrasts creates moments of high drama in the outer movements, as does his understanding of Mahler's very particular articulation.' (6/13)

Symphony No 2

City of Birmingham SO / Sir Simon Rattle
Warner Classics

Gramophone Award

'No matter which recording of this great work you already possess, you must have this one too. It is, like Tennstedt's of No 8, in a spiritual class of its own, a Mahlerian testament.' (10/87)

Symphony No 2

London PO / Vladimir Jurowski
LPO

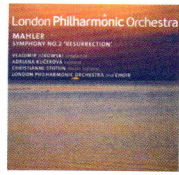

'A performance of revelations, big and small, and easily the most illuminating to have appeared on disc in a very long time ... You may think you know how Mahler's Second Symphony goes. Think again.' (2/11)

Symphony No 2

Budapest Festival Orchestra / Iván Fischer
Channel Classics

'He has a keen nose for Mahler's particular brand of tempo rubato – the ebb and flow of the music, the way it speaks, or rather sings; the bucolic and melodramatic elements of the score are vividly conflicted, and best of all Fischer really breathes in the atmosphere of Mahler's precipitous flight to eternity.' (AW/06)

Symphony No 3

New York PO / Leonard Bernstein
Sony Classical

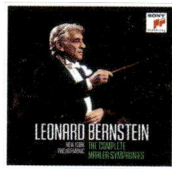

'The vast Third Symphony – which is becoming something of a musical best-seller – receives here a performance which, if far from orthodox, is deeply thought out and extremely compelling in its own right.' (12/62)

Symphony No 3

Royal Concertgebouw Orchestra / Riccardo Chailly
Decca

'Riccardo Chailly's Mahler Third offers us a graphic narrative, a fantastical refuge, cosseted and balanced so even the standard CDs sound three-dimensional.' (8/04)

Symphony No 3

Pittsburgh SO / Manfred Honeck
Exton

'The great cinemascopic vistas that are summoned up by those eight unison horns at the start are quite remarkable for their depth, breadth and thunderous immediacy.' (11/11)

Symphony No 4

Miah Persson; Budapest Festival Orchestra / Iván Fischer
Channel Classics

RECORDINGS

Leonard Bernstein is to be found 'at his exciting best' in Mahler's Fifth Symphony

'Some maestros choose between neo-classical modernity and old-world Gemütlichkeit. Fischer gives us both and more: he gives us instability.' (4/09)

Symphony No 4

Elsie Morison; Bavarian RSO / Rafael Kubelík

DG

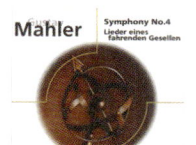

'[Kubelík's] first movement is delightful, fast and pointed; while the sharp edge for the *Ländler* is also most effective.' (10/71)

Symphony No 4

Chen Reiss; Czech PO / Semyon Bychkov

Pentatone PTC5186 972

'The conductor, not always considered a Mahler specialist, has known the music since childhood and is now embarked on a complete cycle for the Pentatone label: you may have caught one of his recent live performances of this seemingly modest work. Smaller in size is not the same as smaller in meaning and Bychkov plainly knows what he wants and how to get it.' (5/22)

Symphony No 4

Hanna-Elisabeth Müller; Düsseldorf SO / Adám Fischer

AVI-Music

'The intricacy of detail here (balance, phrasing, dynamics) makes even the familiar sound new and unexpected. And taking Mahler at his word, edging him out of even his comfort zones, is the key to rekindling its newness.' (01/17)

Symphony No 5

Philharmonia / Sir John Barbirolli

Warner Classics

'If the aching tragedy of the opening "Trauermusik" is more deeply conveyed by Barbirolli than his rivals, so is the buoyant optimism of the final movement.' (12/69).

Symphony No 5

Vienna PO / Leonard Bernstein

DG

'Best of all is Bernstein himself, here at his exciting best, giving daemonic edge to the music where it is appropriate and building the symphony inexorably to its final triumph'. (8/88)

Symphony No 5

Düsseldorf SO / Adám Fischer

AVI-Music

'There's a stylistic and emotional understanding which goes beyond the precisely annotated scores.' (7/18)

Symphony No 5

Swedish RSO / Daniel Harding

Harmonia Mundi

'Harding's strategy is not to duck the composer's frequent recourses to extremity but to meet them head-on.' (11/18)

Symphony No 6

London PO / Klaus Tennstedt

LPO

'Tennstedt exposes every nerve-ending of the piece from start to finish. Big sounds, big rubatos, big everything'. (8/09)

Symphony No 6

San Francisco SO / Michael Tilson Thomas

SFS Media

'Less mannered than Bernstein, and more emotionally engaged than Karajan, this is an exceptionally intense and ... remarkably coherent performance that isn't to be missed.' (5/02)

Symphony No 6

Berlin PO / Claudio Abbado

DG

Gramophone Award

'I can't remember hearing a tauter, more refined performance than this, nor one that dispenses so completely with the heavy drapes of old-style Mahler interpretation.' (9/05)

Symphony No 7

Bayerische Staatsorchester / Kirill Petrenko
BSORecordings

'Petrenko has a way of hearing deep into textures and harmonies that is at times really quite startling. He gives us X-ray ears.' (8/21)

Symphony No 7

LSO / Michael Tilson Thomas
RCA

'[Tilson Thomas] is very much alive to its "concerto for orchestra" potential, but he emphasizes also its radical discontinuities. Contrast, parody, and even brashness, are paramount.' (1/00)

Symphony No 8

London PO / Tennstedt
Warner Classics
Gramophone Award

'This is the finest of the Tennstedt cycle and one of the superlative Mahler performances on record.' (3/87)

Symphony No 8

Staatskapelle Berlin / Pierre Boulez
DG

'I have to say that I enjoyed the experience more than I would have thought possible and certainly more than anything else in this now complete Mahler cycle' (13/07)

Symphony No 8

Chicago SO / Sir Georg Solti
Decca

'Now at last Mahler's Symphony of a Thousand can be heard on record at something approaching its full, expansive stature.' (10/72)

Symphony No 9

Berlin PO / Herbert von Karajan
DG
Gramophone Award

'Karajan's reading and the Berliners' playing of it — the *Adagio* in especial but much else besides — is one of the seven wonders of the modern musical world.' (7/84)

Herbert von Karajan's Mahler Ninth: 'one of the seven wonders of the modern musical world'

Symphony No 9

Leipzig Gewandhaus Orchestra / Riccardo Chailly
Accentus

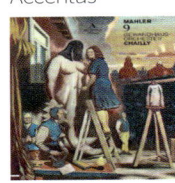

'Under Chailly's direction the finale's hymn-like opening is beautifully played, the colossal final climax overwhelming, the quiet close held as if on a single breath.' (2/15)

Symphony No 10

Berlin Philharmonic Orchestra / Sir Simon Rattle
Warner Classics
Gramophone Award

'A thrilling recording of what was clearly an electrifying event. Rattle and the BPO are set to be a combination that will hold the attention of the musical world ... a major event.' (May 00)

Symphony No 10

Berlin Radio SO / Riccardo Chailly
Decca

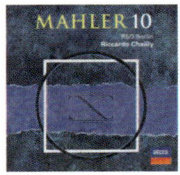

'This is a worthwhile addition to the collection – a Tenth to live with.' (12/00 – reissue)

Das Lied von der Erde

Kathleen Ferrier; Julius Patzak;

Vienna PO / Bruno Walter
Decca

'Bruno Walter's deep understanding of Mahler is given every chance to show itself in this carefully balanced recording with its sense of space; and one can appreciate to the full Mahler's wonderful handling of his large orchestra in its most delicate as well as in its most strenuous moments.' (10/52)

Das Lied von der Erde

James King; Dietrich Fischer-Dieskau; Vienna PO / Leonard Bernstein
Decca

'Bernstein's lithe, agile, and sophisticated, yet eagerly responsive to the two widely-separated emotional poles of the music - desperate passion and poignant charm.' (2/67)

Das Lied von der Erde

Dame Sarah Connolly; Robert Dean Smith; Berlin RSO / Vladimir Jurowski
Pentatone

'I cannot stress enough how effectively Jurowski conveys the ethereal "natural world" beauty of the score. It is cool and lucid and thoroughly autumnal.' 09/20)

The Songs

Kindertotenlieder

**Anne Sofie von Otter ; Vienna PO /
Pierre Boulez**

DG

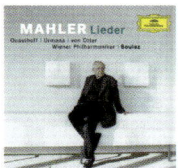

'Anne Sofie von Otter's long-awaited recording of the Kindertotenlieder is deeply felt and notable for its nobility.' (3/05)

Rückert-Lieder

Christiane Karg; Malcolm Martineau

Harmonia Mundi

'Karg's artistry, distinguished by natural intelligence and vivid sense of communication, is an ideal complement to Martineau's. Her voice is beautiful, more velvety than diamantine, and, with her supremely sensitive partner she never has need to push it ... This is lieder performance of wonderful freshness and intelligence; a delightful album, highly recommended.' (11/20)

Rückert-Lieder

Jamie Barton; Brian Zeger

Delos

'The voice is rich, generous and vibrant, big but beautifully controlled, impeccably smooth throughout its range. It's the sort of instrument you could listen to all day, in any sort of repertoire...' (2/17)

Rückert-Lieder. Kindertotenlieder. Lieder eines fahrenden Gesellen.

**Dame Janet Baker; Philharmonia Orchestra /
Sir John Barbirolli**

Warner Classics

'Baker and Barbirolli reach a transcendental awareness of Mahler's inner musings'.

Rückert-Lieder. Kindertotenlieder. Lieder eines fahrenden Gesellen.

**Christian Gerhaher; Montreal SO /
Kent Nagano**

Sony Classical

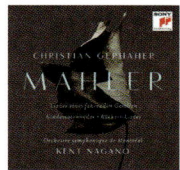

'As ever, Gerhaher combines vocal beauty and acute sensitivity to verbal and musical nuance with a certain patrician restraint ...The Montreal orchestra (superlative wind solos) match the baritone in their sentient, compassionate playing, while Nagano keeps textures lucid ... one of the finest baritone versions of these cycles since Fischer-Dieskau.' (6/14)

Des Knaben Wunderhorn

Elisabeth Schwarzkopf; Dietrich Fischer-Dieskau; LSO / Georg Szell

Warner Classics

'Few command the musical stage as Fischer-Dieskau does in a song such as "Revelge", where every drop of irony and revulsion from the spectre of war is fiercely, grimly caught.'

Rückert-Lieder. Lieder eines fahrenden Gesellen. Des Knaben Wunderhorn (selection)

Christian Gerhaher; Gerold Huber

Sony Classical

'Christian Gerhaher's all Mahler disc has a rare eloquence.'

Des Knaben Wunderhorn

Anne Sofie von Otter; Thomas Quasthoff; Berlin PO / Claudio Abbado

DG

'A performance that is predictably – given the BPO/Abbado partnership – shipshape in execution, nothing in Mahler's highly original scoring overlooked.' (9/99)

Dame Janet Baker, whose Rückert-Lieder with Sir John Barbirolli has become a catalogue classic

My Music

Every month, for 20 years, Gramophone has interviewed a famous figure from outside the world of classical music for our final page, about the composers and artists which mean the most to them. Some have talked about Mahler, and here is a selection of their reflections on his music.

Will Self, novelist

'Of all the great symphonists, Mahler is the most literary. His music is strongly expository at the same time as being highly self-critical. Yes, this is beautiful, but why is it beautiful? What happens if I introduce some dissonance? Is it still beautiful for you? If I chuck in another 80,000 violins and a choir does that help? This music is about the loss of the sweetness of life, a sense of lost profundity which is why, I think, he resorts to sweetness – is that going to help you cope with the bitterness of life?'

Gemma Whelan, actor

Every interviewee each issue names a recording they couldn't live without, and the Game of Thrones star named Mahler's Symphony No 5, by the New York Philharmonic Orchestra, conducted by Leonard Bernstein (on Sony Classical). 'The way he conducts is alchemy!' *she told us.* 'He's like a vessel for this music, which is both alarming and exciting.'

Howard Brenton, playwright and screenwriter

The prolific playwright also chose a Mahler recording, in his case the Symphony No 9 from the New Philharmonia Orchestra under Otto Klemperer (available on Warner Classics). 'As a student, I'd go to the student union and listen to records for free,' *he recalled.* 'This one had a great effect on me.'

Douglas Kennedy, novelist

'I discovered early on that if you heard Mahler, say, conducted by Boulez and Bernstein, you were hearing two radically different soundworlds. An extraordinary Mahler First conducted by Bernstein made a vast impression on me: Bernstein was looking on Mahler as the first great 20th-century exponent of the self against the world – which was Bernstein's own self image. I also remember a fantastic Mahler Seventh from Boulez in Chicago: what you hear there is "the next stop on this train will be the Second Viennese School".'

Alec Baldwin, actor

Alec Baldwin also opted for Mahler's Symphony No 9 for his choice of recording: 'I love the power, the searing quality, of Mahler so much, in all of his symphonies but especially in this one. The whole universe of emotion is contained in this piece.'

Alan Hollinghurst, novelist and poet

'I got very interested in Mahler – being a schoolboy in the 1960s Mahler was becoming more available. There was a sort of revolution in taste that made it possible. Mahler was thought to be bad taste for a composer and I suppose he is "impure", in the sense of his eclecticism. And that must have reverberated a lot with the preoccupations of the time. There was something thrilling about the performance of a Mahler symphony as an event in those days not only in its rarity but also in its sense of theatre. All that seemed to me to be so much more profoundly rooted in things that mattered than Strauss.'

Rufus Wainwright, singer, songwriter and composer

'If the world were to end today (and sometimes it seems like it is), it would be all right, because Mahler wrote his symphonies. I don't think anything encapsulates the end of humanity the way Mahler's symphonies do. I listen to the Bernstein recordings, and I love Georg Solti's Mahler, too.' **G**